RELIGION, REASON
and
REVELATION

Duane E. Cory

UNIVERSITY SERIES, Philosophical Studies
Dr. Gordon H. Clark, Editor

RELIGION, REASON
and
REVELATION

By

GORDON H. CLARK

THE CRAIG PRESS

Nutley, New Jersey

Contents

Contents

RELIGION, REASON
and
REVELATION

1.

Is Christianity a Religion?

Is there such a thing as *religion* of which Christianity is one manifestation? This question is important for two reasons: its answer will influence and reveal what a person believes Christianity to be; and on a broader scale it will determine the method that ought to be used in formulating a philosophy of religion. Therefore let us ask the question a second time in a slightly different form. Is Christianity a species of a genus? Whether this is answered affirmatively or negatively, certain further problems are introduced. If Christianity is a species of the genus religion, how is religion to be defined and what are Christianity's differentiating characteristics? If it is not, what sort of philosophy of religion can there be and what sort of philosophy of Christianity can there be? Apparently the first step in examining these questions must be the definition of religion. What is religion?

Unity and Multiformity

Religion is familiar to the common man in every age and nation. He performs its simple or complicated rites; he believes its doctrines. However justified may be the orthodox complaint or the atheistic exultation that a particular religion is losing its hold on the people, the ineradicable experiences still remain a familiar force. Among the learned too, it is a familiar subject of discussion. Of the making of many books on the general subject of Religion, the Psychology of Religion, the Philosophy of Religion, and the History of Religion, there is no end. But although religion is a phenomenon as multiform as it is familiar, both these characteristics contribute to the difficulty of understanding it.

No one denies the multiformity. There is Christianity, and there is Mohammedanism; and further there are Judaism, Hinduism, Buddhism, the religions of the interior of Africa, and of the isles of the seas. Yet notwithstanding their great differences, they are all popularly unified under the single term religion. Can such a unification survive scholarly analysis? Is it really possible to gather all these under one definition so that they can be discussed together as one subject? In Botany, for example, the Nightshade, the Indian Cucumber-root, the Bellwort, the Lily of the Valley, Solomon's Seal, Asparagus, and the Star of Bethlehem are all gathered together and discussed under the lily family. All the members of the lily family have certain characteristics in common, characteristics which tie them together in one family, and at the same time differentiate them from other families. Cannot the same thing be done for religions?

As may be expected, this way of looking at the matter has been tried. Not only so, but it is the usual method of procedure. It seems to be only common sense. For example, Winston L. King, in his *Introduction to Religion*, writes that religions are one as well as many. Although he makes the obscure denial that they have any common denominator "of a neutral sort," there is "some sort of unity" and there are "actual likenesses." At the end of eighty pages he concludes, "We have been trying to use the term 'religion' as well as 'religions' with the confidence that it has some distinguishing meaning." Such phrases as these in an eighty page attempt to define religion indicate the presence of difficulties. Apparently botany is an easier subject than religion. But another author shows more confidence.

Professor William E. Hocking, in *Living Religions and a World Faith,* commences by asserting that "In its nature religion is universal and one." As a matter of fact, Hocking means more by this assertion than that religion is one in the sense that all the members of the lily family are one family, for he goes further and complains that the plurality of religions is a scandal to the religious man himself, to the philosopher, and to the statesman who wishes to unify his community. But why should it be scandal? The plurality of lilies is no scandal to the botanist. Should the plurality of religions be scandalous to the philosopher? And however scandalous the plurality of religions may be to the "statesman" who wishes to unify his community, this very plurality may seem a blessing to freedom loving individuals who think that some societies have been too thoroughly unified already. What can religion be, if it is a more perfect unity than the generic unities of botany? Why should the unity of religion exclude specific differences?

In a later volume, *The Coming World Civilization*, Professor Hocking repeats his vigorous assertions of unity. In the fifth section of the book, to justify the identification of all religions in essence, he argues that "affirmation is not exclusion" (p. 137). The Christian faith, and *a fortiori* the Buddhist doctrine, do not offer themselves as hypotheses competing with other hypotheses. Each one says, This is a Way to peace; and such an affirmation does not exclude other Ways. In a sense there is an Only Way, but it is not the Only Way of a particular religion. It is a universal way. The essence of the precepts and doctrines that mystics in all religions have discerned is the same. The agreements are not even mere similarities; they are identities. Thus the Only Way is not the Way that marks off one religion from another, but "it is the Way *already present in all* . . . The several universal religions *are already fused together, so to speak, at the top*" (ital. his; p. 149).

Naturally such a view stimulates many questions. For example, it may be asked, Does Hocking base his statements on an empirical study of the several religions? Is this what the religions assert or admit? How does Hocking obtain the conclusion that the doctrines of all religions are essentially identical? If this is only what some mystics in every religion say, can the student of religion accept the mystical evaluation and disregard what other members of the same religions assert? It is undeniable at least that Hocking's principle, "affirmation is not exclusion," is in conflict with the explicit teachings of some religions. Christ's statement in the Gospel, "No man cometh unto the Father but by me," is decisively exclusive. Similarly, the Apostle said, "There is none other name under heaven given among men whereby we must be saved." Hocking would have to hold that Christ is not essential to Christianity. But of course this criticism is premature, for at the beginning it seems reasonable, especially for one who is writing a book on religion, to assume that there must be some sort of unity, either a generic unity or some still deeper kind, that makes religion a single subject of discussion.

A Disconcerting Disjunction

Promising and even necessary though this principle may appear, its application is already seen to be attended with great difficulty. Perhaps the very familiarity of religious experience is one cause of its stubborn defiance of analysis. At any rate, a comparison of the many volumes on religion discloses a disconcerting disjunction. Either, in spite of the similarity of titles, the authors are not writing about the same subject, or, in spite of the length of the books and their learned vocabulary, they do not know what they are writing about.

The first half of this disjunction reflects those authors who, like King, frankly, courageously, and commendably formulate an explicit definition of religion. A frank attempt is reasonable because one expects a writer to state what subject he intends to study. But a quick survey of these definitions shows that the more definite the authors are, the more obviously they are not talking about the same thing. King virtually includes a belief in God in his definition—at least he spells Object of devotion with a capital O, and further emphasizes it in the following chapter (pp. 74 ff.) . Julian Huxley, on the other hand, in *Religion Without Revelation*, says that the essential religious reality is not God, but a sense of the sacred, which like the feeling of hunger or the emotion of anger, is irreducible. Although this latter definition is not so definite in its affirmation as in its denial, it is still definite enough to see that King and Huxley are not talking about the same thing when they use the term religion. There are other humanistic definitions of religion that may be taken as vague or definite, depending on how one looks at them. The *Humanist Manifesto* constitutes religion of those actions, purposes, and experiences which are humanly significant. Now this may be vague and meaningless; but if it is taken at literal face value and assigned an intelligible meaning, an interesting question comes to the fore. Is not an appendectomy humanly significant? Then it follows that appendectomies are religious exercises. It is evident therefore that what the humanists call religion is not the same thing that other authors are discussing. Once more, William James was definite enough when he spoke of religion as the experiences of men in their solitude; but other writers are definite in defining religion as social. And the devout worshipper in any of the several religions might not like any of these definitions. Clearly what one man calls religion, another does not recognize as such. The more definite the definition is, the more clearly the writers are not writing on the same subject.

This difficulty gives rise to the second half of the disjunction above: some writers do not know what they are writing about. They recognize the impossibility of defining religion and rely on its familiarity to satisfy the reader. L. W. Grensted, in *The Psychology of Religion*, remarks in his Foreword that the subject is nebulous and ill-defined; no one part of it has any clear logical or scientific priority; "there is always a lurking doubt whether religion is a proper study for psychology at all." And a few pages later he admits that "The definition of religion is impossible . . . Thus the only means of saying what we mean by religion must be empirical, descriptive, and accumulative. We must in fact return to . . . what ordinary folk understand by religious behavior" (p. 15.) This initial admission of failure, however, does not prevent the gentleman from writing his book —a humorous paradox that he himself seems to enjoy.

Now, there are powerful reasons for accepting the position that religion cannot be defined. In fact, such is the main conclusion of this chapter. It will be shown definitely that we cannot with confidence, to repeat a phrase from King, assume that religion has a distinguishable meaning. This conclusion sometimes leads to the clear-sighted muddle-headedness of Grensted. There is, however, another alternative to be mentioned later. But, for the moment, and particularly at the opening of the discussion, one should not merely assume the impossibility of defining religion. It is better to examine the two chief methods used in attempting to frame a definition; and, if in doing so, we are fairly convinced that the problem is insoluble, we shall have learned the precise reasons for the failure.

THE PSYCHOLOGICAL APPROACH

In general two methods have been used to distinguish religion from other subjects of study. The second method, based on examining the multiformity of Mohammedanism, Shintoism, Brahminism, and so on, may be named the comparative method. But first to be considered is the psychological approach, based on the intimate familiarity of the experience.

Emotion versus Intellect

There are many persons, both scholars and others, who believe that the essence of religion, the common factor in all religions, is some sort of emotional experience. In one way or another they minimize the intellectual content. Although Hocking speaks of a search for righteousness, and righteousness no doubt is something other than emotion, Hocking's stress falls on the passionateness of the search, rather than on the contents of righteousness. He does not make an outright denial that there are intellectual factors in religion, but he asserts that no theoretical proposition is true apart from feeling. This seems to imply that even the truth of mathematics depends on passion. Perhaps he would not say that all passion is religious or commendable, but passion is so much the medium of religion that whatever is of passion "tends to be" religious. King also emphasizes the emotional nature˜of religion and disparages the intellectual. In his Foreword he refers to "the bare bones of the intellectual statements of religious dogma" as opposed to "the vital phenomena of breathing and moving religions themselves."

Or, consider a little more at length the views of another well-known scholar who places the emphasis on emotion. James Bissett Pratt, in *The Religious Consciousness,* aware of the difficulties in framing a definition, admits that in many respects his own definition is probably as bad as any other; but he holds that one word in it hits the mark pretty accurately. Religion, he says, is a serious attitude toward those powers which people believe control their destinies. It is the word 'attitude' which he stresses, and by which he plays down the intellect. In his study of conversion he states that "the essential thing about conversion is the unification of character," and that this is "the really important and the only essential part of it . . ." (p. 123). This involves will, emotion, and thought, but it is primarily "moral." "Nor is the intellectual side of the process to be neglected, though it is frankly the least noticeable of the three. In most cases it seems to play but a negative part."

Preconceived Notions

At the risk of anticipating too much of the later argument, it might be best even at this point to question whether all unification of purpose or character is religious. As one example of conversion, Pratt chooses the experience of a certain Ardigo who renounced the Roman Catholic priesthood to become a positivistic scientist. Now, this is no doubt a conversion of a sort; but is it a religious conversion? Of course the answer to this question depends on one's definition of religion. Pratt defends his choice of examples on the ground that he has not permitted preconceived notions derived from Christian theology to influence him. Presumably to choose as examples of conversion only those instances which accord with Christian theology would be to forfeit the claim to scientific objectivity. At the same time, although Pratt may not have selected his material from the standpoint of any one of the well-known world religions, he nonetheless has made his selection on the basis of other preconceived principles, which can be thought of as his private religion. From a logical standpoint it is equal whether one's assumptions are philosophical or theological, Christian or not. If it is reprehensible to operate on Christian presuppositions, is it any less so on other presuppositions? The only difference would seem to be that the writer with Christian principles is probably more aware of the fact, while the scientific writer sometimes claims that he has no preconceived notions at all. In other words, Pratt attempting to avoid the bias of a Christian view of conversion does not seem to be aware of his own bias in assuming Ardigo's conversion was a religious conversion and that the essence of religion is the unification of character.

Bunyan and Edwards

Pratt's interest in conversion further reveals the importance he assigns to emotion. In addition to the doubtful case of Ardigo, he relates the more obviously religious experiences of Brainerd and Bunyan. In these two instances the process was essentially the same. When they began to think of the condition of their souls, their previous neutral state of mind gave way to increasing depression. They felt themselves entirely helpless. Desirous of salvation, they were convicted of sin and could not rid themselves of temptations. The impossibility of recommending themselves to God by their unaided human efforts increased their despair. Then suddenly there came a great peace of mind. And, concludes Pratt, "the whole drama was one of feeling, and all that was accomplished was the substitution of one feeling for another" (p. 147). Feeling is further elevated in the following chapter by a serious misinterpretation of Protestant theology. From the thesis that man by his own efforts cannot satisfy God's requirements, Pratt draws the erroneous conclusion that "the attention of everyone desiring salvation—since it was vain to center it on thought or deed or will—was inevitably fixed on feeling. Feeling indeed could help—the feeling of one's own devilishness and despair—and nothing else could" (p. 149). With this interpretation of the situation Pratt disparages Bunyan's conversion.

To straighten out Pratt's misunderstandings of Protestant theology would complicate the discussion too greatly. One point that lies on the surface is enough to mention. Since the Protestant thesis is that man by his own efforts cannot satisfy God's requirements, it would follow that feeling and emotion could be of no more help than thought or deed or will. Thus the need of gracious divine help would of itself no more require attention to feeling than to thoughts and deeds. However, rather than to correct Pratt's views of evangelical religion, it is more to the point to see how he uses his interpretation to disparage Bunyan's conversion. He complains that Bunyan gained no new insight through his experience; no change of character or will had been wrought; no new unification of purpose had been achieved. Now, this complaint involves Pratt in a curious inconsistency. If no change of will or character had been wrought, Pratt should not have included this experience in a list of conversions, for he had previously said that "the essential thing about conversion is the unification of character" (p. 123). As in the case of Ardigo Pratt stumbled upon a conversion that was not religious (at least in the popular sense of religious), so here he blunders and contradicts himself by selecting an experience that is religious, but on his own showing is not a conversion. The confusion is an evidence of a poor method.

Furthermore, Pratt is not justified in his disparagement of Bunyan's emotions, even if they do not constitute a conversion. From a psychological point of view, a point of view that stresses the description of phenomena and boasts that theology has had no influence on its conclusions, a sequence of emotions is as legitimate a subject of study as the unification of character. In the descriptive method disparagement is out of place, whether the subject be emotions or nuclear physics. Particularly for one who thinks of religion as primarily an attitude or feeling, Bunyan ought to be a most happy example of religious experience. But the contemptuous style rather indicates that Pratt surreptitiously accords more value to the intellectual contents of religion than he explicitly admits and that he evaluates Bunyan from a position that does not lack theological bias.

Evidence of this one-sided procedure is again seen in his reference to Jonathan Edwards. This great New England Puritan is also assimilated to the general phrase that "feeling could indeed help . . . and nothing else could." Now, it is true, as Pratt points out in his footnote (p. 150), that Edwards said "religion consists much in holy affection," and no one who reads Edwards' explanation could disagree. But first, note that Edwards said *much*; he did not say that religion or even conversion consists altogether in affections. Then, second, the term *affection* in Edwards does not mean what Pratt says it means. Pratt had said that "it was vain to center it on thought or deed or will." But for Edwards the term affection includes the will and in fact has more to do with will than with pure feeling. Third, Edwards spends most of his book in warning his readers not to trust their feelings. And fourth, far from saying that nothing but feeling can be of help, far from belittling intellectual content, Jonathan Edwards put great emphasis on doctrine. Indeed, his stress on theology is more frequently the object of secularistic displeasure than his actual or even his alleged approval of emotions. It would seem therefore that these inaccuracies are the result of a poor method and of a prior decision to define religion in terms of emotion.

On the other hand, one who wishes to lay some or even great emphasis on the intellectual side of religion need not conclude that it is worthless to study the emotions. Jonathan Edwards studied them and on the basis of his theology gave certain warnings against them. William James' intensely interesting *Varieties of Religious Experience* proceeds on a different theological basis. The New Testament itself, of course from its own point of view, describes the very different emotional circumstances of a number of conversions. But one's evaluation depends on one's theology. Doubtless religion includes emotions; but it does not follow that will and intellect are negative factors, unessential, least noticeable, and bare bones.

Does Description Explain?

In general, whatever the value or even the undisputed importance of such psychological studies, one may wonder whether strictly psychological descriptions are of much help in explaining religion or even in discovering its nature. First, as to explanation. To be sure, the philosophy of logical positivism holds that description is explanation. No statement of causality is permitted; no statement of purpose is permitted; no possibility is allowed of saying that a phenomenon must be as it is; not even an evaluation is permitted; the only legitimate statement is that the phenomenon is as it is observed. Since a critique of logical positivism cannot be undertaken here, it must suffice to point out that the logical positivists constantly violate their prescription. Besides that, the identification of description and· explanation is tantamount to denying explanation. No doubt this fact is as it is described: a golf ball rises and falls; a painting or a sonata is pleasing to me; Congress enacts a new law. But even more than the description of the event, we want an explanation of it. Why did this event occur? Under what generalization can it be subsumed? What was its purpose and what will be its effects? And should we, if possible, try to repeat it or to prevent its recurrence? The logical positivists go beyond their own principles when they limit explanation to description, for the limitation itself is not a description of anything observable other than their own conduct. Admittedly, description provides some elements that contribute to an understanding; at least description provides material to be explained. But it is *prima facie* unreasonable to confuse the two.

Now, if understanding goes beyond the range of description, should we explain religion as the opiate of the people? Or should we be a little less radical and explain it as the result of parental compulsion and social pressure? Or, again, is the cause of religion either some innate aesthetic response to the sublime or an abject fear of the unknown? Or, finally, does an adequate explanation transcend these factors and demand God as the cause? No psychological description can give any one of these answers nor choose from among them.

Does Description Discover?

Just above it was questioned whether the psychological method could explain religion or even discover its nature. There are several reasons why psychology cannot discover what religion is. One reason, but not the deepest or most independent, is that the descriptive accounts of emotions are concerned only with surface phenomena. As the following considerations will show, these descriptions do not grasp what is essentially religious. That the same emotions are found in different religions would not disturb but would rather be welcomed by a writer like Hocking, who insists on the unity of all religion and is not interested in distinguishing one religion from another; that there are different emotions found in the same religion might merely result in increasing the difficulty of finding the one complex emotional state by which religion is to be defined; but what is fatal to this method of procedure is the fact that these emotions are found in experiences that are not usually regarded as religious at all. For example, love is currently emphasized by some religious writers as the religious emotion par excellence. It has been regarded as the sum and substance, the inner nature and deepest spring of true religion, and the essence of God himself. But when left undefined, the emotion of love is hardly restricted to religious situations. So far as the emotion per se is concerned, the psychological description would be the same, no matter what the causes, the object, the circumstances, or the value might be. Some love is quite human, some is irreligious or even unholy. Yet, if religious love is to be defined so as to exclude the unwanted examples, the procedure becomes logically circular. Love is first used to define religion and then an independent concept of religion is used to differentiate among loves. Then again, not only is it impossible to confine a given emotion like love, or a complex of emotions, to religious experience, it is equally impossible to confine religious experience to a given emotion. The emotion of anger is usually thought of as an anti-religious emotion; but Jesus' anger (Mark 3:5) was preeminently religious. Such considerations as these show that no purely psychological description of experiences, no emotion, no particular state of the affective consciousness, nor any combination of them, can be singled out as the uniform and definitive element in religion. There can be a sequence of a calm mind, then depression, with elation following, as Pratt notices in the case of John Bunyan; but the same sequence occurs regularly on election night in the case of politicians also. There is nothing distinctively religious about emotions.

Description and Presupposition

The keener writers recognize the deficiencies of purely psychological description. Grensted says openly,

"Ultimate questions about the real existence of the constituents of our experience, in their own right and apart from their setting in that experience, cannot be decided or even discussed by psychological methods . . . Psychology cannot even choose its own objectives, which are selected by the psychologists on the basis of values of which psychology can give no complete account" (op. cit., pp. 3, 5).

Nonetheless there are a few, even though they are not professedly logical positivists, who write as if psychological description answers all questions. Yet it will be found that their volumes, no less than the works of the better authors, contain many presuppositions and judgments of value that cannot be obtained by observation. At the very beginning, though these writers do not recognize it, a normative or non-descriptive principle is needed for the selection of what to describe. It is very plausible to argue that no one should philosophize about religion before he describes the phenomena which call for explanation. The facts, so it is said, must precede the theory. But the trouble is that a descriptive procedure can never isolate what must be described. A theory must precede the choice of facts. Pure description could never decide to place the emphasis on emotion rather than on intellection. According to the vague popular connotation of the term, religion is a most complex phenomenon. Some religious services are quite emotional and the people shout and sing, stamp on the floor, wave their arms, and act in a most undignified manner. Other people, like the Presbyterians and Puritans, used to sit quietly, trying to understand a two hour doctrinal sermon. There are groups also, both within and without the sphere of Christendom, who limit themselves almost entirely to an elaborate ritual. And still others equate religion with social service. Therefore only a non-observational judgment of value could motivate the assertion that the intellectual tenets of a religion are not worth investigating. And only the same a priori judgment could select which part of the complex phenomenon to describe.

Each author therefore decides what he thinks is important and significant, whether it be ritual, dogma, or emotion. Such a decision cannot be avoided; but it should not be hidden. It should be made consciously. It should not be put forward as an objective, descriptive discovery. The most deceiving and the most deceived author is the one who thinks he is simply describing what is there. The *there* itself cannot be selected without presuppositions. If a given emotion or some other affective state of consciousness, however complicated, is selected as the essence of religion, the implication is that another state is not religious. Thus religion is sharply separated from sport or politics or other human activities considered non-religious. This is the psychological counterpart of the common distinction between Sunday religion and week-day practice. Undoubtedly there are persons who have a Sunday religion for public display, if indeed it can be called their religion. Similarly there may be persons whose professed religion is some isolated emotion. But could there not be others whose religion permeates all their activities? For them, politics, prayer, and procreation are all religious duties. Is it possible to bring these two types of religion under one description? By what right is the latter ruled out when the attempt at isolation is made? Obviously therefore the psychologist must have a philosophy of religion of his own which controls his psychology of religion; and it is this deeper material which the present chapter believes to be the more significant.

Integration of Personality

To this point the discussion has emphasized the view that emotion is the essence of religion. However, this restriction does not do justice to the psychological method nor to the general exclusion of intellectual definitions. The explanation of religion as a nonrational experience allows of another possibility—a possibility that was evident in the material from Pratt, but which has not yet been examined. Pratt spoke about the unification of character and used the secular conversion of Ardigo as an example. This is a theme popular with the modern humanists. Confining religion to one emotion, such as Schleiermacher's feeling of dependence, they say, is too narrow a view; and though religious experience may sometimes be characterized by this feeling, other equally religious experience may not. A sense of dependence is not essential to religion. The humanists generally therefore try to locate religion in the more universal needs of man—not the non-religious needs of food and shelter, but in particular the need of integrating one's scattered and conflicting impulses, emotions, and desires. This means that religion is the process of achieving a unified, coherent, and effective personality. The consciousness of sin, as the Christians call it, is the consciousness of failure to achieve this unified self; and redemption is the subsequent success. But success is not dependent on Christian ideas. This was the mistake of Protestant liberalism, commonly called modernism. Rejecting traditional theology, this religious movement still sought the solution of life's problems within a Christian framework. But this restriction is inconsistent with the substitution of religious experience for an authoritative book. Humanism, consistently empirical, insists that integration of character is often obtained by other methods. If we should examine all the methods of successful integration, it will be clear that Christianity is not unique or even superior. The main goods are the pursuit of truth, the creation of beauty, and the realization of love and friendship. Whatever methods are used to attain these goods may be equally called religious, if one wishes to speak of religion.

There are two chief difficulties in this humanistic thesis. The first is the establishment of truth, beauty, and friendship as goods. Nietzsche denied that truth is always good. Can humanism, especially a tentative and relativistic humanism, defend itself against Nietzsche's arguments? Perhaps the good is even less to be found in beauty and friendship. Is it possible then on humanistic presuppositions to justify these preferences or indeed to show that any definite line of conduct is good or evil? This question, since it raises the general problem of ethics, will be examined in a later chapter. The point here simply is that it is a difficult question. It is so difficult that sometimes the humanists shy away from it and embrace another difficulty. All the more do they shy away because the selection of particular goods, such as truth and beauty, and the stress laid by the humanists on society, on cooperation, on collectivism, leading them at times to speak even of reverence for the social good, is inconsistent with their view of religion.

If personal integration is the essence of religion, if, as one of their number says, the empirical method cannot demonstrate that the non-christian solution is inferior to the Christian, if therefore true religion is just wholehearted absorption in whatever envisioned greatness empirically brings integrity of selfhood (and the humanists use all these phrases), then it follows that the integration of purposes, emotions, and sentiments achieved by Hitler and Stalin cannot by any empirical method be judged inferior to any other. These two dictators could say with as much truth as the apostle Paul, "This one thing I do." All three men were characterized by complete unity of mind. The examples of misers and hermits who also have achieved great integration of emotions and sentiments are only slightly less embarrassing to this view of religion.

The disadvantage of this attempt to define religion should now be clear. The definition is so broad and vague that it covers an unmanageable variety of experience. The Hindu mystic, the apostle Paul, the dictator, and the miser are equally perfect examples of religion. But while they are undoubtedly equally perfect examples of integral personality, the types of personality are so incompatible with each other that if one is called good, another must be called evil. No one, not even a humanist, would admit that he has no preference among these manners of living. And in this case, one cannot say *tout court* that integration of personality is good. This conclusion is an essential point in the message of a Christian evangelist. Many of the people to whom he preaches are integrated personalities: that is just what is the matter with them. Their desires and interests are thoroughly harmonized into a naturalistic system of values. They are altogether satisfied with themselves. No sense of guilt disturbs their equanimity. The Christian message must destroy this integration; and even if the message does not succeed in providing them with as perfectly harmonized a substitute, the semi-integration so produced is better than the previous complete integration.

The psychological method therefore fails to discover, to define, and to explain religion; and at the same time it fails to justify its claim to scientific impartiality. It is not by pure description that psychology over-emphasizes emotion: this is a normative judgment. And it is a judgment which precludes distinguishing between religion and other emotional experiences like politics. The controlling influence of non-descriptive, philosophical presuppositions is also revealed by the disparagement of certain types of conversion. Disparagement is obviously evaluative. If, now, these presuppositions are made definite and

specific values are elevated above others, the general problem
of ethics is inescapable. But if specific values are left vague and
every type of integration is allowed, the general problem of
ethics is evaded because incompatible types of life are put on
the same level. Since this method results in these confusions,
since the terms are left without definite meaning, it seems therefore that some other method is imperative.

THE COMPARATIVE METHOD

The ideal of classifying religions as the members of the lily
family are classified in botany is too attractive to be discarded
because of the failure of one attempt. Another method of approaching the problem is the method of comparative religions.
If similar emotions blossom in different religions, and divergent
emotions within one religion, and all of them without benefit of
any religion, perhaps the nature of religion is to be found in its
intellectual aspect. Surely the systematic exclusion of the "bare
bones" of intellectual content is an extreme position. A study
of the beliefs or theology of a religion is indispensable to an
understanding of it. Only by grasping the doctrinal or intellectual system of each faith, can one avoid vague and misleading
abstractions. And in spite of the first impression of incompatible
differences among religions, must there not be some basic similarities? Otherwise, why should they all be called religions?

Is God Essential to Religion?

At first sight it would seem that there was a greater variety of
beliefs than of emotions, and that the nature of religion could
never reside in any theological formulation; but the hope of
comparative studies is of course to find in this welter of beliefs
some common denominator, some minimal consensus, some
general agreement. No doubt Mohammedanism and Christianity
have different conceptions of God, but they both believe in some
sort of deity. Perhaps then this is the common element and
essential nature of all religion.[1]

Karl L. Stolz in *The Psychology of Religious Living* argues that humanism is not a religion because it "invests the word 'religion' with a connotation that is absolutely foreign to it . . . A godless religion is a contradiction in terms" (pp. 75-76). For the moment let us grant that Stolz and King are right in denying that a religion can be godless. We are now confronted with the philosophy of Spinoza and with the superstitions of savage tribes. Did Spinoza have a religion? Did Spinoza have a God? Some people have called him an atheist; and if this is the truth, he could not have had a religion in Stolz' sense of the word. But others have called him a *Gottrunker Mench*—a God-intoxicated man. He spoke frequently of God, of *Deus sive Natura*. Therefore he must have been very religious. Unfortunately, however, if God and nature are identified and if Spinoza's God is the universe itself, can it be said that he believed in God? Isn't God something other than the universe? What is meant by the term God? Or, to turn from the complicated philosophy of Spinoza to the superstitions of uncivilized peoples, clearly whatever God the Inca religion acknowledged or whatever gods are worshipped in the various animistic cults, it is not the God of Christianity. If the term God is so broadened as to include the usage of both Spinoza and the animists, the term and the definition of religion in which it is used become meaningless. Therefore, if religion is to be defined in terms of belief, perhaps it must be a belief in spirits, or merely in immortality, or some other wide-spread belief that examination will show to be the uniform ingredient of every religion.

Yet this expedient of substituting the more inclusive term spirit for the more definite term God faces exactly the same difficulties. Spirit would have to be defined, and one would have to question whether Spinoza's *sub specie aeternitatis* could properly be included under the notion of immortality. But beyond these detailed difficulties, there are decisive reasons why the method itself, the very search for a common element, is unsatisfactory.

The Hunting of the Snark

The method is unsatisfactory because it requires at the outset the knowledge it aims to obtain at the end. In order to discover the common element in all religions, it would first be necessary to distinguish religions from all non-religious phenomena. If there were an authoritative list of religions, a student could begin to examine them for a common element. But before the common element is known, how could an authoritative list be compiled? If Lewis Carroll tells Alice to examine all Snarks and find the common nature of the Snark, Alice, at least in her waking moments, would not know whether all the objects before her were snarks, or even whether any of them were. Now, we are not in a much better position than Alice would be. In our attempt to find the common nature of religion, we believe we are safe in assuming that Christianity and Mohammedanism are religions. But is Hinayana Buddhism a religion? If it is, then a belief in God is not essential to religion; but if a belief in God is essential, then this form of Buddhism is not a religion. Should we examine Buddhism or not? Should we include Buddhism on our list? To answer this question, one would first have to know the essential nature of religion, and yet this essential nature is the still unknown object of search. It does not help to advise us to begin with a smaller undisputed list. In the first place, there is no undisputed list at all. Until religion is known, nothing can be placed on the list. And in the second place, even if we had a small undisputed list, its common elements could not be assumed to be the nature of religion, for with religion, even more than with botany, the common element of a longer list is not likely to be the common element first observed in the shorter list.

Nor is Buddhism the only or most embarrassing difficulty. Consider communism. Ostensibly it is the enemy of all religion, fundamentally and vociferously anti-religious. Indeed, it is religiously anti-religious. Its anti-religious zeal makes it a religion for its adherents. Should the student of religion therefore list

communism as one of the world religions and search for the
common denominator of communism, Christianity, and
Buddhism? How could the student decide what to do? Unless he
first knows what religion is, he will not know whether or not to
examine communism along with the others in the hope of discovering the essential nature of religion.

In addition to this objection to the method, there is also an
objection to the usual conclusions it offers. Let it be assumed
that Christianity, Mohammedanism, and even Buddhism have
been examined. Perhaps it is claimed that the common element
is a belief in an Original Being. The phraseology in which such
common elements are stated must be so general and is interpreted by the various religions in such incompatible and antagonistic ways that nothing common seems to remain but a
name or empty form of words. Original Being for Buddhism
may be Nirvana; for Christianity it is the Trinity; for communism it is the atoms. But if the Trinity is spirit and not
matter, if the atoms are matter and not spirit, and if Nirvana is
neither, it is hard to see that there is any real element in common. Original Being is just a name, a name of nothing, a sound
in the air.

Common Human Needs

If in answer to this criticism it be said that the three original
beings perform analogous functions in the three systems, and
that this function is a real common element, the reply will be a
repetition of the argument. The defense often speaks of the
several religions fulfilling the needs of their adherents, and thus
the common factor in all religions is that they satisfy certain
needs. However, this answer will not do. It will not do because
the several religions do not agree on what a man needs. Of
course there can be verbal agreement that men need what is
good for them, but when the specific contents of the good or the
need are spelled out, they will be found to differ. Does man
need the heaven where Christ sits at the right hand of the
Father, or does man need Nirvana and personal extinction? No

devout Christian will admit that Nirvana, or atoms, can perform the same function that the Trinity does; nor will the communist or Buddhist admit that the Trinity can do what Nirvana or atoms can do. Only the critics who have no religion can so light-heartedly identify them. The adherents themselves do not claim that their Original Being performs the same function that is claimed for the Original Being of other religions. Function and need, like Original Being, are nothing but empty names. There is therefore no element in common among those phenomena that are popularly designated as religious.

What then is religion? Colloquially the word is applied to Mohammedanism, Buddhism, and Christianity. But because it is vague, it can be applied to communism also. Then the definitions of religion take on the form of "what a man will live and die for." Such definitions are completely without content and do not specify any definite subject of scientific investigation.

Meaningful Words

Conversely, to have a definite and meaningful subject of study, the colloquial and empty word must be relinquished, and some specific contents must be selected. For example, the word God cannot be just any first principle. The *Deus sive Natura* of Spinoza and the God of Abraham, Isaac, and Jacob, as Pascal saw so well, are not the same thing. Nor can salvation mean both Nirvana and heaven. Therefore, if we wish to use the word religion, we must define it particularly. We may wish to discuss Mohammedanism, or we may wish to discuss Christianity. In this sense there are religions, even though there is no religion. True, it may be difficult to define Christianity or Mohammedanism, but it is not impossible. We may have to alter the colloquial meaning somewhat in the interests of precision, but the technical definition will not be so far from the common meaning as to be absurd. At any rate, we need clear-cut concepts to avoid confusion. When a term like God is stretched to include every first principle that anybody has ever thought of, and every fetish, spirit, and superstition, though these are not first principles, the term means nothing. As Hegel insisted, every determination is a negation. Or, as Aristotle argued, a term not only must mean something, it also must mean not-something. After centuries of philosophic discussion it ought not to be necessary to defend the indispensability of unequivocal language; but such is the chaos in discussions in religion and such is the antipathy toward taking a particular point of view that the disastrous results of vague generalities call for emphasis. Let us therefore try to avoid confusion by being explicit. Most words in the dictionary have three, four, or even five somewhat different meanings; but if any word had a thousand meanings, or better, if any one word could stand for every other word in the dictionary, nobody could tell what it meant. If a word means everything, it means nothing. To have no definite or limited meaning is to have no meaning at all.

CHRISTIANITY

From here on the discussion will proceed from the viewpoint of Christianity. The term Christianity is far more definite than religion. Christianity has certain doctrines about a personal God, Christ the Redeemer, heaven and hell, that cannot be confused with communism, Mohammedanism, or Spinozism. But if definiteness of intellectual content is a virtue, why should one stop with just a little? Even the word Christianity is used colloquially in various senses, and one is forced to admit that professing Christians themselves often have inadequate ideas of what Christianity is. Surely the images, medals, beads, and other paraphernalia of Romanism is not the same religion as iconoclastic Puritanism.

Definition of Christianity

It is essential therefore to define Christianity more exactly by a specific doctrinal system. Romanism is not what is meant. By Christianity we shall mean, to use common names, what is called Calvinism. Or, to be most specific the definition of Christianity shall be the articles of the Westminster Confession. With such a definite basis it will no longer be necessary to spin dizzily in a whirlpool of equivocal disputation. Now we can know what we are talking about.

Since the cause of confusion in the philosophy of religion has been empty and meaningless terminology, the hope now is that this avoidance of ambiguity will contribute to the solution of several problems. The main subjects, the relation of reason and faith, inspiration and revelation, the basis of morality, will be considered in the following chapters. An attempt will be made to show that, because of the basic doctrinal position, it is possible to arrive at definite and consistent conclusions. There is no hypocritical claim that the argument is without presuppositions. On the contrary, only because the Westminster Confession is consciously adopted can progress be expected. But before the main questions are put, certain minor points prove to be satisfactory examples of the procedure, and may be used to conclude this introduction.

The Religions

First of all, a definite Christian standpoint can furnish the solution to the paradox of the present chapter. How can there be religions, yet no religion? If there is no common quality, emotional or intellectual, why are these phenomena uniformly classified together and called religion? Why are there also doubtful cases which sometimes seem to be religions and at other times seem to be "merely" philosophy, or maybe politics? Of course, one can simply appeal to the ignorance and stupidity of the populace and their lack of clear thought. But there is something more. The Christian answer begins with God's creating Adam in his own image and giving him a special revelation. Here was the beginning of religion. With the fall, however, and the resultant depravity, men became estranged from God and distorted both the revelation and their reaction to it. As generations came and went, these distortions diverged in many directions, giving rise to all forms of idolatry, animal worship, fetishism, and witchcraft, not to mention the more blatant rebellion of atheism. Thus there was no possibility of any intellectual content remaining the same in all these developments. The religions of today therefore are descendants of the one original religion, and because of this common origin they are colloquially called religion. If the divergence is not so great as to obscure this origin, people do not scruple to call the phenomena religions. Thus Islam is always called a religion because of its inheritance from Judaism. When the divergence becomes greater, hesitation and perplexity set in. This is seen where people wonder whether Buddhism is a religion or merely a philosophy. And if it becomes extreme, people will usually be quite sure that it is not religion. But logical classification fails because the divergences have occurred through no logical principles. Uninhibited inspiration has ridden off in all directions at once. Therefore the only comprehensive result of attempting to define religion is now the vaguest of meaningless statements.

Christian Conversion

A second example of the confusion engendered by vague notions has already been seen in the discussion of conversion. But take another example: Strickland (*Psychology of Religious Experience*, pp. 113-115) remarks that psychology should not attempt to say what must be, but in keeping with scientific ideals should simply try to find out what is. Applying this principle to conversion experiences, Strickland will not prescribe any necessary or essential elements without which conversion cannot occur, but rather he will collect data from accounts of conversions and make whatever generalizations these data permit. As was explained before, this is equivalent to hunting the snark before one knows what a snark is. Therefore Strickland continues by pointing out that the cases he has collected do not always exhibit sorrow for sin. This, he says, is evident from accounts both of Christian experiences and of modern Hindu experiences. In this line of argument Strickland assumes that the Hindu experiences are cases of conversion. But what is the

definition of conversion? Acknowledgment of the Westminster
Confession as one's presupposition provides a definition and a
solution of the problem. On this basis conversion is a sinner's
initial turning to the mercy of God in Christ upon an apprehen-
sion of sin as contrary to the righteous law of God. Although
this is not a verbatim quotation from the Confession, it is a
fairly close approximation of the Puritan or Calvinistic meaning; and if this is what is meant by conversion, it is clear that
Hindu experiences cannot be called experiences of conversion.
It is only slightly less clear that many experiences called Christian by careless thinkers are not conversions and may not even
be Christian at all. The confused state of mind of secular psychologists who mix together all sorts of experiences, which at
best have only the most superficial similarity, renders their investigations almost completely useless. One might as well an-
nounce as a great discovery that coxcombs, the light from the
planet Mars, and communists are all red. If psychologists are
not supposed to legislate, nevertheless Christianity should.

Sin

A third and final example of misapprehension resulting from
poorly defined terms, also arising in connection with the phenomena of conversion, is the sense of sin. To return for the last
time to Pratt, we note that he hardly disguises his antipathy
toward Bunyan's experience. The objection he expresses is that
Bunyan suffered under a sense of sin without particularizing one
or a few definite sins. Pratt gives the impression that Bunyan
would be more understandable if he had shown sorrow for some
obvious act of wrong-doing. Had he committed murder, or theft,
had he maligned or injured his next door neighbor, then he
would have had something to be sorry for, and his depression
might have been somewhat justified. But, says Pratt in disparagement, Bunyan suffered merely from a sense of sin rather than
from any definite acts. The reason why Pratt passes from simple
psychological description to open condemnation is not hard to
see. He has tacitly defined sin as an overt and voluntary act,

possibly restricting it to fairly serious acts, and he shows no understanding of the view of sin as any falling short of God's standards. In his non-Christian view peccadilloes possibly and certainly inherited, involuntary character are not regarded as sin. Thus Pratt with his presuppositions can neither appreciate nor even understand the Christian doctrine of human depravity. He is trying to apply a secular notion of sin to the Christian experience of Bunyan, and the result is no more relevant than it is impartial.

Time and time again this is what happens. In the following chapters with respect to several important problems it will be seen at great length how the ambiguous and misplaced terms of the comparative method either produce insoluble difficulties and paradoxes, lead to obvious absurdities, or come illogically to conclusions inimical to Christianity. The non-christian arguments regularly assume the point in dispute before they start. The questions are so framed as to exclude the Christian answer from the beginning. Examining this procedure to see how it works, we shall also see how unambiguous Christian concepts combine into a consistent system.

NOTES

1. Cf. Karl Barth, *Church Dogmatics,* II 1, p. 449: "It is therefore unthinking to set Islam and Christianity side by side, as if in monotheism at least they have something in common. In reality, nothing separates them so radically as the different ways in which they appear to say the same thing—that there is only one God."

2.

Faith and Reason

Throughout the history of theology and philosophy, both in all the "war between science and religion," and as well in more devotional writing on the relation between God and man, the antithesis of faith to reason has been a frequent focus of discussion. But are faith and reason antithetical? In the sense in which these terms were used by St. Augustine, they are virtually identical. In some contexts certainly they are arranged in friendly co-operation. But of course they have frequently been set in opposition.

The present discussion will be condensed under four easily remembered sub-headings. First, the Roman Catholic view will come under the heading of *Reason and Faith*. Second, *Reason without Faith* will summarize modern philosophy from Descartes to Hegel. Third, the outbursts of irrationalism that followed Hegel, including mysticism, neo-orthodoxy, as well as Nietzsche and instrumentalism will be taken as examples of *Faith without Reason*. And fourth, the only remaining combination is *Faith and Reason*.

REASON AND FAITH

Natural Theology

That true religion is preceded by or in some way founded on the activity of natural reason is an idea that has been and continues to be widely prevalent. The proper procedure is pictured as beginning with a proof of the existence of God. When the unbeliever is convinced by an argument drawn from nature, then he may next be shown the antecedent probability of a special revelation, and finally the reasonableness of the Scriptures. Not only has this natural theology in its Medieval form been adopted as the official position of Romanism, but many Protestant theologians also accept it in some form or other. Not all, to be sure: A. H. Strong, *Systematic Theology* (Vol. I, p. 71), says "These arguments are probable, not demonstrative." However, the Lutheran professor, Leander S. Keyser, expounds the rational arguments for the existence of God in *A System of Natural Theism*. His analysis and rejection of the ontological argument only underscore his dependence on the others. A. E. Taylor is more ambiguous in his ecclesiastical position, in his concept of God, and even in the precise force he assigns to his argument; but he wrote a book, *Does God Exist?*, to which question his answer is certainly not negative. J. Oliver Buswell, Jr., Stuart Hackett, and in his own way Edward John Carnell ally themselves with several Protestant writers who accept the theistic proofs. Prior to all these men, however, and in a much more elaborate and systematic form than any of them, Thomas Aquinas stated the natural arguments for God's existence, on the basis of which he then erected a revealed theology.

The Thomistic view distinguishes between the process of arriving at truth by man's unaided natural reason and the voluntary acceptance of truth on the authority of divine revelation. The former is demonstrable philosophy; the latter, accepted without demonstration, is the sphere of faith. Faith and reason are, therefore, in one sense, incompatible. This sense is of course not that in which humanists or materialists make them mutually antagonistic. Rather, they are psychologically or subjectively incompatible. If we have rationally demonstrated a proposition, it is impossible for us to believe it on bare authority. We now have the proof, and this leaves no room for faith. For example, a high school teacher may tell a pupil that plane triangles contain 180 degrees, and the pupil, if he has some idea of what a degree is, may believe what his teacher says. But after the pupil has understood the proof, he no longer believes the theorem on the authority of the teacher, he knows the theorem because he has proved it. St. Thomas and Aristotle would even allow an example from sensory experience. An American might tell a European that Denver is west of St. Louis; but if the European should come to America and visit the cities, he would no longer believe on authority, he would know by experience. It is thus impossible to know and to believe the same thing at the same time. The principle holds equally for the proposition that God exists.

However, the subjective incompatibility of knowing and believing the same thing at the same time does not prevent the same proposition from being a part of one man's theology and another man's philosophy. God has accommodated himself to human frailty, and because the Christian religion is not to be restricted to scholars, God has supernaturally revealed some truths which scholars can discover of themselves. Thus God has revealed his existence so that peasants and morons may believe on him; and they have faith. But Thomas no longer believes in God's existence; he knows that God exists because he has proved it.

In another and more important sense, reason and faith are not incompatible. They are complementary. There are many truths about God that are indemonstrable. Yet, though they cannot be obtained naturally, they are necessary for positive religion. Therefore, God has graciously revealed them. For example, it can be demonstrated that God exists and that he is the cause of the world, but the doctrine of the Trinity cannot be demonstrated. Nevertheless the doctrine of the Trinity is not incompatible with reason; it does not contradict any proposition demonstrable in philosophy. On the contrary, the doctrines of revelation complete what philosophy had to leave unfinished. The two sets of truth are complementary.

True faith and true reason cannot contradict one another. Natural knowledge and the truths of faith both come from God —though in different ways. But as they both come from God, they must be consistent. Because of this it follows that faith is often an aid to reason. Whenever a thinker in his speculative reasonings arrives at a proposition inconsistent with faith, as Averroes did when he concluded against individual immortality, he should accept the warning of revelation that he has made an error in his argumentation. Faith is never a hindrance to reason; one should not picture the believer as a prisoner who ought to be given his freedom; faith restricts only from error. Thus reason and faith are in harmony.

In this Thomistic representation of affairs, the meaning of faith and reason should be noted. These key terms are not used in the same sense by all authors, and therefore the historical discussions have not always concerned the same subject. Faith for Thomas Aquinas refers to truths received by the supernatural impartation of information, but this is not what Jacobi and Schleiermacher later meant by faith. Reason in the present context means a process which begins with sensation, passes through imagination, makes use of abstraction, and arrives at conceptual knowledge. But in seventeenth century philosophy reason was sharply set apart from sensation. Reason then meant logic alone. Because of such variation in usage, caution is necessary. One author's strictures on faith may indeed apply to one meaning of faith, while at the same time they may be entirely irrelevant to another. Failure to observe this, not only by the readers, but more especially by the authors, has been a source of endless confusion.

Before examining the cosmological argument itself, to determine whether or not reason can fulfill Aquinas' expectations, it will be best to consider some objections to the general program as outlined. Edwin A. Burtt in his *Types of Religious Philosophy* seems to approve of the following criticism: If man's reason is naturally incompetent to arrive at the doctrine of the Trinity or at other truths of faith, it must be incompetent to prove God's existence in the first place. Why should one truth be demonstrable and not others? And further, even if God's existence and goodness are proved, it does not follow that a supernatural revelation is needed. God could show his goodness in other ways.

The Romanist, he says, faces this dilemma:

"If man's reason is competent to tell that God's goodness implies the provision of a supernatural revelation, it needs no such revelation, being able to decide equally well what man's own attainment of good requires; if it is incompetent to point the way to human salvation, it is still more incompetent to conclude anything about infinite providence" (p. 454, first edition).

Now, there may be flaws, and serious flaws, in the Thomistic philosophy; but Professor Burtt's criticism seems to miss the mark. It may seem strange that a discussion which will arrive at a thorough-going rejection of Thomism should pause to defend it against contemporary attacks. Yet not only should one try to be fair, but even self-interest cautions against relying on defective criticisms. And indeed it seems that Professor Burtt has placed a burden on Thomism that it need not bear.

In the first place, it is not necessary to hold that God's goodness *implies* a supernatural revelation. It is enough that God's goodness permits the possibility of a revelation. Of course, God might show his goodness in other ways, as Burtt contends, but this does not rationally exclude a special revelation.

Then in the second place, even if God's goodness implied a special revelation, it by no means follows that unaided reason could discover the contents of that revelation. Granting unreservedly that from God's goodness we could validly infer that there must be a revelation; granting, that is, that we recognize the need of further information as to the method of obtaining our ultimate felicity; there is still no reason to conclude that this information is discoverable by our unaided efforts. Quite the contrary, would it not be largely our own inability to discover God's requirements for us that led us in the first place to conclude for the necessity of revelation?

Burtt's criticism relies wholly on the principle that if it is possible to demonstrate any one proposition, it is possible to demonstrate all others. This is implausible. There is nothing irrational or self-contradictory, certainly nothing obviously self-contradictory, in maintaining the demonstrability of some truths and the indemonstrability of others. Even Hegel, who by the exigencies of his system should have made everything demonstrable, admitted the existence of contingencies in nature. In Hegel's construction this admission may indeed be a flaw. Absolute idealism presupposes that all knowledge is so interrelated that every part entails the whole. All nature is supposed to be grasped through a dialectical manifestation of concepts that is completely under our control. But Thomism is not Hegelianism. If with Thomas, the premises of demonstration are to be sought in sensory experience, each man is limited by the relatively narrow range of his own experience, and all mankind would be limited by a universe of experience that does not include premises for all truths. Without these premises we cannot possibly arrive at the desired conclusions. Intricate epistemological considerations enter here that cannot be discussed just now, but at least from a more ordinary point of view the inability to demonstrate the events of history does not seem to invalidate the proof of the theorems in geometry.

Burtt then makes the supposition that the Romanist, in answer to the criticism that any rational competency makes revelation unnecessary, would point to the Bible as being in fact a revelation. But, Burtt holds, this is an inadequate reply to the criticism. "Acceptance of any supposed revelation as an actual fact depends upon the prior conviction that there is in the universe a God able and willing to supply it," (p. 406, revised edition.) This assertion also is wide of the mark, but in one respect it better describes the position than the earlier dilemma. The dilemma depended on the point that an argument for God's existence would *imply* a revelation. That is to say, Burtt first contended that a demonstration of God's existence, if further continued, would also demonstrate the existence and the contents of a revelation. This later remark merely insists that a conviction of God's existence must precede the acceptance of a revelation. Here it is not a question of God's existence implying a revelation, but it is the more modest position that a revelation presupposes a God able and willing to reveal himself. Obviously Thomas claims that he has demonstrated the existence of such a God. Therefore, the next step is to search through the world to discover whether or not an actual revelation has occurred. And again, obviously, Thomas finds the Bible. Now, Burtt asserts that this discovery is an inadequate reply to the criticism; but if we accept the first part of Thomas' philosophy, it is not easy to see why this step should be called inadequate.

However, there is still one further source of confusion. As a matter of fact, acceptance of a revelation may not depend on any prior conviction of the existence of God. To be sure, a revelation presupposes God; but the acceptance of a revelation does not require a previous belief in God. A man might accept the Bible and in that very act be for the first time convinced of God's existence. That is, he might find God in the revelation. Indeed, since not many people are competent to understand the proofs of God's existence, and since many who are competent do not study the proofs, it would seem that most people who accept revelation have not first convinced themselves intellectually of the existence of God. They take both the existence of God and the contents of the Bible equally on faith.

Logically, of course, the fact of a revelation presupposes that there is a God. To this extent Burtt is obviously correct. But this is not a damaging criticism, since Thomas would admit as much. It is entirely in accord with the distinction made by Thomas, but rather ignored by Burtt, between the order of reality and the order of knowing. In reality God comes first and everything else comes later; but the human process of learning, according to Thomas, starts with other things first and arrives later at God as a conclusion. For these reasons, complicated though they may be, Burtt's criticism of Thomas must be judged unsound.

Reflection on Burtt's criticism may suggest that the matters he discusses are after all of secondary importance. The crux of the matter lies in the demonstration itself. If the demonstration is valid, objections automatically fail. But is the demonstration valid? Has Thomas actually proved the existence of God? This is the important question.

The Cosmological Argument

On this argument hangs the fate of all natural, as opposed to revealed theology; and its force will decide whether the labors of centuries have been worthwhile or whether they have been misdirected. Now, if the cosmological argument (leaving the ontological argument out of consideration) is invalid, either Christianity has no rational foundation, or a meaning for reason must be found that is independent of Thomistic philosophy. To point out the direction which this discussion will take, it may be said that Thomas' argument will prove to be invalid, and his use of reason indefensible; then an alternative meaning of reason will be proposed which, in addition to any Thomistic reference, will also reveal the ambiguity in modern humanistic charges that Christianity is irrational.

The cosmological argument for the existence of God, most fully developed by Thomas Aquinas, is a fallacy. It is not possible to begin with sensory experience and proceed by the formal laws of logic to God's existence as a conclusion. The terms fallacy, formal laws of logic, invalidity, demonstration, and so on refer to those rules of thought which admit of no exception. They refer to necessary inference. Some of the Protestant theologians describe valid reasoning as mathematical. For example, David S. Clark (*Syllabus of Systematic Theology*, p. 62) wishes to "distinguish between proof and mathematical demonstration." By the term *proof*, he means evidences, such as are used in law courts. The reason that the term *mathematical* is used with demonstration is that algebra and especially geometry consist of necessary inferences. The demonstrations of geometry are clearly valid. They are outstanding examples of correct thinking. If the premises be admitted, the conclusions cannot be avoided. In a law court a piece of evidence and often all the evidences together do not necessitate the decision. The use of the term *mathematical*, however, is unfortunate, for the proof of geometrical theorems is no more valid than the non-mathematical syllogism used for centuries in logic textbooks. All men are mortal; Socrates is a man; therefore, Socrates is mortal. This, too, is a necessary reference. Now Thomas Aquinas intended, and natural theology demands, that the argument for God's existence should be a formally valid demonstration. The conclusion must follow necessarily from the premises. In this, I maintain, the argument fails.

The first reason it fails is too complicated to spell out here. As summarized in the *Summa Theologica* I, Q. 2, the cosmological argument depends on an extensive philosophical background borrowed from Aristotle. It includes a theory of motion which asserts that nothing can move itself. This thesis rests on the concepts of potentiality and actuality. Thomas defines motion as the reduction of potentiality to actuality. The cause of a motion must be actually what the thing moved is potentially. And since nothing can be both actual and potential in the same respect, it follows that nothing can move itself. Unfortunately, the concepts of potentiality and actuality remain undefined. Aristotle tried to explain them by an analogy. In the context motion is used in the explanation and then the concepts of potentiality and actuality are used to define motion. The argument therefore is circular. Behind this stands a mass of metaphysics and epistemology. Such intricacies cannot be discussed here, but it should be noted that if any essential syllogism in all the extensive argumentation is invalid, the whole system and the proof of God's existence collapses.

A second reason for repudiating the cosmological argument can be better pin-pointed. In his attempt to conclude with a first Unmoved Mover, Thomas argues that the series of things moved by other things in motion cannot regress to infinity. The reason Thomas gives for denying that moving causes can regress to infinity is that this view would rule out a first mover. But this reason that Thomas gives is essentially the conclusion he wishes to prove. Of course, an infinite series of moving causes is inconsistent with a first Unmoved Mover. But if the argument is designed to demonstrate the Unmoved Mover, its existence cannot be used ahead of time as one of the premises in the argument.

A third reason of a slightly different sort concerns the identity of the Unmoved Mover. Suppose that all the syllogisms to this point were valid. Suppose the existence of the Unmoved Mover had been demonstrated. Yet, when Thomas adds, "this (first mover) everyone understands to be God," we may demur. The argument taken at its full face value would prove the existence merely of some cause of physical motion; one might even say that it could prove the existence only of some physical cause of motion. To avoid this, Aristotle goes to some trouble to prove that the Unmoved Mover has no magnitude; but this is one of the most unsatisfactory parts of his argument. At any rate it is quite clear that the Unmoved Mover of the proof has no qualities of transcendent personality. There is nothing supernatural about this cause. In fact, if the argument is valid, and if this Unmoved Mover explains the processes of nature, the God of Abraham, Isaac, and Jacob is superfluous, and indeed impossible.

This is a point on which a great contemporary theologian commands attention. Karl Barth, the founder of Neo-orthodoxy, in his *Church Dogmatics* II, 1, pp. 79 ff., gives some of his reasons for rejecting the Roman Catholic viewpoint. In contrast to the decision of the Vatican Council, April 24, 1870, that God, who is the beginning and end of all things, can certainly be known from the phenomena of created nature by the natural light of human reason, Barth declares that God can be known only through God. The main reason for this, says Barth, is that we are talking about the Christian God, the Triune God. Admittedly the Vatican Council did not intend to speak of another God, nor about only a part of this one God. But its method, nevertheless, leads to a partitioning of God, and therefore to another God. The decree uses the appelation "Our Lord," but the argument concerns only "the beginning and end of all things." Now, says Barth, Christianity holds that God is the beginning and end of all things, but it also holds that God is the Redeemer; and if we take the unity of God seriously, we shall not be able to separate the one from the other so as to make one knowledge of God, as beginning and end of things, dependent on nature and another knowledge of God as Lord and Redeemer dependent on revelation. No, says Barth; the knowledge of God cannot be so partitioned. A knowledge of God as the beginning and end cannot exist without a knowledge of God as Redeemer; nor can we know God as Redeemer without knowing him as the beginning and end of all things. "Is not the *Deus Dominus et creator* of this doctrine," Barth asks, "the construct of human thinking—a thinking which in the last resort is not bound by the basis and essence of the Church, by Jesus Christ, by the prophets and apostles, but which relies upon itself? And although the knowability of this construct can rightly be affirmed without revelation, do we not have to ask what authority we have from the basis and essence of the Church to call it 'God'?"

Perhaps it is impossible to follow Barth in every line of his objection here quoted. Very likely Pascal put the matter more accurately in his paragraphs contrasting the God of the philosophers with the God of Abraham, Isaac, and Jacob. But in any case, the gap between the "Unmoved Mover" and the Living God is underscored.

Now, fourth and last, Thomas' argument is invalid because one of its chief terms is used in two senses. Is it not obvious that a valid argument requires its terms to bear the same meaning in the conclusion that they started with in the premises? Unfortunately Thomas very clearly argues in other places that no term when applied to God can have precisely the same meaning it has when applied to men or things. When we say that God is wise, and that Solomon is wise, the term *wise* is not univocal. Not only the term *wise*; the term *exist* also. In the proposition *God exists*, the term *exists*, has a meaning different from its use in the proposition *man exists.* Thomas is very emphatic on this point. But if a term is not used univocally throughout the syllogism, if a term does not bear precisely the same meaning, the syllogism is invalid. The rules of logic have been violated.[1] Those who today accept the cosmological argument will immediately deny that its fortunes are indissolubly connected with its formulation by Thomas. There are other ways of stating the argument, they claim, so as to avoid any error that Thomas may have stumbled into. If this were true, one would expect to find this unimpeachable formulation somewhere in the published writings of its defenders. But the fact of the matter is that no such formulation can be found. There are references to the cosmological argument, there are discussions of it, and there are summaries of it; but the full argument itself, with none of the steps omitted, seems never to have been put into print.

Hume and Hodge

Therefore, those who defend a cosmological argument without stating what it is must be challenged to answer several objections that would seem to apply to any formulation. No doubt it is Hume who, quite apart from his strictures on the principle of causality, has best expressed those objections. But since Hume was such a vicious antagonist of Christianity, his name is anathema to believers, and they are irrationally inclined to assume the falsity of all he said. The reverse may be closer to the truth. It may be that his conclusions are validly drawn from his premises; he may be perfectly correct in arguing that the existence of God cannot be demonstrated on the basis of sensory experience. And if this is so, Christians should thank him for pointing out a procedure that ends only in embarrassment for them. Hence Hume's arguments should be examined without any prejudice that he could not possibly have been right.

Hume's rejection of natural theology depends chiefly on two points. The first point is this: if it is valid to conclude the existence of a cause from observation of its effects, it is nevertheless a violation of reason to ascribe to that cause any properties beyond those necessary to account for the effect. For example, if we see the score and hear the music of Beethoven, and if all our knowledge of Beethoven depends on this observation, we may perhaps conclude that there existed a man with a great degree of musical ability; but it would be irrational to conclude that this musician was also the star quarter-back of Bonn University. Similarly the cosmological argument, if otherwise sound, might give us a God sufficiently powerful to be the cause of what we have observed; but no more. In spite of the remark of some orthodox theologians that that is already a good deal, one must reply that it is not the omnipotent creator described in the Bible.

What is worse, the argument is not otherwise sound. Paley's famous analogy assumes that the universe is a machine like a watch, and hence needs a divine watchmaker; but Hume questions the analogy. Is the universe a machine? In many natural processes the universe resembles an organism more than a machine. And if the universe is an organism in spontaneous movement, the analogy of a divine watchmaker falls away. The objection may be stated in still more general terms. Whether the universe is a machine or a living organism, the cosmological argument assumes that it is an effect. As an effect it needs a cause. But how can it be shown that the world is an effect? Of course there are causes and effects within the universe. One part causes another part to move, just as one wheel in a watch causes another wheel to move. Even vegetables have causes and effects within them. The cosmological argument, however, requires that the universe as a whole be an effect. But no observation of parts of the universe can give this necessary assumption. To be quite clear about it, no one has ever seen the universe as a whole.

Then next, even if it could be proved that the universe is an effect, there is another and extremely serious difficulty, though it is but a particular application of Hume's first point. The first point was the principle that no characteristics can be ascribed to the cause beyond those necessary to produce the effects by which alone the cause is known. Now, the observed effects include many evils, disasters, tragedies, and what the Christian calls sin. These can be listed in terrifying profusion. They have been so listed and used against Christianity both by Hume and Mill, as well as by more cynical writers like Voltaire. These manifest evils, from congenitally deformed infants to the torture chambers of Nazis and Communists, prevent a conclusion that the cause of the world is good. The cosmological argument totally fails to prove the existence of a just and merciful God. To be sure, it allows, though it does not prove, the existence of a good God, but only on the assumption that he is neither omnipotent nor the cause of all that happens. But the cosmological argument was supposed to deal with the universal cause. As a recourse for Christian theism, therefore, the cosmological argument is worse than useless. In fact Christians can be pleased at its failure, for if it were valid, it would prove a conclusion inconsistent with Christianity.

It is most unfortunate that a large section of conservative Protestantism is unwilling to discuss the justice of God and its relation to the evils of the world. There are devout individuals who seem to suppose that a discussion of evil may put wrong ideas into young heads. Any attempt to explain evil, they hold, is unsettling to the faith. In this they are disobedient to their own standard, the Bible; and beyond this, their viewpoint implies that Voltaire, Hume, Mill and other opponents of Christianity are, and will remain, unknown. These well meaning individuals do not realize that Hume's arguments have been public property since 1776; that millions of people have rejected Christianity because of them; and to stop this loss it is a Christian duty to meet them squarely. This, I believe, can be done. The problem of evil is not insoluble. But the solution does not depend on rehabilitating the cosmological argument.

Charles Hodge tried to do so. Hodge is one of the princes of historic Christianity. As a theologian and exegete he has had few peers since he left for glory. One might even venture to say that without reading his *Commentary on the Epistle to the*

Romans, it is impossible to understand Romans. Though such praise may be a bit of exaggeration, nevertheless his high standing as a theologian must be admitted. But his philosophy is deplorable, particularly his treatment of the cosmological argument.

In his *Systematic Theology* (Vol. I, p. 211) he attempts to prove that the universe is an effect. He argues that since all its parts are dependent and movable, the whole must be dependent, because "a whole cannot be essentially different from its constituent parts." This is not true. For example, Rembrandt's painting called the Night Watch is made up of various pigments and canvas, but the whole is essentially different from its parts. The whole is essentially an aesthetic object; the parts are not. If, instead of identifying the parts as pigments in their tubes, we speak of the whole as made up of two inch squares of painted canvas, the same remark holds true. None of the two inch squares is an aesthetic object, but the whole is one of the greatest paintings in the world. Or, for another example, we may select common table salt. It is good to eat—on eggs at least; it is a preservative of pork and olives; it is also, essentially, a chemical compound. But its constituent parts are sodium and chlorine. These are essentially elements. They are also essentially poisonous to the human system. The salt on pretzels tastes good, but who would put a piece of sodium on his tongue? It simply is not true that parts singly have the same characteristics as the wholes of which they are components.

Hodge continues by saying that "an infinite number of effects cannot be self-existent. If a chain of three links cannot support itself, much less can a chain of a million links. Nothing multiplied by infinity is nothing still." Let us look closely at what Hodge has said. The first of his three sentences, viz., an infinite number of effects cannot be self-existent, is the conclusion Hodge should prove. It offers no reason on its own behalf. The second, which presumably is intended as a part of the proof, is an analogy. Hodge supposes that the events of history and nature are like links in a chain, and if a chain of three links cannot support itself, much less a chain of a million links. Analogies, however, are never valid arguments, and this analogy is particularly bad. In the first place, the picture of a chain whose first link is held by a hook is a far from adequate picture of the connections among the parts of nature. Second, whether it is three links, a million links, or just one link, the fact that it cannot float by itself in the air provides no rational basis for concluding that the universe is not self-existent. Eternal self-existence is quite a different concept from that of a link hanging on a hook. Finally Hodge's third sentence, which seems to bear the form of the main argument, does not clearly attach to the preceding. He had just said that what is true of three links must be true of a million; now he adds that nothing multiplied by infinity is nothing still. Aside from its doubtful connection with the preceding, for he had not mentioned zero or multiplication, the sentence is bad arithmetic. It is not true that zero multiplied by infinity is zero, as one can easily see by realizing that the fraction two over zero and the fraction three over zero are both infinity. Let this much suffice as a horrible example of defending natural theology.

Let this suffice also to refute the claim that God's existence can be demonstrated on the basis of observation of nature. The cosmological argument is invalid, and a different type of philosophy is called for. One possibility would be to hold to Christianity at the cost of being irrational. Another possibility, and the one next to be discussed, is the attempt to follow reason even if it should lead to a repudiation of Christianity and revelation. Thus *Reason and Faith* gives way to the new rubric, *Reason without Faith.*

REASON WITHOUT FAITH

The Medieval, that is, the Roman Catholic world-view lost its monopoly over men's minds in the fifteenth and sixteenth centuries. Two powerful movements combined, or at least competed, to form modern civilization. One of these, Protestantism, renounced scholastic reason and based itself on revelation; the other, the Renaissance, gave itself over wholly to reason and would have nothing to do with faith. This latter alternative will be discussed first, and its development may be conveniently arranged by prefacing the account of the main philosophical theories with a few notes on its form in popular culture.

Early Irreligion

The effect of "reason" on the broad aspects of culture, since it includes the many-sided developments of the Renaissance and extends its influence over several centuries, let us say to the French revolution, is entirely too large a subject for adequate treatment. Certain evidences of hostility to Christianity are all that is pertinent and manageable here.

The fortunes of Christian faith had been at low ebb for centuries. A few pious souls, like the Waldensians, John Huss, and Wycliffe, barely kept the gospel alive, while the great mass of people were sunk in superstition. Yet there probably would have been no surging revolt against the dead forms of Christianity, had it not been for the invention of the printing press in the middle of the fifteenth century. It was the printing press that brought to the people both the New Testament and the Greek and Roman classics.

In Italy where the classical literature first arrived as the Eastern Empire crumbled under the pressure of the Turks, the time was ripe for an intellectual revolution, for it was in Italy that the corruption of the papacy was most evident. When therefore the glories of Greece and Rome became known, when, that is, a civilization that had not been dominated by the idea of God was brought to light, society quickly shed its hypocritical Christianity and became openly pagan.

Of course, not all scholarship became pagan. The idea of God was not universally discarded. Not only were the classical authors studied, but New Testament scholarship also was advanced both by the cowardly Erasmus and the courageous reformers. But the Renaissance as distinct from the Reformation was essentially pagan. And if this was true of the scholars, particularly the Italian scholars (Pico della Mirandola, † 1494; Marsilius Ficinus, † 1499; and later, Telesius, † 1588; Giordana Bruno, † 1600), it was all the more true of Benvenuto Cellini, Machiavelli, and the Borgias. Artistic brilliance, intense conceit, political power, and dissolute riches were not compatible with Christian doctrine and morality. It is not necessary to maintain that the Medieval ignorance of the classics was an advantage, nor that the Medieval art form was superior to the new techniques. A knowledge of Homer and Virgil and the discovery of the laws of perspective must not in themselves be considered inimical to faith; but the content of art was changing, and the religious themes became less Christian while the pagan themes became more frequent. In literature Boccaccio, Rabelais, and the cut-throat Villon combine contempt for ecclesiastical duplicity with a disinclination to personal morality. Not all of this paganism, however, should be attributed to a philosophic decision on the merits of faith and reason. Villon and Rabelais are simply the ordinary results of human depravity. Indeed, extenuating circumstances can be alleged for the revulsion from what went under the name of Christianity. Nonetheless all these men were representative components of the new culture. They were the spokesmen and mirror of their time, both influenced and influencing. But the type of more thoughtful writer, who without being a systematic philosopher would in the long run exercise a wider influence, may be found in Michel de Montaigne.

Strange to say there is a notable contrast between Montaigne and the others in the Renaissance tradition, both earlier and later. Renaissance humanism was optimistic. It did not worry itself with the limits of man's reason. In denying the need of God's grace, it assumed that human resources were adequate for all our needs. The philosophic development, yet to be discussed, and the burgeoning scientific advances anticipated no checkmate. But Montaigne was not so sure.

In fact, Montaigne was not sure of anything. He was a skeptic.

This is first to be seen in his attitude toward morality and religion. Far from being willing to die for any dogma or even to be inconvenienced by any scruple, he advises us in his essay on *Custom* to conform ourselves to our time and society. There are no universal moral principles binding upon all men; and still less can anything be known about God, salvation, and a future life. Wisdom therefore consists in having no personal conviction and in deferring to common opinion so as to avoid trouble. When in Rome do as the Romans do.

The Romans, that is the Romanists, were at that time busily massacring the Protestants in France. Well, the Calvinists had it coming to them. They were opinionated people who violated accepted customs. Neither they nor the Romanists had any reason to believe as they did, but as Romanism was on the ground first, the Reformed people were clearly wrong in creating a disturbance. Of course, the Romanists were wrong too in murdering the Protestants, for no belief is worth killing or being killed for.

Montaigne's skepticism, however, goes deeper than these moral and religious matters. Although the Renaissance was optimistic, although the seventeenth century in France was to exalt reason, and although Montaigne himself exercised some influence over the seventeenth century writers, still he expresses grave doubts as to the powers of reason.

"If you say, 'The weather is fine,' and you are speaking the truth, then the weather is fine. Is that not a way of expressing a certainty? And yet it will deceive us. To see that this is so, follow up the example. If you say, 'I lie,' and you are speaking the truth, then you are still lying. The art, the reason, the force of the conclusion in this case are the same as in the other. Nevertheless you find yourself bemired. I observe the Pyrrhonian philosophers who cannot express their general notion by any manner of speech, for they would have to have a new language. Our language is entirely made up of affirmative propositions, which are wholly hostile to them; so that, when they say, 'I doubt,' we have them immediately at our mercy, if we force them to admit that at least they assert and know this, that they doubt."

Although the last lines of this paragraph point the way to a dogmatism immediately utilized by René Descartes, the main thrust is skeptical and as such contrasts sharply with the views of the following three centuries. With the sole exception of David Hume, the philosophic and scientific development that formed modern European culture showed no anxiety relative to the competency of the human mind. It is the thought of these major philosophers to which most attention must be given. But first one later continuation of the Renaissance, a continuation on the level of the popular viewpoint, should receive brief mention. This is the so-called Age of Reason, including both the French Enlightenment and English Deism.

The French Enlightenment will be condensed into a reference to Voltaire and the Encyclopedists. It was not any great philosophical movement, but thoroughly popular. Voltaire was as shallow as he was prolific. Anyone who spent his time writing so many volumes and pamphlets cannot have spent much time thinking, though anyone with more than average wit who has been in and out of prison, honored, exiled, insulted, and flattered could no doubt write a great deal. Yet Voltaire presents no consistent system of thought. At one time he favors free will, at another determinism; there are and there are not innate ideas; the world had a beginning and the world is eternal. Or, again, the teleological argument for God's existence is valid, but noses were made for spectacles and so we have spectacles. However, consistency and profundity are not the prerequisites of popularity.

The French people, with Protestantism virtually extinguished, were groaning under the autocratic power of the aristocracy and clergy. Voltaire was their spokesman. From the beginning of his literary activity he made war on the Christian religion as he knew it. With the passing of time his attacks became more direct and more bold. Writing on *God and Men*, and *The Bible Finally Explained,* he does not attack the foibles and hypocrisies of priests and believers, but rather the Gospel itself. His conclusion is that whenever the Scriptures are neither apocryphal, fraudulent, nor altered, they are immoral and absurd.

Unlike Diderot, however, and the majority of the Encyclopedists, Voltaire was not an atheist. He believed that morality requires a finite God who rewards and punishes. Yet the idea of reward and punishment conflicts with the basic tenet of Deism that God does not intervene in human affairs; and if these rewards and punishments are supposed to be distributed in a future life, one must remember that Voltaire ridiculed the idea of soul by saying: either admit that a flea and a grub have a soul, or say that man is a machine.

English Deism, from which Voltaire picked up many of his ideas, was a relatively distinguishable phenomenon that can be located in the eighteenth century. Naturally, its roots were in the past, the Renaissance, and even on back to Celsus and Porphyry. In England Lord Herbert of Cherbury (1583-1648) first collected the set of ideas later to be known as deism; but perhaps it is Charles Blount (1654-1693) who may be best identified as a full fledged deist. After him come the main representatives of the movement: John Toland (1670-1722), the Earl of Shaftesbury (1671-1713), Anthony Collins (1676-1729), Thomas Woolston (1669-1731), Matthew Tindal (1656-1733), and, not to mention lesser figures, Viscount Bolingbroke (1672-1751).

In the main, deistic writing attacks Christianity. The authenticity and authority of the Bible are denied, and its accounts of miracles are discredited. Anti-clericalism is not limited to the Romish variety, but the Protestant clergy also are described as venal and greedy; in fact deism goes further, for Shaftesbury and most deists were anti-semitic also. Frequently there is a tendency to depend on ridicule, and even the friends of deism acknowledge that Thomas Woolston's writings were coarse and ribald.

The generally negative strategy, the use of ridicule, and even the centering of attention on particular details are conducive neither to positive construction, philosophic profundity, nor to systematic and consistent comprehensiveness. The best representative of deism, from the point of view of calm temperament and breadth of statement, is Matthew Tindal.

His work, *Christianity as Old as Creation,* synthesizes the ~~Deism~~ main deistic themes. First of all, there is a natural religion discoverable by reason. No special revelation is needed and nothing mysterious or supernatural is to be accepted. Reason supports a belief in a God who rules the world rationally. Being perfect and immutable, God does not violate the laws of nature by any miracle. For the same reason the religion he gave to man at creation is perfect and needs no supplementation. The perfect rationality of God is likewise incompatible with his choosing and favoring a particular people. Special revelation would also be an instance of partiality. On the contrary all men have a sufficient means of knowing what God requires, for we could not conceive of a just God requiring of all men the information he had given to only a few. In any case the Bible is not a special revelation because it is full of superstition and error. The Old Testament is immoral and Christ himself is to be censured for making salvation to depend on beliefs of which most men have never heard. All that God requires is that we should promote the common good. Tindal also believed in a future life, though some deists did not.

In addition to its being the most comprehensive and worthy expression of deism, Tindal's book achieved another distinction, for it stimulated Bishop Butler to produce that famous *Analogy* which so successfully put an end to deism.

Now, perhaps it is exaggeration to say that Butler's *Analogy* destroyed deism. The deists themselves were beginning to feel the difficulty of defending their negations in the face of orthodox replies and their affirmations in the face of more radical arguments. Deism, in spite of its profession of an ethical religion, was also accused, and with some show of justice, of fostering widespread public immorality. On this point the Methodist revivals changed popular opinion. Perhaps, too, political and military events tended to crowd deism off the front page.

Interesting as all this is, English Deism and the French Enlightenment are essentially popular results of the Renaissance. These men, though they wrote voluminously, were more followers than leaders in the formation of European culture. Their arguments are sometimes inconsistent and their terms ambiguous. In particular the term *reason* shifts its meaning, if not always in a single author, yet certainly from one to another. Behind these men stand the major philosophers. Therefore it is necessary to examine the source of that faith in reason which holds that reason has no need of faith.

The direction in which the culture of an age develops is, humanly speaking, chosen by a few exceptionally intelligent men. The popular authors then pick up some of the main ideas, usually distorting and diluting them considerably, and finally fifty years or a century later the general viewpoint has seeped down to the whole populace.

The clearest ideas therefore on reason versus faith must be studied first in the major philosophers, viz., the Rationalists—Descartes, Spinoza, and Leibniz—the Empiricists—Locke, Berkeley, and Hume—and finally Kant and Hegel.

Rationalism

Descartes might be introduced as a wise father who tut-tuts the foolishness of his little boy, Montaigne. One can imagine him saying, Don't be so pessimistic; I know that philosophy is too hard for you; let me do it. Or, to put the matter in Descartes' own more dignified language: while sensation and experience repeatedly deceive us and furnish us no indubitable foundation for a firm superstructure, yet if only a single point be found solid, then like Archimedes we can move the universe. Descartes went to extreme lengths to give doubt the benefit of doubt. Because of optical illusions, which are more frequent than one might first suppose, we cannot begin by trusting sensation.

For that matter, we cannot be sure that we are awake. On a

number of occasions I have intended to take a nap but seem to have failed; then when I remarked that I did not get to sleep, my wife would smile and tell me I had been snoring loudly. Dreams prove the same point, for dreams are often as vivid as supposedly waking experience; and while we are dreaming we do not suppose it is a dream.

Finally, to push doubt to the limit, what if there be an omnipotent demon whose chief delight it is to deceive us? He makes us believe that two and two are four, when the answer is really five; and how he chuckles over our confusion! To be sure, this sounds like an absurd supposition. How could anyone take it seriously? But, on the other hand, how could one decide what is absurd and what is not absurd, unless some assured knowledge provides the basis for the decision? In the absence of all knowledge, when one knows nothing at all, nothing at all can appear absurd. Therefore, for all we know, i.e., nothing, there might exist an omnipotent deceiver.

Yet there is one thing that not even an omnipotent demon can do. He cannot deceive us without allowing us to think. If we are deceived, we must be thinking; and if we think, we exist. Here then is an indubitable truth, a firm fulcrum by which we can move the universe of philosophy.

It is necessary to note just how Descartes has defeated the omnipotent demon. Had he said, I walk, therefore I exist, he would have failed. I can easily deny that I am walking without actually walking. It would be enough to sit in a chair and say, I am not walking. But it is absolutely impossible to deny I am thinking without thinking. Since doubting is a form of thought, I cannot doubt that I think without thinking the doubt. I think, therefore, is an indubitable truth.

How Descartes proceeded to build up his world-view from this point does not concern us here. What is important is his method. One must not suppose that the certainty of thought depends on any experienced vividness of thinking. If certainty depended on vividness, then lightning and thunder would serve to outwit the demon. Obviously they do not. The proof of the *cogito* depends on logic alone. 'I think' is a proposition such that if it is denied, it is proved true. If I say, I think, it follows that I think; but just as well if I say I do not think, it follows that I think. This is not a matter of experience but of logic alone.

Because of this method Descartes and his followers are called rationalists. They depended on reason. But note, the reason on which they depended is not in the first instance a reason that is antithetical to revelation. This is not to say that a rationalist, or rationalism as a system, is the bulwark of revelation. Spinoza in particular had no love for the Bible. But the reason of rationalism is in the first place a reason that is antithetical to and exclusive of sensory experience. Here reason means logic.

All knowledge, on this rationalistic theory, is to be deduced as the theorems of geometry are deduced from their axioms. No appeal to sensation is permitted. The consistent application of the laws of logic is alone sufficient. Reason therefore bears the meaning of logical consistency. This explains why the rationalists adopted the ontological argument for God's existence. They needed God's existence not only to rid themselves of an omnipotent devil, but, more seriously, to prove the existence of a world. Now, to fit their principles, the argument for God's existence had to be so construed as to make a denial of his existence self-contradictory. As a person who denies that the interior angles of a triangle equal two right angles simply does not know what the concept of a triangle means, so anyone who denies God's existence simply does not understand the term *God.* Thus God's existence is proved by logic alone.

When this meaning of reason is coupled with the principle that all knowledge can be deduced by reason alone, it follows that revelation is at best unnecessary.

Spinoza, who applies the principle of rationalism more consistently than Descartes, draws out the inference explicitly.

"The truth of an historical narrative, however assured, cannot give us the knowledge of God nor consequently the love of God, for love of God springs from knowledge of him, and knowledge of him should be derived from general ideas, in themselves certain and known, so that the truth of an historical narrative is very far from being a necessary requisite for our attaining our highest good."[2]

The Christian reply to a rationalistic rejection of revelation should not concern itself too much with archaeological evidence that the Bible is historically accurate. Spinoza, to be sure, was an early member of the long line of higher critics who delighted to find blunders in the Old Testament. And no harm has come to Christianity through the archaeological investigations that have discomfited the critics by showing that writing had been invented in Moses' day, that the nation of Hittites actually existed, and that all the other stupidities of Wellhausen's school are but the wishful thinking of the Bible's enemies.

But Spinoza's argument was that an historical narrative, even if perfectly accurate, is valueless in religion. A Christian reply therefore must be directed against the epistemology that underlies Spinoza's statement. The important question is not whether or not the Bible is true, but whether or not all knowledge is deducible by reason, i.e., by logic alone.

Now, the history of philosophy, that is, the secular scholars themselves—for it is not necessary to consult Christian writers —have convincingly answered in the negative.

Kant did his best to explode the ontological argument; and since this argument is rationalism's only hope of making contact with real existence, without which philosophy would be merely a game of words, such a refutation, if sound, would annihilate rationalism altogether. But even if the ontological argument should be valid, no one has ever succeeded in deducing the precise number of planets, or the actual species of japonica, from the existence of God by logic alone. And if astronomy and botany must progress apart from rationalism, it is inconsistent to demand that religion should be so confined.

Rationalism therefore, in the seventeenth century meaning of the term, is a failure. So construed, reason without faith not only provides no religion, it supports no knowledge of any kind. If this were the only possibility, the Christian could offer the world a choice between faith in revelation or abysmal ignorance.

Empiricism   Reason = Sensation

The next attempt in European philosophy to build on "reason" without faith was British Empiricism. This is the philosophy which the later deists, if not the earlier, came to adopt. But it must be noticed that the term *reason* has taken on a very different meaning. Without much distortion it may be said that reason now means sensation. That is, whereas rationalism attempted to base all knowledge on logic alone, empiricism depends on experience alone. The famous line from John Locke reads, "whence has it (the mind) all the materials of reason and knowledge? To this I answer in one word, from experience; in that all our knowledge is founded, and from that it ultimately derives itself."

Locke's view of revelation may be a little too complicated, or possibly too disguised, to describe accurately. Although he seems to have admitted the fact of revelation, some interpreters judge it to be a grudging admission. In one place he raises the question whether or not we can be sure that anything is a revelation, and seems to suggest that probably we cannot.

But however it may be with Locke himself, and more pointedly however it may have been with the devout Bishop Berkeley, Hume showed that empiricism, consistently maintained, cannot provide room for revelation. There is no need to balance the Christian Berkeley against the secular Locke and to stress Locke's deficiencies to the advantage of Berkeley's more acceptable attitude toward revelation. The important thing is to discover what results from the principle that all knowledge is based on experience, chiefly sensation.

According to empiricism, knowledge begins with what Locke calls ideas, notions, or phantasms, what Hume calls impressions, or what most people today call sensations. By combining, transposing, augmenting or diminishing these sensory materials, we

develop all, even our most abstruse, knowledge. The most
complicated of Einstein's relativity equations, though this is
not the example Hume used, can be resolved into memory
images that were copied from previous sensations.

Now, how far will experience take us? Do these inner sensations give any knowledge of external bodies? Can we discover
the causes of these impressions? Berkeley had already showed
that the sensations of red, hard, bitter, etc., give no evidence in
favor of the existence of an external material world. Hume,
following him, gives the example of a table. Suppose we see a
table. We have a sensation of a table. If we walk away from it
down a long hall-way, what we see appears smaller than what
we saw when we were closer. An external table is supposed always to maintain the same size. Therefore what we actually saw
was not the alleged external table, for what we actually saw
changed in size. What we actually saw was an image or phantasm
in our own mind, and hence our sensations furnish us with no
evidence for the existence of an external world. Even if we
should suppose that our image had some external cause, we
could not know that the image resembles the cause, for we have
seen nothing but images. In fact, if the word *image* connotes a
similarity to something external, we have no reason to believe
that our sensations are images.[3]

Hume, however, goes further than Berkeley in reducing
knowledge to experience. Locke had accounted for the idea of
matter by abstraction; and Berkeley had shown that experience
provides no instance of an abstract idea. Ideas of blue, red, and
green, we have in abundance; but the abstract idea of a color
that is neither blue, red, nor green, an idea of color that is no
color at all, simply does not exist. Similarly "matter" does not
exist; it is merely the sound of our voice, nothing more than an
empty word. But if the abstract idea of material substance is
nothing, it follows with the same necessity that experience can
give us no idea of spiritual substance. The one is as abstract as
the other. That is to say, a mind or soul does not exist. Experience gives us ideas only. There are reds, greens, bitters, sweets,

roughs, smooths; and their compounds, rivers, trees, and tables; but there is neither matter nor spirit, for perception can never furnish evidence for anything imperceptible. We ourselves are nothing but a collection of sensory perceptions.

Next, if it is obvious that perception can furnish no evidence of any imperceptible entity, it is only a little less obvious that perception can furnish no evidence for what is unperceived.

If I offer a perceived letter as evidence that my unperceived friend is in France, I am assuming that there is a necessary connection between the letter and my absent friend. Were there no necessary connection, had my friend not written the letter, were he not the cause and it the effect, then I could not know that he was in France. All questions of history therefore, in fact all alleged knowledge of facts beyond present sensation and the records of our own memory, depend on the principle of causality.

An examination of experience, however, shows that a knowledge of cause and effect is not to be had. We may have the sensation of red and a moment later a bitter taste; or the sensation of a loud noise may be followed by a sweet smell. Experience provides the succession of ideas; but we never see, smell, taste, or hear a necessary connection. There is no reason to believe that red causes a bitter taste or that a noise causes a smell. Quite the contrary, no one can imagine how or why a color might cause a taste. This remains true for compound ideas as well as for simple ideas. The combination of white, a cubical shape, and a crystalline structure that we call sugar may precede a sweet taste. But can anyone show a necessary connection between the first set of ideas, singly or together, and the sweet taste or the feeling of a full stomach after eating quite a bit of it? Experience accustoms us to expect certain sequences. They become so familiar we take them for granted. We call them causes and effects. But in it all we have no understanding of the sequence and no experience of any necessary connection. A knowledge of history is therefore impossible.

Now, finally, if it is impossible to know the imperceptible

[margin note: Exp. never provides us w/ a necessary connection.]

by perception, and if it is impossible to know the unperceived by perception, is it even possible to know what we now see? Granted that there is no evidence in experience of an unexperienced table whose size does not change, can we have even the image of a table, composed as it is of sensations of color, shape, and hardness?

Here is the difficulty. At any finite time, no matter how short, we experience a multitude of sensations. We see dozens of colors, we may hear two or three sounds, we could smell several odors, and even if we have no tastes at the moment, we always have a number of tactual sensations. From this manifold of sensations we select a few and combine them to make the image of a table. But why is it that we combine the color brown, a somewhat rectangular shape, and the sensation of hardness to make a table, instead of selecting from our many sensations the color pale green, the sound of C sharp, and the smell of freshly baked bread to combine them into the idea of a jobbleycluck?

Locke had tried to justify the connecting of certain ideas on the ground that they were qualities inhering in the same material substance. But as material substance does not exist (even if it did we could not know it until after we had combined simple ideas into things and then done some abstracting), this explanation is not available to empiricism. Berkeley and Hume give the impression that our selections for combinations depend on the fact that the ideas selected occur at the same place and time. Time, however, is unimportant, for at any time we are experiencing many ideas that we do not combine into a table. Then, must an empiricist say that the particular combination depends on the space in which the simple ideas are perceived?

Whether this answer is satisfactory or not depends on the empirical account of how we can recognize space.

Do we see space? Do we hear space? Do we smell space? Not only is this impossible, but even when we see a single object in space, we cannot see the distance between it and us. We judge distances by comparing known objects. Since we have previously seen and touched a particular table, and thus know its size at close range, we can judge how far away we are when it appears half its previous size. Or, we can judge that a house down the road is a mile away because on other occasions we have walked the distance. Space and distance therefore are matters of judgment and comparison, not of simple sensation.

But if space is learned by comparing houses and tables, we must first be able to perceive the table before we can compare it with a house and learn of space. That is to say, space is an idea of comparison. But if the idea of space cannot be had until after we have compared tables and houses, we cannot produce tables and houses by selecting simple ideas through the use of space.

Empiricism therefore has blundered fatally. It has surreptitiously inserted at the beginning of the learning process an idea of space which does not exist until after the process has been well nigh completed. Once again, then, the attempt to found knowledge on "reason" as distinct from revelation has failed. If this were the end of the story, the Christian could offer the world a choice between faith in revelation or an abysmal skepticism.

Immanuel Kant

Immanuel Kant, awakened, as he says, from his dogmatic slumbers by David Hume, promptly set about to remedy empiricism's defect. If all knowledge is based on experience alone, then there can be no knowledge of any necessary truth. At most, experience could reveal that such and such is so, but not that it must be so. For example, sensation might tell us that doors have two sides, but it cannot teach us that doors must have two sides. Doors might, somewhere, someday, have only one side. No experience can disprove this possibility. Similarly empiricism cannot substantiate universal propositions. We might possibly know that all the doors we have seen have two sides, but, without any reference to future inventions, even for the past we cannot know that all doors have had two sides. Or, again, everytime we have added two and two, the answer has been four;

but so far as experience goes, we cannot say that two and two are always four. Experience cannot tell us how much two and two are in those instances we have not experienced. Briefly, without necessity and universality, and these are inseparable, there can be neither mathematics nor physics.

By one stroke Kant is able to rehabilitate necessity and universality, and to account for the perception of individual objects like chairs and tables. The mind of man at birth is not just a sheet of blank paper, as Locke said it was. It possesses characteristics, forms, or notions in its own right. Space and time are two such forms. The knowledge of space and time does not depend on experience; rather, the reverse is true: experience depends on our knowledge of space and time. These two forms make the perception of things possible.

In colloquial discourse we speak of railroad tracks converging in the distance. They do not really converge. The railroad tracks themselves do not converge; but we see them converging. This perspective is our form of seeing. The tracks in themselves exist independently of our seeing them, but when they enter our vision they take the form of our perspective. Thus we make them converge by looking at them.

This illustration of tracks in perspective must be extended to cover all objects in space. The tracks stand for any object, such as a chair or a table; and the perspective of the illustration stands for the spatial characteristics of every visible object. Chairs and tables themselves, or generally things in themselves do not exist in space; it is we who see them that way. Therefore, just as we know ahead of time, before experience, or to use Kant's term, a priori, that all seen railroad tracks must converge, always have, and always will converge, so on a more profound level we know a priori that doors must have, always have had, and always will have two sides. That is to say, the doors of experience, doors as seen, must have two sides. But what doors in themselves are like, doors not appearing in our perception, doors not conformed to our mind's a priori form of space, we have not the least idea.

Knowledge, however, is not restricted to the bare perception of objects. In addition to sensation there is thought. Thought combines sensations into judgments. We may say, this door is thick, or, some cats are black, or, every change must have a cause. In such judgments many perceptions are summarized and joined together. Now, obviously, the things of experience do not do the joining themselves. Framing judgments is something that is done by thinking beings. Therefore the mind, far from being a passive recipient of knowledge, is an active manufacturer of knowledge; and as such it has definite methods of procedure. It joins or unifies experiences in a definite number of ways. These methods of unification are not learned from experience; on the contrary, they make experience possible. If we did not possess this equipment, we could no more begin to think than we could begin to see objects without the a priori form of space. Since therefore thinking or judging consists in arranging perceptions under concepts (this visible kitty belongs to the species cat, or to the class of black objects), it follows that meaningful experience is possible only on the basis of certain a priori concepts or categories.

The identification of the categories is accomplished by noting that the forms used in organizing experience are the forms of logic. Since all knowledge consists of judgments, the forms of knowledge are the forms of judgments, and the forms of judgment are the forms of logic. The categories therefore are the basic concepts without which we could not think at all. The categories are the ways in which the mind synthesizes the diversities of experience. The categories produce judgments. Since, on Kant's theory, there are twelve logical elements in the aggregate of judgments, there are twelve categories. The concepts of unity and plurality are categories. Without the concept of unity we could not think at all. A more complicated form of judgment is implication. We say, since this is true, that must be true; or we could say, that must be true because this is true. Note the *because*. Implication therefore depends on the category of causality. Causality therefore is a category, an a priori concept, a form of knowledge which, instead of being learned from experience, must be known prior to experience so as to make experience possible. Thus by making the knowledge of causality prior to experience, Kant believes he has escaped the skepticism of Hume. If he has really done so, then he has established knowledge without an appeal to revelation, and reason without faith would be successful.

However, it was no Christian trying to defend revelation that questioned Kant's success. Christians are sometimes accused of being biased and of forcing their arguments to foregone conclusions. Yet this is no more true of Christians than it was of Kant or of anyone else. Kant knew that he wanted to work out a theory of categories, and he made repeated attempts to deduce them before he hit upon his final formulation. The conclusion was decided upon before the argument was worked out. This is true of every philosopher, although Christians are more often castigated for it than are other writers. And those who do the castigating are more pointed examples than those they deride. But anyway, as a matter of history, the failure of Kant was not exposed by a Christian trying to defend revelation.

Certain basic defects in Kant's system are universally recognized. Kant had explained his categories as the mind's methods of unifying experience. Unity, plurality, causality and the others were forms by which experience could be put together. But if there were no sensory experience to put into these forms, the categories would remain empty and would not of themselves be knowledge. Furthermore, the categories have no further use whatever. They can be applied to experience but cannot be applied beyond experience. A concept without its sensory content is empty. Similarly empty is the a priori notion of space. Unless sensations appear in space, we can have no contact with reality. Knowledge requires the combination of a priori forms and a posteriori experience. Either one without the other is not knowledge.

This construction makes Kant's problem an impossible one. He sought the pre-conditions of experience while denying that these conditions are objects of experience. If our knowledge is always a combination of form and content, we cannot know the form without the content. Yet Kant professed to have deduced the categories.

This criticism can be expressed in other and perhaps clearer terms. Kant had in effect argued that before we attempt to study physics and theology, we must determine whether or not the mind is capable of investigating physical things and God. But if this is so, can it not be maintained with equal plausibility that before we attempt to study the limitations of the mind, we must determine whether or not the mind is capable of investigating its limitations. Therefore Kant's *Critique of Pure Reason* should have been preceded by a Critique of the Critique of Pure Reason, and so on backward for quite a while.

Another standard objection to Kant, though perhaps it is simply the same objection again in a different form, has to do with things-in-themselves. On Kant's theory things-in-themselves must stand behind things-as-they-appear-to-us. It is assumed, to make use of the previous illustration, that behind the converging railroad tracks, there are real tracks that do not converge. These non-converging real tracks are presumably the cause of the tracks that appear and converge. The convergence occurs only in experience; the non-convergence does not occur in experience. But, very unfortunately for Kant, categories cannot be used outside experience. Causality is a relationship existing only between two objects of experience. The category of causality cannot be appplied to non-converging tracks. Or to repeat the clever remark of F. H. Jacobi, "Without the thing-in-itself one cannot get into Kant's system, and with it one cannot stay in."

These objections to Kant do not depend on the fact that he failed to establish a theology. God cannot be the cause of the world because God is not an object of sensation; and causes must be confined within sensory experience. But this failure to arrive at a theology would not destroy Kant's philosophy. The objections depend on the fact that Kant has failed to find a basis for physics. He has failed to explain sensation. He has failed to give an intelligible account of the relation of form to content. He has failed to make knowledge possible. Therefore the question still remains whether knowledge can be achieved apart from revelation.

Hegel and His Critics

There is one more, one magnificent, let us say, one final attempt in secular philosophy to establish the claims of Reason spelled with a capital R. Though the seventeenth century exhibited a rationalism in a very definite sense of that term, no one is more of a rationalist, no one exalts the powers of reason, more than G. W. F. Hegel.

To show therefore that the attempt, begun by the Renaissance, to establish the possibility of knowledge apart from divine revelation is a failure, it will be necessary, in the last place, to indicate the flaw in Hegel's system. This is not easy. An exposition of Hegelianism would become intolerably technical; and yet without it the locus of Hegel's inadequacy could not be intelligibly indicated. To be sure, it is all but universally admitted that Hegelianism cannot be successfully defended; and perhaps it would be the part of wisdom, as it will be to a large measure the part of necessity, to rely on this consensus and proceed. Nevertheless something of the line of argument ought to be given.

Kant, as has been shown, compounded knowledge of form and content. The form is the contribution of the mind, while the content comes from an independent, external thing-in-itself. Yet, since the categories do not apply beyond sensation, the thing-in-itself remains unknowable; but if unknowable, its existence and necessity could not be asserted. Hegel makes quite a point of the absurdity of asserting an unknowable; then he tries to remove the opposition between consciousness and its object by showing that on a higher level they are both within consciousness itself. Nature, the given, the contributions of sense, are one with mind or spirit. There is no ultimate disparity. This unity, however, must be shown in detail. Hegel refuses to rely on any mystic experience or ecstatic trance to gain the One; on the contrary he proposes a new logic by whose dialectical procedure the required unity can be developed step by step.

*Aristotelian logic in its insistence on clear cut distinctions is good so far as it goes. A cat is not a dog, and a sense object is not the self: they should not be confused. Unless thought marks one thing off against another, there can be no thought. But thought not only distinguishes one thing from another, it also relates and conjoins them. Both dog and cat are species of mammals; and the recognition of one species makes use of the contrast with the other. Without such relations it would be impossible to think; just as impossible as it would be to think without distinctions. Every object must be differentiated from every other object, but no object can be so totally differentiated as to exclude the identity that transcends the difference. The differences are expressions of unity.

Every definite thought excludes other thoughts, excludes especially its opposite thought; yet every thought has a necessary relation to its opposite or negative. It cannot be detached from its negative without losing its own meaning. Its negative is a part of its meaning, and is therefore included within it. To see that each opposite includes the other is to see that both are included in a higher unity. This is true not only of cat and dog, but also of consciousness and thing.[4]

For all of Kant's efforts, his theory of the self is not too great an improvement over Hume's. Self-consciousness, he said, was not a concept but a consciousness that accompanies all concepts. The ego remains unknown in itself and is known only through the thoughts that are its predicates. But this is as much as to say, concludes Hegel, that we cannot see the sun because we cannot throw the rays of a candle upon it. Kant has declared intelligence itself to be unintelligible! He did so because he

*The next few paragraphs follow *Hegel*, by Edward Caird, pp. 134ff.

presupposed that only abstract identity, without difference, is entirely intelligible.

The old logic assumed that each object is an isolated identity, a pure this and not that. Relations were regarded as external, as outside of the real nature of things. On the contrary, it is essential that a dog be not-a-cat. The meaning of every object is implicated in the meaning of every other. Nothing is isolated or purely one. In particular the isolationist procedure stumbles at self-consciousness because in it true unity is essentially complex. Mind and object, subject and substance, and the particular selves form a unity. Nothing is outside or independent. Nature and man are identical. Yet this identity is not abstract or empty. All the differences are preserved. Unity and plurality are so blended that neither has meaning without the other.

In Descartes and surely in Locke thinking was regarded as the activity of an individual person. But if thinking is essentially and exclusively an individual capacity, it seems impossible to avoid solipsism. There is no escape from one's own mind. And in any case, whether there are many minds or my own only, the objects of experience miraculously become real time and time again in separate, casual acts of perception. Kant thought he had avoided solipsism, but he failed to give a satisfactory account of how one object could appear to many persons. Undoubtedly he intended the categories to be the same in all minds and to apply to a common world of objects. But no purely individual experience could reveal a world common to other centers of experience. Therefore, concludes Hegel, there must be a universal mind in which all persons and objects participate.

To apply these principles in detail, to show precisely the unified differences of the Absolute Mind, Hegel works out a system of categories. Instead of Kant's twelve, Hegel has a hundred or more. These categories are the concepts that apply to and constitute everything. The first, the simplest, the most abstract, the emptiest is pure Being. Every object is a being. Being contains everything—implicitly. The implicit must now be made explicit by a dialectical process. Since everything is determined by its opposite, Being cannot be thought apart from non-being. When we have said of an object that it is a being, the very universality and emptiness of Being has left us saying nothing. We have not said it is green or heavy; we have not determined it in any way. Being therefore is the equivalent of Nothing. But since by this dialectical process of thought, Being has become Nothing, the category of Becoming has emerged. Becoming is the synthesis of Being and Nothing. For a thing both is and is not, when it is becoming.

By such a dialectical procedure Hegel deduced a long list of categories. The final category contained explicitly all that the first contained implicitly.

Undoubtedly Hegel was a genius, and in spite of his frequently cumberous jargon there is a great deal of worth-while profundity in his *Phenomenology* and *Logic*. In particular he often puts his finger on the sorest spots of previous systems, so that it may well be said that to understand Kant, Descartes, or the ancient Stoics, one must first read Hegel. The accidents of Prussian politics, to which someone might want to credit his immediate popularity in Germany, cannot explain his long ascendency in Great Britain nor his vogue in the United States. Nevertheless, since World War I, Hegelianism has become all but extinct; and in Germany it began to suffer eclipse even in the middle of the nineteenth century. This reversal must be taken as evidence of some philosophic flaw or flaws in Hegel's construction, and where the trouble lies must be discovered.

One particular point of criticism was early singled out by Hegel's immediate followers. If the universe is this system of categories, they argued, if the real is the rational and the rational is the real, then clearly all reality can be dialectically deduced and every item must find its clear place in the system. Hegel had made a point of preserving differences; he did not favor empty abstractions nor the night of mysticism in which all cows are black. To make good his claims therefore, Hegel ought to deduce some one individual cow, that very real black and white Holstein in the pasture over yonder.

But this is precisely what Hegel did not and could not do. As Plato never satisfactorily connected his Ideas with individual sense objects, so too, and even all the more so, Hegel could not rationally deduce an individual object from the Absolute. To be sure, Hegel was not unaware of this criticism. When faced with it, he replied that he had dissolved the individual, the this, the here and now, and the individual ego as well, in the very first chapter of his *Phenomenology,* but whatever reality they have, he had preserved in the dialectical process. This is of course in keeping with the denial of an unknowable *Ding-an-sich* and the removal of that sharp separation between the mental form and the sensory given which plagued the post-Kantians.

Now, it seems impossible to defend the *Ding-an-sich;* but it also seems that Hegel's claim to preserve the differences in his dialectical ascent cannot be substantiated. With respect to zoology Hegel admits with commendable candor that the deduction not only fails to reach the individuals but even fails to reach some sub-species. The concept *animal* might perhaps be deduced, and even the species *cow;* but not Holstein-Friesian, let alone Pieterje van Rijn III.

Hegel's candor removes the sting of the criticism, but it cannot be maintained that his natural willingness to give himself the benefit of the doubt has diminished its force. One wonders whether the species *cow* or even the concept *animal* can be deduced. And so far as physics is concerned, it is clear that no deduction of determinate being, quality, or quantity can give us knowledge of the quality of sulphuric acid or the atomic weight of gold. Can it not therefore be concluded that Hegel failed to find the concrete universal he sought and has offered us only empty abstractions?

Absolute Ignorance

There is a second criticism, and on these two the present refutation of Hegelianism must depend. It was seen above that for Hegel the truth is the whole, every determination is a negation, and an object's relationships are logically internal to its meaning. A cat is not a dog; it is a part of the essence of a cat to be not-a-dog. But to be not-a-dog is to be related to dog; and this relation is internal to the meaning of cat. Thus cat and dog, sense object and self, are included in a larger whole. The All-Inclusive is the Absolute.

That relations are internal and especially that the truth is the whole are themes hard to deny. Yet their implications are devastating. So long as you or I do not know the relationships which constitute the meaning of cat or self, we do not know the object in question. If we say that we know some of the relationships, e.g., a cat is not-a-dog, and admit that we do not know other relationships, e.g., a cat is not-an-(animal we have never heard of before), it follows that we cannot know how this unknown relationship may alter our view of the relationship we now say we know. The alteration could be considerable. Therefore we cannot know even one relationship without knowing all. Obviously we do not know all. Therefore we know nothing.

This criticism is exceedingly disconcerting to an Hegelian, for its principle applies not merely to cats, dogs, and selves, but to the Absolute itself. The truth is the whole and the whole is the Absolute. But obviously we do not know the whole; we do not know the Absolute. In fact, not knowing the Absolute, we cannot know even that there is an Absolute. But how can absolute idealism be based on absolute ignorance? And ours is absolute ignorance, for we cannot know one thing without knowing all.

The rationalism of the seventeenth century, British empiricism, the critical philosophy of Kant, and now Hegelianism have all tried and have all failed to justify knowledge. Reason apart from revelation has come to grief. The only remaining possibility of escaping revelation now is to abandon reason. It is a bitter pill for man to swallow, but some men would rather wallow in abysmal ignorance than accept information by the grace of God.

FAITH WITHOUT REASON

Throughout the history of the Christian church there have appeared from time to time individuals and groups who look with disfavor on reason, intellect, and higher learning. From the Patristic period Tertullian is often quoted as saying, "I believe because it is absurd." Although this is not precisely what Tertullian said, his opposition to pagan culture is well known. What has the Christian in common with the philosopher, he declaims; the Church with the Academy; revelation with reason? Yet, because he did some philosophizing himself, perhaps he should be understood as deprecating, not reason in general, but pagan reason only. Nonetheless there remains a suspicion that his is a faith without reason.

Types of Mysticism

There are other cases also where, although the phrase cannot be applied with complete literalistic vigor, there is a suspicion and more than a suspicion that faith without reason is the ideal. The mystics form a particularly noteworthy group.

Dionysius the Areopagite was a Christian Neoplatonist of the fifth century. A few words of his will show, not that he utterly despised reason, but that at least he placed a realm above reason. It is a realm in which the categories of thought and of language are so strained that intelligible meaning seems to have escaped. For example,

"Triad supernal, both super-God and super-good, Guardian of the theosophy of Christian men, direct us aright to the super-unknown and super-brilliant and highest summit of the mystic oracles, where the simple and absolute and changeless mysteries of theology lie hidden within the super-luminous gloom of the silence, revealing hidden things, which in its deepest darkness shines above the most super-brilliant, and in the altogether impalpable and invisible fills to overflowing the eyeless mind with glories of surpassing beauty" (*Mystic Theology* 1:1) .

Neoplatonic mysticism, from which this Dionysius took his inspiration, told of trances in which one's personality merged into the perfect simplicity of an original One. In this One the simplicity is so perfect that there is not even the dualism of subject and predicate. Therefore in this realm knowledge is impossible, for all knowledge consists in the attribution of predicates to subjects: the cat is black, the number four is even, or William was a conqueror. But in the trance or absorption there is not even an I and thou. There is only the pure simplicity of the One. For this reason, not only is there no knowledge during the trance, but even upon recovery a man can say nothing true about it because he would have to use the duality of sentences to speak or to know.

Although this characterization is taken from Plotinus and pagan mysticism, it applies to the Christian mystics as well. Bernard of Clairvaux, the devout opponent of proud Abelard's dialectical skill, speaks of becoming penetrated with God as air is penetrated with light. Meister Eckhart and Nicholas of Cusa use many expressions that parallel those of Plotinus. It is a matter of common agreement that the mystic consciousness is not clearly differentiated into subject and object. The experience is not sharply focused, if focused at all. Subject and object, I and thou, are fused or confused in an undifferentiated one. With enthusiasm, but in unintelligible phraseology, the mystic speaks of being flooded with an inrush from the abysses of inner life; or he says that transcendental energies invade the soul, and the whole being in an integral and undivided experience finds itself.

There are gradations of mystical opinion. The Neoplatonic type, whether in Plotinus or in Nicholas, did not forego the rigorous use of reason in ordinary philosophical and ecclesiastical problems. But they agree that the soul's union with Absolute Reality is not intellectual. God can be known only negatively. No finite qualities, that is, no definite qualities, can be ascribed to him. He is not good, not just, not wise, not anything. We unite with him, we merge ourselves in him, in wordless communion, in a consciousness that transcends ideas.

Other mystics, or, if the term mystic is not applicable here, others who speak of a faith without reason, diverge from the Neoplatonic standard in two ways. They have no liking for philosophy nor do they rest upon wordless trances. This negative description, admittedly broad, includes groups otherwise quite dissimilar. It includes not only the anarchical prophets of Zwickau, who did not need to study Greek or Hebrew because God would speak to any excited peasant, but also the later devout, sober, and earnest pietists. And who can be too hard on the pietists? Living a moral, godly life, they see the cold formalism of the educated classes and repudiate systematic theology in favor of a simple and warm-hearted devotion.

In the twentieth century the fundamentalists, in varying degrees, advocate a faith without reason. Although they stress Bible study more than the pietists and the anarchical prophets did, they frequently inveigh against philosophy and "mere" human reason. Even in doctrine they do not ordinarily go beyond a half a dozen fundamental beliefs. Anything further is dry-as-dust theology.

If it is inaccurate to categorize the positions of these groups as that of faith without reason, it is because the disparagement of the intellect always involves a certain amount of inconsistency. It takes a little intellectual argument to justify the disparagement. And particularly in the case of the fundamentalists with their zealous defense of a few doctrines reason cannot be wholly abandoned. Some use and acknowledge more, some less. Such variation and inconsistency make it difficult accurately to classify all these groups under one heading. Nevertheless, the mystics, at least in what they consider most important, the pietists and fundamentalists, and still more another viewpoint to be mentioned in a moment have the common tendency of a faith without reason.

This other viewpoint, so popular and powerful at the present time, is often called by the name of Neo-orthodoxy. It is even more anti-rational or anti-intellectual than either pietism or fundamentalism. Its background and motivation are also different. Instead of being a dilution of original Protestantism as fundamentalism is, Neo-orthodoxy descends from post-hegelian philosophy. To understand it therefore, and to see where anti-intellectualism may lead one, it will be necessary briefly to trace certain strands of nineteenth century thought, even though it is not all distinctly religious.

In the previous chapter the Renaissance attempt to justify knowledge without appeal to revelation has been quickly surveyed. The rationalism of Descartes and Spinoza, British Empiricism, Kant and Hegel have been adjudged failures. Though their brilliance evokes our admiration, their results cannot be accepted. The judgment that Hegel failed is not a biased judgment of a Christian whose ulterior motive is to defend revelation; it is also the judgment of those who were more eager to destroy Christianity than Hegel was.

The contemporary rejection of Hegelianism was begun by two of Hegel's students, Karl Marx and Soren Kierkegaard. As Marx had the greater immediate success and because he was less radical than Kierkegaard, Marx will be briefly discussed first.

To a certain extent Marx profited from the work of a lesser contemporary, Ludwig Feuerbach (1804-1872). In opposition to Hegel's idealism, Feuerbach held that reality consists of individual material things. As a student he had noted the epistemological difficulties of materialistic behaviorism, but now he decided to ignore them. Sensation and sensation alone can disclose real existence to us. The deduction of existence from essence is a dream, and therefore Hegel's operation with concepts lost contact with reality. In particular, Hegel's philosophy lost contact with individual human beings. Men were considered as essentially intellectual and cognitive, whereas a man, that is, a human body, is fundamentally emotional and is determined not by idealistic fancies but by what he eats. *Der Mensch ist was er isst.*

Marx continues this materialistic behaviorism. Thought is a product of the brain. And because the universe is physical, all is in constant flux—nothing is fixed. It is thus that Marx transforms Hegel's dialectic of concepts into the physical process of dialectical materialism. Indeed, the great merit of Hegel, in contrast with Spinoza for example, was to acknowledge flux and process; while at the same time the great self-contradiction of Hegel was to end this process in a fixed Absolute.

With the economic and political aspects of Marx's philosophy the present discussion can have nothing to do. The one point to be emphasized is Marx's abandonment of intellectualism. Epistemology, mathematics, and ethics are cases in point. Like Feuerbach he virtually ignores epistemology. At best, he disposes of solipsism on the basis that it is a mockery of the efforts of the working class to liberate itself. The philosophical problems relative to the foundations of mathematics are pushed back into the obscurity of an unknown evolutionary past. In ethics Marx espouses a relativistic theory. Rights become class demands that are to be enforced rather than proved by rational argument. The claim of one class must give way to another; only force decides which; and success is the test of truth.

To be sure, in speaking of the physical constitution of nature, in spite of his insistence on universal flux, Marx seems to admit the fixed truth of materialism. It is not necessary for the present purpose to contend that Marx was free from such self-contradictions. The point of this brief account is that modern philosophy's reliance on human reason is called into question. This is one of the first two attacks on intellectualism. The second is far more radical and thorough-going.

Soren Kierkegaard

Soren Kierkegaard (1813-1855), although he would not be classed with Karl Marx by the superficial reader, is nonetheless in certain basic respects a typical representative of the mid-nineteenth century. In his revolt against the systematic rationalism of Hegel, in his attack on official Christianity, and in the anti-intellectualism that permeated the Romantic movement, this melancholy Dane expressed the widely held opinion that there was something rotten in the state of Denmark, i.e., Europe or Christendom. He also largely agreed with Feuerbach and Marx as to the symptoms of rottenness; but with respect to the cause and the cure he diverges from them radically.

Marx had diagnosed the sickness of society as an economic malady; but, asserts Kierkegaard, the social reform which the time demands is the opposite of what it needs. The malady is not economic; it is spiritual and religious. The Spirit of the age has been substituted for the Holy Spirit, man has taken the place of God, and time has swallowed up eternity. If Marx, in his erroneous diagnosis, had criticized Hegel for being too Christian and too abstract, Kierkegaard attacks them both: Hegel for not being Christian enough and Marx (or at least socialism, for it is not clear how definitely S. K. had Marx in mind) for being too Hegelian. Their common flaw, for after all Hegel was a socialist in fact if not in name, was their disregard for the individual. Any object, for instance a pen, is enough to confront abstract thinking with the problem of individual existence; but individual persons are more important than pens. Persons are important: in particular, I am extremely important to me; and my problem, i.e., the problem of the person in his individuality, is basically religious. Now, Hegel had lost the person, not merely the pen, in the universality of the world process, for systematic rationalism cannot give an account of real individual existence.

It is not true that the real is the rational. Reality, asserts Kierkegaard, cannot be grasped by reason. In spite of the argument in the *Phenomenology*, the immediate, the now, the this, and especially the mine cannot be "aufgehoben" or suppressed. Hegel tried to explain the world by the movement of the idea; but there is no motion in logic, nor is there logic in motion. Motion is illogical; becoming is open, not closed; reality is chance, and chance cannot be put into logic. By his identification of essence and existence Hegel got conceptual existence only, while real existence eluded him. His inability to see the difference between thought and being was a result of his thinking as a professional thinker rather than as a man. Perhaps for philosophy existence and non-existence are of equal worth. The System (and the proletariat as well) is not concerned with a single person. But for the existing individual, e.g., for me, I and my existence are of greatest value. Contrary to all abstractionism, whether of Plato, for he was a communist too, or of Hegel, or of Marx, the *what* is unimportant and the *that* is essential. Therefore the duty of man is not exemplified in the studious activity of Professor Hegel. Reality cannot be taught or communicated rationally and academically. It must be grasped personally, passionately, anti-intellectually. It is not conclusions that are needed, but decisions.

This same criticism applies to Marx and Feuerbach also. They are scarcely less abstract than Hegel. In Humanity as well as in the Absolute Spirit the individual cannot be found. Mass movements of faceless men undoubtedly have the strength of numbers, but such leveling and amalgamation weakens the individual ethically. The mass man has lost responsibility and the power of making decisions. To face the confusion of the times and to stand before eternity requires, not human similarity, but Christian individuality. In nature the individual is merely an instance of the species; anyone who improves a breed of sheep changes every individual. But religion is not a matter of the species, and it is foolish to suppose that Christian parents automatically produce Christian children. Spiritual development is radically individual; and the cure for society is the cure of individuals. Because society is afraid of individualists, this cure will not be easy. There will be bloodshed: not the bloodshed of communistic revolution and battle, but the bloodshed of individual martyrs.

Anyone but an Hegelian or a socialist must feel a measure of sympathy for this rugged individualism; and they can applaud the sarcasm that S.K. directed against an empty and insincere religious formalism. But when one turns from the negative to the positive, from the destructive to the constructive, can one seriously conclude or decide that Kierkegaard's statements are true?

For Kierkegaard God is truth; but truth exists only for a believer who inwardly experiences the tension between himself and God. If an actually existing person is an unbeliever, then for him God does not exist. God exists only in subjectivity. This emphasis on subjectivity and the corresponding disparagement of objectivity result in the destruction of Christianity's objective historicity. The historical is not religious and the religious is not historical. If Christ were an historical figure who lived a long time ago, he would have no religious significance now. Conversely, if Christ is a religious figure, the historical interval must be cancelled by an inner contemporaneity. Real religion does not consist in understanding anything. It is a matter of feeling, of anti-intellectual passionateness. The acceptance of any objective historical truth depends on historical methods; and the objective student of history is too modest to put his own feelings into his conclusions. Speculative thinkers are not personally interested in suffering; they do not study the subjective truth of appropriation.

But Christianity has always been regarded as an historical religion, not merely in the sense that it has had a history of nineteen hundred years, but specifically in the sense that it is based on historical events that happened that long ago. For Hegel these events and their significance were integral parts of universal history regarded as the developing expression of the Absolute Spirit. But for Kierkegaard the relation between the process of history and eternal truth is a paradox. In the language of Kierkegaard and his twentieth century followers the term paradox indicates something more embarrassing than those queer puzzles which after some difficulty can be solved and understood intellectually. An elementary student of physics is puzzled when he is told that the water pressure at the bottom of one container is twice that of another even though the former container has but half the weight of water. This is a paradox. It is solved by learning the relation of height to pressure. But an existentialist paradox is insoluble. It is a contradiction to suppose that eternal blessedness can be based on historical information. Therefore the subjectivity of appropriation is not continuous with, but stands in opposition to, an historical dissemination of Christian teaching. Passionate appropriation, the moment of decision, does away with the interval of history and makes one inwardly contemporaneous with Christ. The method is not intellectual; it is an experience of suffering and despair. The detached objective truth of Christianity is not to be had. Beginning with the preaching of the Apostles, all the centuries of history are worthless as a proof of it. The objective truth of Christianity is equivalent to its subjective indifference, its indifference to the subject, i.e., to me.

This type of thought provokes an obvious question. If there is no objective truth, if the How supersedes the What, then can truth be distinguished from fancy? Would not a suffering Satan be just as true as a suffering Savior? Would not an inner, infinite, decisive appropriation of the devil be as praiseworthy as a decision for God? The philosophy of William James will later raise the same question though James does not seem to be aware of the question; S.K. notices the dilemma, but can hardly be said to solve it. There is a half-hearted effort to distinguish between the inwardness of infinity and the inwardness of the finite; and he seems to say that the infinity of Christian inwardness is based on God, whereas the inwardness of finitude relates to some other object. Now, if there were objective knowledge of God and of other objects, an individual could judge the quality of his passion on the basis of its objective reference; but if God and perchance the devil also are hidden, and if one is limited to a subjective, passionate appropriation, there would seem to be no distinguishable difference between the truth of God and the truth of Satan. Objectively it is indifferent whether one worships God or an idol. Whether God exists or not is immaterial. What counts is the individual's relation to an unknown Something.

In his vivid style Kierkegaard describes two men in prayer. The one is in a Lutheran church and he entertains a true conception of God; but because he prays in a false spirit, he is in truth praying to an idol. The other is actually in a heathen temple praying to idols; but since he prays with an infinite passion, he is in truth praying to God. For the truth lies in the inward How, not in the external What. Or, again, Kierkegaard says,

"An objective uncertainty held fast in an appropriation process of the most passionate inwardness is the truth, the highest truth attainable for an existing individual."

Finally, another statement, also found in his *Concluding Unscientific Postscript,* a statement just as definite as the preceding, expresses Kierkegaard's subjectivity. After remarking that a search for objective truth takes no account of the relation of the individual to that truth, S.K. continues,

"If one asks subjectively about the truth, one is reflecting subjectively about the relation of the individual; if only the How of this relation is in truth, then the individual is in truth, even though he is thus related to untruth."

Suppose now that there are serious flaws in Hegel's "System"; suppose too that the communistic mass man violates the prerogatives of the moral individual; suppose in the third place that the Danish Lutheran church was formal, hypocritical, and dead; suppose therefore that S.K. has made some telling criticisms of his contemporaries. Does this then imply that the cure can be effected by a suffering or passion, a subjective feeling, to which objective truth and untruth are equally indifferent? If this were true, not only would an idol be as satisfactory as God, but Hegel or Marx would be as satisfactory as Kierkegaard.

Through the nineteenth century and down to World War I, S.K. remained unknown. The revolt against reason, however, continued. Though much must be omitted, the advance made by Friedrich Nietzsche is particularly worthy of mention.

Nietzsche

Friedrich Nietzsche (1844-1900), so far as German philosophy is concerned, was the culmination of the nineteenth century. Its second half had brought great advances in science. Physicists considered that they had completely demonstrated the truth of mechanism. Fechner, although he attempted to found an empirical psychology, rejected mechanism under the inspiration of grand romantic ideas and peopled his universe with souls, angels, and gods. Lotze made the intellect, not an instrument for representing things, but for transforming them. Being is in flux, and reality is richer than thought. Wundt abandoned monism and pictured the universe as a plurality of wills. And Darwin, though not a German, revolutionized, not only biology, but all phases of philosophic thought. From these sources Nietzsche took what appealed to him and completed the nineteenth century's atheistic, materialistic, anti-hegelian world-view.

Nietzsche's theory of evolution, his Superman, his eternal recurrence, his transvaluation of all values, must be omitted. Attention is restricted to his opinions on the powers of reason. In Nietzsche's view there is no such thing as mind; the proper starting place is the body as it has evolved. What Descartes and Kant mistook for an ego, instead of being a simple subject, is a multiplicity of conflicting desires or urges. Therefore the notion that the world proceeds so that human reason must be true is down-right simple-minded. Everything that reaches our consciousness is simplified, adjusted, and interpreted. We never find a fact in nature; we never grasp things as they are. The whole apparatus of knowing is a simplifying device, directed not at truth but at the appropriation and utilization of our world. Philosophers have believed that in the forms of reason a criterion of reality had been found; whereas the only purpose of these forms is to master reality by misunderstanding it intelligently. This means that the will to logical truth presupposes a fundamental falsification of all phenomena. What we now call truth therefore is that kind of error without which a species cannot live. The object of mental activity is not to know, in any scholastic sense, but to schematize and to impose as much regularity on chaos as practical needs require. After all, why should we be so greatly interested in truth? Falsity is no objection against an opinion; the important question is, Does this opinion sustain life? Indeed, to understand how the abstrusest metaphysical assertions of a philosopher have been arrived at, it is always well and wise to first ask oneself, What morality does he aim at? Behind all logic there are physiological demands for a mode of life.

Logic depends on the law of contradiction, but instead of this law's being necessary it is only a sign of inability—our inability to affirm and deny one and the same thing. We cannot talk without using it. But for this very reason it should be examined the more carefully. The law of contradiction claims to be ontological as well as logical. It assumes something about Being. But to suppose that logic is adequate to reality requires a knowledge of reality prior to and independent of the law. Obviously then the law of contradiction holds good only of assumed existences that we have created.

These ways of thinking have been bred in us through the long evolutionary process, and they are now so ingrained that no amount of experience can change them. They are indeed a priori for the individual, but for the human race they are evolutionary end-products. Belief in causality and contradiction may be and is useful; but this does not make them true. In fact, they must be false, for knowledge and evolution are mutually exclusive. The character of the world in process of becoming is not susceptible of intellectual formulation. Parmenides said, One can form no concept of the non-existent; we are now at the other extreme and say, That of which a concept can be formed is certainly fictional.

William James

After Nietzsche the American school of pragmatism continued the attack on reason. William James, inspired by French as well as by these German developments, made a vigorous onslaught on Hegelian absolutism and fixed truth. As before, only

the barest essentials and most pertinent points can be crowded
into this short account.

Over the domain of theism and absolutism, writes James,
"you will find the trail of the serpent of rationalism, of intellectualism " (*Pragmatism, p.* 19). Intellectualism is a serpent because its transcendental principles are useless. "You can deduce
no single actual particular from the Absolute . . . And the theistic God is almost as sterile .ˑ. . Theism is more insipid, but
both are equally remote and vacuous." James also repeats the accusation that Hegel confuses conceptual flux with physical flux,
for which reason the conceptual treatment of the flow of reality
is inadequate. Inadequate, that is, to the reality itself. Knowledge must come through experience: not experience consisting
of discrete, atomic simple ideas, but experience as an ever flow-
ing stream of consciousness. There are no discrete data; nothing is separate or distinct; things are constantly merging into
each other; there are no distinctions such as matter and form,
substance and relation. To be sure, concepts have a practical
value; we select portions of experience and arbitrarily set them
off; this process serves our purposes well, but such concepts are
far from satisfying the demands of rationalistic speculation; they
are purely practical. Our fundamental ways of thinking, the
categories and the law of contradiction, are discoveries of exceedingly remote ancestors. Lobsters and bees no doubt have
other modes of apprehending experience. Children and dogs do
not use our adult categories; their experience is virtually chaotic. Space and time are not Kantian intuitions but patently
artificial constructions, for the majority of the human race uses
several times and several spaces. Although our categories are
very useful, we cannot dogmatically deny that other categories,
unimaginable by us today, might have proved just as serviceable
as those we now use.

If this is the case and if we may apply James' principles to a
selected example, the syllogism called *Barbara* might have
evolved as a fallacy. All Athenians are Greeks and all Greeks
are human beings might have implied that some Athenians

are non-human. Similarly, asserting the consequent could have formed a valid argument, and we would have reasoned: all numbers ending in zero are divisible by five, therefore twenty-five, since it is divisible by five, must end in zero.

William James cannot dismiss these examples on the ground that they are illogical, for, according to him, the present forms of logic are not fool-proof. Logic is too pat. It cannot grasp reality. So great is its failure that when the rationalists came to recognize that the real world escapes their neat formulas, they invented unreal worlds from which these stubborn facts were barred. Kant's rational will emigrated to the world of noumena; Bradley escaped all contradictions somehow in the Absolute; and Green relied on a transcendent Mind. But this is only to say that human concepts falsify reality.

Unlike Nietzsche, however, James utilizes his irrationalism to support a certain type of religion and ethics. Some notice of this must be taken, both for its own importance as well as in preparation for what follows.

Absolutism and Pragmatism, says James, signify two different religious attitudes. One man insists that the world must be and shall be saved; the other believes that it may be. There is also another view; namely, the world cannot be saved. Pragmatism therefore is an attitude midway between pessimism and optimism; it may be called meliorism. The world may become better because we can make it better.

James then offers this choice. Suppose the world's author came to you before creation and said, I am going to make a world not certain of being saved; it can be saved only if every agent does his level best; [if any eases up on the job, the result will be unfortunate;] now, then, do you want the chance of taking part in this world, with its real dangers, with no guarantee of safety, or would you prefer to relapse into the slumber of nonentity from which I have just aroused you?

Note that God or James does not offer us a choice between this dangerous world and one in which the good is absolutely guaranteed. Absolutism seems here to have been forgotten. The choice is between danger and Nirvana. And James is ready to make the choice for us. Any "normally constituted" person with his "healthy-minded buoyancy" would find such a universe exactly to his liking. Only a few "morbid minds," "Buddhists" who are "afraid of life," would refuse the opportunity. These latter may be religious in a sense, but they are not moral. "In the end it is our faith and not our logic that decides such questions." It is a faith in our fellow men, that they will all do their level best. It is also a faith in superhuman forces, for there is a God, not an Almighty God who controls the outcome, but a limited and finite god who helps along; in fact he is such a help that the danger is considerably reduced. Belief in this type of a god is true because it works. Of course we do not know certainly that this god exists, "for we do not yet know certainly which type of religion is going to work best in the long run." It is a matter for personal decision. "If radically tough, the hurly-burly of the sensible facts of nature will be enough for you, and you will need no religion at all . . . But if you are neither tough nor tender . . . the type of pluralistic and moralistic religion that I have offered you is as good a religious synthesis as you are likely to find."

In the section on Soren Kierkegaard the question of personal decision was also acute—a decision apart from any objective knowledge. Kierkegaard personally made a choice that is not too different from James'; although S.K.'s Christianity is not what James would have preferred, still both of them, along with Nietzsche, say Yes to the universe. But when James calls his choice moral and other choices morbid, he seems to imply that it is more than a personal choice. How can James distinguish between a moral and an immoral choice? If he says that truth is that which works, and that which works is that which gives personal satisfaction, then the man who chooses Nirvana to danger seems to have achieved more satisfaction than a Pragmatist is likely to. Is it likely that all men will do their level best? Faith in mankind is an inspiring slogan, but the tough facts suggest that one or two men in history have not worked full time to make the world better. Assuredly James is consistent in choosing danger for himself, since his theory depends on his personal decision; but precisely for this irrational reason he cannot conclude that anyone else ought to make the same choice.

Unfortunately this intellectualistic objection is based on the law of contradiction. It assumes that a principle of philosophy should apply consistently to all men. If success in satisfying personal preference justifies the choice of one man, success in satisfying a different preference should equally justify the opposite choice of another man. But it is consistency and logic that James disallows.

Although Nietzsche and James stand outside the Christian tradition and are thus examples of the collapse of human reason apart from knowledge given by divine revelation, it was seen in the case of Kierkegaard that even the religious thinking of the post-hegelian era had turned toward irrationalism. Therefore to conclude the analysis of faith without reason, mention must be made of Kierkegaard's influence on the twentieth century, and for this purpose the thought of Emil Brunner shall be made to serve.

Emil Brunner

It is impossible and fortunately unnecessary to summarize all of Brunner's publications for our purposes. But even with the restriction of subject matter to irrationalism, one must break in to the middle of things somewhat arbitrarily. An interesting discussion of error is a good beginning.

Unlike those philosophers who stand so definitely outside the Christian tradition, Brunner, in common with the main neo-orthodox position, recognizes that sin is a pervasive power in human life. Sin not only breaks out in gross crime, but it affects our inner thinking as well. Since sin alienates man from God, the mental effects of sin are seen more clearly and more frequently when we try to think about God than when we think about mathematics or physics. Not only does Brunner say that error due to sin is more obvious in theology than in physics;

but he adds that mathematics and logic are so far removed from the religious center of life that in them there is no error at all.

This observation, which at first sight may seem so plausible, is in fact a confusion between the objective and the subjective. In it, Brunner, following S.K.'s emphasis on subjectivity, seems to have denied the distinction between the knowing person and the truth known. It is a confusion between the how and the what.

Let us more carefully examine the nature of error in mathematics and theology. Subjectively the noetic deterioration caused by sin produces mistakes in arithmetic and geometry as well as in theology. We all have trouble with the stubs in our check books. No doubt blunders in theology are more serious, but it is plainly false to say that there is no error in our mathematics.

Now, if Brunner should reply that although you and I make mistakes in mathematics, mathematics itself, mathematics objectively considered, contains no error, the answer is that theology itself, theology objectively considered, contains no error either. Subjectively we make mistakes in both; objectively the one is as true as the other. Hence Brunner's assertion that theology contains the most error, physics less error, and mathematics none at all is plausible only by confusing the objective and the subjective, that is, only by erasing the distinction between the thinking person who may make mistakes and the objectively true propositions. Or, better, it is a denial of objective truth. This is consistent with Kierkegaard's anti-intellectual passionate appropriation. God is the truth, S.K. had said, but God and truth exist only for someone who believes; an unbeliever need not fear divine penalties because for an unbeliever God does not exist. Truth is entirely subjective.

The subjectivizing of truth has serious consequences. For Brunner, propositions, or abstract truths as he calls them, are merely pointers to a so-called but poorly defined personal truth. Not only do words as sounds have a merely instrumental function, but the conceptual content itself is only a framework or receptacle for something else. Propositions are merely pointers; and pointers can be effective whether they are true or false. Brunner states very clearly that a pointer need not be true. Even a false proposition points, because God is free from the limitations of abstract truth and can reveal himself in false statements as easily as in true.

Gott kann (says Brunner in *Wahrheit als Begegnung* p. 88), *wenn er will, einem Menschem sogar durch falsche Lehre sein Wort sagen.*

Now, if we put aside the amenities of oblique expression and speak pointedly and clearly, are we not forced to conclude that Brunner's words point to a God who tells lies?

Could anything more clearly indicate that Neo-orthodoxy is more Neo than orthodox? Brunner certainly does not stand in the tradition of Calvin. To be sure, he uses the words revelation, transcendence, sin, and incarnation, but their intellectual similarity to the Calvinistic concepts is nil. One hesitates to classify Brunner with Nietzsche, but if they are not brothers, their common irrationalism makes them at least cousins.

This is the point at which to stop. Although Brunner has published many books, it is not profitable to examine any language unless truth is distinct from error. A writer who gives them equal authority has repudiated the law of contradiction and meaningful conversation ceases.

It is time therefore to draw a conclusion. Under the heading *Reason Without Faith* the history of modern philosophy was seen to fail in its attempt to base knowledge on unaided human resources. Even the secular philosophers, those who have no interest in divine revelation, admit that Spinoza, Kant, and Hegel did not produce a sound epistemology. In the present chapter both secular and religious irrationalism have been examined. Not only Nietzsche and James leave us in intellectual anarchy, but Neo-orthodoxy also has concluded that human reason is a failure. Although these latter writers have a doctrine of revelation, even in it they fail to distinguish truth from falsity. Instead of saying, Let God be true, but every man a liar;

they say, Let God be false, and every man will be a liar too. This type of philosophy is self-contradictory, self-destructive, and intellectually stultifying.

Therefore I wish to suggest that we neither abandon reason nor use it unaided; but on pain of skepticism acknowledge a verbal, propositional revelation of fixed truth from God. Only by accepting rationally comprehensible information on God's authority can we hope to have a sound philosophy and a true religion.

FAITH AND REASON

In the foregoing, under the heading *Reason and Faith,* arguments were adduced that led to the repudiation of natural theology and the Thomism of the Roman Catholic church. The Renaissance and modern attempts to base knowledge on *Reason Without Faith* were next shown to result in a disastrous skepticism. And immediately above, the religious implications of irrationalism were indicated. It remains therefore to turn from negative criticism and to provide some constructive view of *Faith and Reason.*

A thorough-going construction would have to systematize a very large number of factors. Unfortunately but necessarily the present attempt will leave many questions unanswered. It is hoped, however, that the line of thought adopted will amply justify two main conclusions. First, in opposition to Deism, the Enlightenment, Spinozism, contemporary scientism and all dogmatic systems that oppose reason to faith, it will be shown that reason and faith are not antithetical but harmonious. True, the harmony will not be of the Thomistic variety. Second, in opposition to secular but chiefly to religious irrationalism, faith will be given an intellectual content. These two conclusions depend largely on acceptable definitions of faith and reason. For Thomas Aquinas and John Locke reason meant the sensory basis of all knowledge. Descartes and Spinoza had another meaning. Several definitions of faith also have occurred in the history of philosophy and theology. This attempt too must choose its own meanings.

In addition to formal definitions, some background, history, and discussion are also needed. This material presents two serious difficulties. First, the history has to do with living religious movements and popular evangelistic preaching. Hence there is a welter of views that defies accurate generalization. If, however, no suggestion of universal agreement is made, fairness requires only that the examples chosen conspire to represent actual tendencies. The second serious difficulty is quite different from the first. Whereas the history centers on popular and therefore superficial phenomena, the discussion turns up exceptionally perplexing technicalities. Reason and faith, since they are human activities, ought to be viewed in the light of human personality as a whole. Some scheme of psychology is required. And the details are endless. In this connection some questions will be raised without being fully answered. They will nonetheless serve as a setting in which the two main conclusions can be amply established.

Popular Religion

The historical background in which these matters become parts of a living religion and find a place in popular preaching can for our purposes be conveniently restricted to fundamentalism in the United States. From the point of view of the Westminster Confession, that is, from the point of view of this entire argument, fundamentalism cannot be entirely condemned nor entirely commended. Most fundamentalists accept important sections of the Westminster Confession and reject other equally important sections. Partly for this reason, fundamentalism does not quite fit into any of the categories of the three preceding chapters. The reference to it at the beginning of the last section might even appear unfair. Admittedly, its classification as a form of mysticism was inadequate. Fundamentalism's firm attachment to a few doctrines saves it from the excesses of irrationalism, but at the same time the fundamentalists can hardly be said to embrace a wholehearted intellectualism. Frequently they deplore reason, knowledge, and scholarship; they sometimes speak contemptuously of "mere human logic"; and one of their complaints against Romanism is that it reduces faith to a mere intellectual assent. Yet, how can fundamental doctrines be defended by a general disparagement of reason? If they insist on any doctrine at all, how can they recommend a faith that is devoid of intellectual content?

They do, however; that is, some do; at least they seem to. It has already been admitted that in a popular movement such as fundamentalism there is a wide variety of views. Perhaps the example about to be given of the irrationalistic strain in fundamentalism is one of the more extreme cases. Even so, an extreme case may be needed to produce the impression that ought to result from a long list of less extreme cases. At any rate the following conversation actually took place. It is neither fiction nor is it exaggerated.

A minister of fundamentalist persuasion and evangelistic zeal asserted that there is little hope of understanding the Bible. Theology is abstruse and doubtful. However, God has given his people the power of discerning the hearts of men, and with this power a minister can decide who should and who should not be admitted to church membership. In the confused and confusing discussion that followed, as this minister tried in vain to list the factors discerned in the hearts of men, Romans 10:9-10 made its appearance. Af first in the rapid exchange of ideas, the minister was inclined to agree that anyone satisfying the conditions of that passage was a saved person. But when it was pointed out to him that belief in Christ's resurrection was a belief about history, an intellectual acceptance of an historical proposition, he quickly corrected himself and denied that a belief in Christ's resurrection entails salvation. Salvation, he asserted, is not a matter of belief at all.

This viewpoint would certainly affect one's exegesis of Romans 10:9-10. It obviously divorces faith from belief, if faith saves and belief does not. But of course no one would expect such a minister to be very consistent in his assertions. The example may be extreme, but it serves the purpose of stressing the undeniable fact that fundamentalism is an inconsistent affair. Nor is it only the fundamentalism of the decades between the two world wars that is inconsistent. The specific inconsistency relative to the intellectual content of faith has descended from earlier forms of Protestantism. Therefore, it is fitting to put the question in terms of a long standing Protestant objection to Romanism.

According to many Protestant writers, Roman Catholicism is seriously mistaken in making faith a mere intellectual assent to certain dogmas. Faith, true faith in Christ, these writers say, is a personal trust rather than a "cold" intellectual belief. On the other side, the Catholic Encyclopedia (in loc., p. 752 edition of 1913) states, "Non-Catholic writers have repudiated all idea of faith as intellectual assent."

Perhaps, however, the truth of the matter is not put accurately in either of these brief characterizations. The Catholic Encyclopedia has substantial grounds for charging Protestantism with anti-intellectualism, but its actual statement is ambiguous and in one of its two senses it is false. On the other side the Protestant complaint about mere intellectual assent is extremely confused. To show this confusion it is necessary to turn from a description of popular religion to a discussion of psychological intricacies. This does not mean that the historical background is to be dismissed with one illustration; other descriptive examples will be cited; but the emphasis will rest more on the academic merits of the case than on examples of rash ministerial assertions.

The Analysis of Personality

In order to define faith, some analysis of personality is needed. Whatever faith is said to be, distinctions among conscious activities are presupposed. According to a very common opinion consciousness consists of these parts: intellect, volition, and emotion. Faith may be placed under one of them, or it may be described as a combination of two of them, or possibly of all three. At any rate, some analytical scheme is required. Now, one of the many difficulties in this procedure arises from the necessity of expressing Biblical truth in non-biblical terminology. In itself, the use of non-biblical terminology cannot legitimately be objected to. The term *Trinity* does not occur in the Bible, but all trinitarians hold that the ideas and relationships for which the term stands are solidly Biblical. Similarly, the word *emotion* does not occur in the Bible, at least not in the King James version. However, in the use of new terminology a certain amount of caution is necessary. In the first place one must make sure that the terms are unambiguously defined. Unfortunately, many discussions of faith fail to define intellect, will, or emotion. Those who use the terms seem to have but a nebulous idea of their meaning, and a little Socratic questioning soon reveals the unintelligibility.

There is also another caution to be observed. After the new term is properly defined, its relation to the Biblical material must be clarified. The use of a non-biblical term in theological discussion is evidence of a technical precision and economy that the Bible itself lacks. No Biblical term corresponds precisely to the new one, and the new term does not exactly reproduce any single term of Scripture. Therefore, complete confusion results if the new term is surreptitiously equated with some familiar term in the Bible. This has happened with great frequency in the identification of the Hebrew term *heart* with the *emotion* of popular psychology. The Biblical meaning of this term will be discussed below; but here emphasis falls on the general principle. When a new term is introduced into theology and is precisely defined, it must never be carelessly assumed, but must always be carefully substantiated, that the new term and definition adequately express Scriptural ideas.

Then, does or does not the Bible support the popular tripartite division of the soul? Obviously, modern psychology offers divisions other than intellect, will, and emotion. Freud specified the id, the ego, and the superego, plus a libido whose relation to them is not too clear. Granted that this Freudian division has an evil odor among the devout; still its very recognition of inherent evil resembles the Christian view of hereditary and total depravity sufficiently to claim a Christian's consideration. Or, perhaps some third analysis is better than either of these two. In any case a hasty assumption cannot be permitted.

Because care is called for, because on principle the analysis finally to be chosen must square with the Bible, and because, as was pointed out a moment ago, the *heart* of the Bible has often been identified with the *emotions* of popular psychology, a brief survey of the Biblical data must be made.

The key term of Biblical psychology, especially in the Old Testament, where the fundamental principles are laid down, is the term *heart*. When contemporary Christians, often in evangelistic preaching, contrast the head and the heart, they are in effect equating the heart with the emotions. Such an antithesis between head and heart is nowhere found in Scripture. On the contrary this usage at once indicates a departure from the Old Testament. In the Psalms and the Prophets the heart designates the focus of personal life. It is the organ of conscience, of self-knowledge, indeed of all knowledge. One may very well say that the Hebrew *heart* is the equivalent of the English word *self*.

To understand Old Testament usage, consider the following few examples:

Gen. 6:5. Every imagination of the thoughts of his heart was only evil continually.
Gen. 8:21. Jehovah said in his heart, I will not again . . .
Gen. 17:17. Then Abraham . . . said in his heart, shall a child be born . . .
Gen. 20:6. In the integrity of thy heart thou hast done this . . .
1 Sam. 2:1. My heart exulteth in Jehovah . . .
1 Sam. 2:35. A faithful priest that shall do according to that which is in my heart and in my mind.
Psalm 4:4. Commune with your own heart.
Psalm 7:10. God, who saveth the upright in heart.
Psalm 12:2. They speak falsehood . . . and with a double heart do they speak.

Psalm 14:1. The fool hath said in his heart, There is no God.
Psalm 15:2. He . . . speaketh truth in his heart.
Isa. 6:10. Lest they . . . understand with their heart.
Isa. 10:7. Neither doth his heart think so.
Isa. 33:18. Thy heart shall muse on the terror.
Isa. 44:18,19. He hath shut . . . their hearts that they cannot under-
stand. And none calleth to mind (heart), neither is there knowledge
nor understanding.

As there are somewhat over 750 occurrences of the word heart
in the Old Testament, these quotations give a meagre sample.
But they are enough to show that many verses would make
complete nonsense if the term were translated emotion. For
example, if this identification were made, it would be necessary
to say, They speak falsehood . . . and with double emotions do
they speak; and, He speaketh truth in his emotions; and, lest
they understand with their emotions. Obviously this substitution results in nonsense. It is not to be denied that the Biblical
term *heart* can and does occasionally refer to the emotions, as in
I Sam. 2:1, though even here there must be some intellectual
understanding. But although the emotions are sometimes referred to, the term *heart* more often signifies the intellect. It is
the heart that speaks, meditates, thinks, and understands. At
the same time, it cannot be uniformly translated intellect as
distinguished from the will or the emotions. This is not because
it excludes or is antithetical to the mind, the understanding, or
the intellect, but because it includes them all and signifies the
total personality. The term *heart* in reality means the self, or,
with some colloquial emphasis, one's deepest self. And as the
self acts emotionally, volitionally, and intellectually, the three
activities are each represented in the several occurrences of the
term. Although the term *heart* includes the emotions and therefore cannot be translated intellect, still the intellectual reference occurs much more frequently than any other; and this
preponderance of the intellectual references shows the preponderance of the intellect in the personality.

It is extremely difficult to appreciate the motives, at least in
the case of those who are attached to the Bible, which lead to a
disparagement of the intellect. Why should emotion be the only
way or even the best way to God? Why is it that thinking, medi-
tating, understanding are to be contemned? Why is knowing,
conceiving, or apprehending God a poor way, an impossible
way, or an impious way of worshipping him? What is wrong
with intellectual activity?

Then too, this denigration of the intellect in favor of the
emotions, and possibly the traditional tripartite division itself,
may entail a so-called faculty psychology that contradicts the
Biblical emphasis on the unitary personality.

Parenthetically it may be noted that this applies to Freud
also. This type of psychology is not to be condemned so much
for its unsavory overtones as it is for its schizophrenic splitting
of the personality. Freudian psychology is faculty psychology
with a vengeance.

The Bible does not suggest a faculty psychology. Although
discussions such as these can hardly avoid using the word *intellect*, let it be clear that there is no "intellect"; there are intellectual acts; there are no "emotions", there are fluctuating
surges of fear, anger, dejection, and exaltation. Similarly there
is no will, no id, no superego, but a unitary person.

Thus the common modern contrast between the head and the
heart is evidently unscriptural. There is a Scriptural contrast.
It is the contrast between the heart and the lips, for Matthew is
quoting Isaiah when he says, "This people honoreth me with
their lips, but their heart is far from me." When the Scriptural
contrast is replaced by an alien faculty psychology, the possibility cannot be ruled out that other Scriptural theses are discarded at the same time.

Trust and Assent

Two examples of this faulty psychology, especially this unscriptural belittling of intellectual activity, will be described.
Neither one is exactly trivial; the second indeed affects one's

total response to Christianity. The first, a common confusion of thought frequently heard from evangelical pulpits, may do less damage because its implications are not so obvious. Yet it too can be symptomatic of wider aberrations.

In describing the nature of faith, fundamentalists, evangelicals, and even modernists in a certain way, stress the element of trust. This is of course what the Catholic Encyclopedia, as quoted above, referred to. A preacher may draw a parallel between trusting in Christ and trusting in a chair. Belief that the chair is solid and comfortable, mere intellectual assent to such a proposition, will not rest your weary bones. You must, the preacher insists, actually sit in the chair. Or, as another minister recently said, mere belief that a bank is safe and sound will not protect your cash or give you any interest. You must actually put your money in the bank. Similarly, so goes the argument, you can believe all that the Bible says about Christ and it will do you no good. Such illustrations as these are constantly used, in spite of the fact that the Bible itself says, "Believe on the Lord Jesus Christ and thou shalt be saved."

There is here at least a lack of analysis, a confounding of something Scriptural and something that is not, a failure to equate two sides of an analogy. The weak point of such illustrations is that they compare faith with the physical act of sitting in a chair and distinguish it from belief. Belief in Christ does not rest your weary bones, for belief is mere assent. In addition you must actually sit down or deposit your money in the bank. But this analogy does not hold. The distinction between believing that a chair is comfortable and the act of sitting in it is perfectly obvious. But in the spiritual realm there is no physical action; there is mental action only: hence the act of sitting down, if it means anything at all, must refer to something completely internal, and yet different from belief. Belief in the chair has been made to stand for belief in Christ, and according to the illustration belief in Christ does not save. Something else is needed. But what is this something else that corresponds to the physical act of sitting down? This is the question that is seldom if ever answered. The evangelists put all their stress on sitting down, but never identify its analogue.

When such one-sided illustrations are not used, the abstract phrases disparaging intellectual assent are equally perplexing. Consider the words of Dr. Thomas Manton in his Commentary on the Epistle of James. Dr. Manton was a devout and pious Anglican, who, although he favored the restoration of Charles II, was one of those ministers who was ejected from his pulpit by the Act of Uniformity of 1662. His Commentary on James is a most admirable and extremely profitable work. Yet when discussing the present subject, he uses phrases that are hard to understand. For example, on James 2:19 he writes,

"This instance showeth what faith he disputeth against; namely such as consisteth in bare speculation and knowledge . . . Such assent, though it be not saving, yet so far as it is historical it is good, as a common work and preparation . . . Bare assent to the articles of religion doth not infer true faith . . . It is not only *assensus axiomati* . . . There is not only assent in faith, but consent . . . True believing is not an act of the understanding only, but a work of all the heart . . ."

In so far as these phrases and the section from which they are quoted indicate the necessity of a faith that produces works, no good Christian could in the least demur. It is Dr. Manton's particular excellence to have emphasized this theme of the Epistle. If by "bare speculation" and "naked illumination" one means a profession discovered to be hypocritical because devoid of virtuous conduct, let us all insist that this is far removed from saving faith. On this point Dr. Manton notices the phrase of James 2:14, "If a man saith he hath faith," and remarks that the man may be supposed to have no faith at all. His profession is hypocritical. He does not necessarily believe any Christian doctrine. This situation is simply the Scriptural contrast between the heart and the lips.

Hypocrisy too is an intellectual act. It is an intent to deceive.

But surely the fact that hypocrisy is intellectual does not imply that faith as an intellectual act is hypocrisy. If one intellectual act is reprehensible, it does not follow that a different intellectual act is.

Now, if Dr. Manton were merely rebuking hypocrisy and insisting that true faith is followed by overt acts of charity, there would be no argument. Nevertheless, although such is Dr. Manton's chief emphasis, there are slight intimations of something further. Aside from the emphasis on good works, bare assent is contrasted with consent. He had said, "There is not only assent in faith, but consent." Consent no doubt refers to some internal rather than overt action. What is this consent? Is it intellectual? If not, is it emotional? Or does Dr. Manton think that it is an act of will? These questions Dr. Manton does not answer. He does not define or explain the term *consent*. He leaves it as a mere word. Hence it is of no help to us.

Again the previous question comes to the fore: if belief is represented by believing that the chair is solid, and this is taken as mere intellectual assent, what is represented by the different and separate act of actually sitting down? Now, in a sense there is another factor; but when it is identified, it will not turn out to be a different and separate act analagous to sitting down. It will still be the same internal, mental act of assent, though viewed in a different light. The difficulty in all this discussion derives from the assumption that an act of "mere" intellectual assent is possible. To this act the zealous evangelist wants to add emotions. Could it not be that what needs to be added is not emotion, but an act of will? Only, this "addition" is not really an addition at all, and a "mere" act of will must be recognized to be just as impossible as "mere" assent. Undoubtedly faith in Christ involves what is ordinarily and confusedly called an act of will. Whether faith requires emotions or not, and if so, which emotions it requires, are unimportant questions. Emotions by definition are fluctuating; an emotional man is unstable and few people have a high opinion of him; whereas throughout our constantly changing emotional states, our beliefs and the volitions founded on them remain comparatively fixed. And, to return, faith surely involves the will.

However, when an attempt is made to use the illustration of the chair, the difficulties of faculty psychology return in full force and the whole collapses. Does not the language that includes such phrases as "mere" intellectual assent betray its unscriptural foundation in the schizophrenic faculty psychology? Certainly intellection and volition do not occur in isolation. There can be no volition without intellection. Even the illustration of sitting in a chair shows this much. A person cannot will to sit in a chair unless he believes that there is a chair to be sat upon. And conversely there can be no intellection without volition, for intellectual assent is itself an act of will.

If the scholastics demur at this last proposition and try to exempt the conclusions of demonstrative syllogisms from volitional acceptance, they do so only by ignoring the voluntary assent required by the premises. The scholastics and possibly more so the seventeenth century rationalists may insist that logic itself is not a voluntary choice, for no one can choose to think otherwise. If someone thinks otherwise, it is an involuntary error. Now, in the following chapter on language it will be strenuously maintained that logic is not stipulative but necessary and irreplaceable. But to argue that the necessary cannot be an act of will presupposes the theory of free will; and free will will be disposed of in the final chapter. At any rate, the use of logic requires a voluntary act of attention, as does every other belief. One may choose simply not to think; or, rather, if he thinks, he must choose to pay attention.

Furthermore, the forms of logic, devoid of other content, do not settle questions of faith. The immediate subject has to do, as will shortly be made still clearer, with theological and creedal propositions. These cannot be deduced involuntarily from the forms of logic. Therefore, within the range pertinent to questions of faith and reason, it may be asserted that there can be no volition without intellection and no intellection without volition. They should not be regarded as two separate faculties, nor even as two separate acts. The common opinion that an act of volition is different from an act of intellection is an illusion which results from the restriction of attention to physical acts such as sitting down. But when the act is not physical, when it is the act of believing a proposition to be true, the supposed two acts so interpenetrate in a single mental state that they become indistinguishable. One can distinguish belief in a chair or in mathematics from belief in Christ, of course; that is, the particular objects thought or willed can be distinguished; but the mental act is equally volitional and intellectual. This is what is implied by saying that the person is a unit. For some superficial purposes, mainly with respect to initiating physical motions, a popular distinction in emphasis is made; but the common threefold division of the person into emotion, intellect and will, is as misleading as the id, the ego, and the superego.

There is also a further complication in the notion of belief or assent that motivates the antipathy to intellectual activity. Those who say that intellectual belief in Christ is of no value, not only fall into the errors exposed above, but they also in some instances fail to distinguish assent from understanding. When they attack "mere assent" they probably mean—though it is rash to guess what some people mean—that salvation is not obtained by knowing the propositions in the Bible and understanding their meaning. Obviously this is true. Many intelligent men know very well what the Bible says; they understand it far better than many Christians; but they are not saved and they are not Christians. The reason is that though they understand, they do not believe. They know what the Bible says, but they do not assent to it. But because understanding and believing are both intellectual acts, those who think carelessly identify them. The distinction between knowing the meaning of a proposition and believing it seems to be too subtle, and therefore some preachers conclude that "mere belief" is of no value. This conclusion is fallaciously drawn. Just because one intellectual act, the understanding of what words mean, is less than faith, it does not follow that faith or belief is not intellectual.

Exegesis will reveal that faith, Christian faith, is not to be distinguished from belief. Consider Hebrews 11:1. "Faith is the substance of things hoped for, the evidence of things not seen." This may not be a formal definition of faith, but it must be accepted as a true statement about faith. The A.R.V. says that "faith is *assurance* of things hoped for, a *conviction* of things not seen." Assurance and conviction are belief, strong belief, voluntary belief, and as intellectual as you please. They are intellectual because their objects are meaningful propositions. Their objects are truths. The heroes of faith, whom the chapter goes on to describe, all believed some definite intellectual truths. In these cases, admittedly, their faith was followed by physical action. Abel offered a sacrifice and Noah built the ark. But the physical actions were not the faith itself. Faith is something internal, mental, intellectual; as Hebrews 11:3 says, "Through faith we understand" something about the creation of the world. Surely this is an intellectual act. And in explaining why "without faith it is impossible to please God," verse six says, "for he that cometh to God must believe that he is." As a reply to those who disparage intellection with the illustration of the chair, the considerations adduced seem to be sufficient.

Anti-intellectualism

The many confusions relative to faith, assent, volition, understanding and so on were used as a first example of a faulty psychology. There is now a second example. Underlying the faulty psychology that gives rise to misleading illustrations about chairs and banks is a distaste for creeds. Creeds are too intellectual, and the type of religion we have been discussing has strong tendencies to the emotional. Sometimes it hardly recognizes a role for volition. But at any rate it exhibits a distaste for creeds. Perhaps, however, this distaste should not be cited as a second example of the faulty psychology. It might be better to take the distaste for creeds and the faulty psychology itself as two examples of an underlying anti-intellectualism.

From the standpoint of Calvinism, anti-intellectualism, a disparagement of creeds, an essentially emotional outlook or a reliance on some ineffable mystical experience is a far more serious error in religion than some unfortunate illustration in popular preaching. It may sound pious to minimize belief in a creed and to exalt faith in a person; but the implication is that it makes little or no difference what a man believes. Religion, I refuse to say Christianity, thus becomes non-doctrinal. This anti-intellectualism, clearly, is a broader theory than faculty psychology; and if faculty psychology conflicts with Christianity at one or two points, the broader theory will conflict at many more—in fact, at all points.

To return for a moment to Hebrews 11:6, we see that faith in God is impossible without a creed. The first article of this necessary creed is that God exists. And how obvious! Can a man come to God if he believes that God does not exist? To turn an illustration back upon its originators, can you take your money to a bank which you believe does not exist? It is not even necessary to put the matter so strongly. The blatant atheist who believes that God does not exist will not come, of course. But what of a man, not a blatant atheist, who merely fails to believe that God does exist? Can such a man any more easily come to God? Hebrews says, No; he that cometh unto God must believe that he is.

This creed has also a second article which must be believed before one can come to God. If a man believes merely that God exists, he will not come: God in this case might be an indifferent Deity with no concern for man; he might even be annoyed at a man's bothering him; or possibly this God might be some impersonal force. Therefore, before a man comes to God, he must believe that he is the rewarder of those who diligently seek him. This, of course, implies that God is personal. What an extensive theology we are getting into! And how intellectual we have already become, for we are now using the logical form of implication.

The slow progress of this argument may provoke an impatient rejoinder that nonetheless intellectual belief is of no value.

Do not the devils believe and shudder? Misinterpretation of this verse in James has gone to the extremity of making it conclusive against any saving efficacy of belief in Christ. Yet the Scriptures say, Believe on the Lord Jesus Christ and thou shalt be saved, for with the heart man believeth unto righteousness. The epistle of James should not be so interpreted as to produce a contradiction with the apostolic preaching in Acts. The belief that causes the devils to shudder is a belief that God is one. Nothing more is said. Certainly it is not a belief that Christ died for them. To show, as James does, that some intellectual belief is inadequate, to show that some is fruitless, or even to show that some is condemnatory is not to show that true faith is not intellectual. The verse in James does not destroy the argument of this chapter to the effect that faith requires a creed and must have intellectual content. So also the points of the creed so far enumerated from Hebrews are not said to be sufficient for salvation. They are said to be indispensable. No one can come to God without this creed. For all its insufficiency, its necessity must be emphasized because of the contemporary disparagement of creeds and intellect by fundamentalists and by the modernists as well.

For the same reasons, faith in Christ, no less than faith in God, requires intellectual assent to theological propositions. The disjunction between faith in a person and belief in a creed is a delusion. None of us proceeds on such a principle in our human affairs. Trust in a person is a knowledge of a person; it is a matter of assenting to certain propositions. Suppose I ask you to lend me a sum of money and to trust me to repay it. On the pleasant assumption that you have the money and do not immediately need it (this is an intellectual belief too), will you make the loan without believing certain propositions about me? Suppose you have heard that I am dishonest? Suppose you believe I will skip out on you? Could you, with these beliefs, say that intellectual assent is trivial and that you will trust me all the same? Not many people are so stupid in business affairs. This stupidity is reserved for non-intellectual, emotional religion. It is of religion that the "heart" is said to be important, but not the head. But if this were true, we could trust Christ for salvation without believing that he is trustworthy, without believing that he can save, without believing that his blood cleanses from all sin. We would need no creed, no statement of the Atonement, no historical information about Jesus; we would need only a comfortable feeling around the non-biblical "heart."

Although there have been mystics and assorted anti-intellectuals in every age, although the influence of Kant, Schleiermacher, and Ritschl have made anti-intellectualism popular in the form of modernism, and although neither neo-orthodoxy nor the ecumenical movement has returned to the historic creeds, or to any creeds, the main current of Christianity has always been intellectualistic. There has been variation of emphasis, of course; but creeds or statements of belief have not been abandoned. There has always been some recognition of the primacy of the intellect. Even the primacy of the will, when in Medieval Augustinianism it was opposed to the Thomistic primacy of the intellect, did not devalue intellectual currency as contemporary irrationalism does. And if, as suggested above, the intellect and the will cannot really be separated, the Medieval controversy militates all the less against the intellect.

This long argument has had to treat of many details, not all taken from the same source. To gather the complexities together, let it be remembered that the Bible teaches the unity of the person; that faculty psychology is unscriptural; that the Old Testament term *heart* is far more intellectual than its use in present day preaching; that faith is an inner or mental act, not properly compared with sitting on a chair; that Hebrews shows the necessity of creeds; and that belief in a creed is both intellectual and voluntary. Woven together like a tartan, some of the lesser strands of the argument may be hard to keep in mind; but the over-all pattern should be obvious enough. However, before a final conclusion can be drawn, the Biblical position on faith and reason should be given a more definite and positive expression. This is all the more necessary because, in addition to the many preceding complexities, there is still another most important factor, so far hardly mentioned.

The Reformed Faith

The clearest expressions of Reformation theology and the most faithful to the Scriptural data are to be found in the Reformed tradition. Three Reformed writers, therefore, will first be cited.

Calvin (Institutes I xv 6-8), after he summarizes some philosophical analyses of the soul's faculties and indicates that they are plausible, but far from certain, particularly because the philosophers ignore the depravity of human nature due to sin, proposes a twofold, not a threefold, division of the soul; understanding and will. There is no power in the soul other than these two. Understanding, he says, discriminates between objects, and the will chooses what the understanding pronounces good. The understanding is the guide and governor of the soul; the will always respects its authority and waits for its judgment. Charles Hodge also (*Systematic Theology*, Vol. II p. 99), speaking of man before the fall, says "His reason was subject to God; his will was subject to his reason." And finally, J. Gresham Machen (*What is Faith* p. 26; cf. pp. 49, 51) states that "it will be one chief purpose of the present little book to defend the primacy of the intellect."

It is significant that these writers say so little about the emotions. The emphasis is on the intellect. Machen in his "little book" speaks of the emotional aspect of faith apparently but once (p. 135); but the word is all that appears, for the context has nothing to do with the emotions.

The quotations just made from the three authors might be taken to indicate that they favor the Thomistic primacy of the intellect rather than the Augustinian primacy of the will. They seem to say that the intellect invariably and automatically dominates the will. Calvin indeed said that it is the office of the will to choose what the understanding shall have pronounced to be good and that the will always respects its authority (*Institutes*

I xv 7). Now, there have been plausible Aristotelian arguments to the effect that the will automatically chooses what appears as good to the intellect. Freedom of the will from the intellect is thus repudiated. And possibly Calvin had this theory in mind when he wrote this section. But if we stress the unity of the person more than Calvin did, and insist that intellectual assent is an act of volition as Augustine so broadly hinted, the radical distinction between will and intellect, necessary if one is to command and the other to obey, falls away. This bears also on the simplicity of the divine nature and will be referred to again in the last chapter.

The primacy of the intellect, then, cannot be a power automatically exercised over the volition regarded as a separate faculty. This would violate the unity of the person. Instead of the phrase 'the primacy of the intellect,' the essential idea might better be expressed as the primacy of truth. And the primacy is one of authority rather than of psychological power. The older forms of expression generate an old perplexity dating from the Platonic dialogues. On the assumption that the intellect dominates the will, it would follow that no one does wrong knowingly. All evil is due to ignorance, and education guarantees correct conduct. The ambiguities hidden in this apparently simple language are enormous. But if we speak of the primacy of truth, we can avoid, even if we do not solve, these perplexities. The primacy of truth will mean that our voluntary actions ought to conform to the truth. Obviously sometimes they do not. If it is true that worshipping God is good, we ought to worship him. Perhaps we choose not to worship God, but the truth is superior in right to our will. This way of putting the matter extends as well to the voluntary choice of belief. We may choose to believe a truth, or we may choose to believe a lie. Both types of choice actually occur. But the primacy of truth means that we ought to believe the truth and we ought not to believe the lie.

It was no doubt the complicated psychological condition of choosing to do wrong that led Hodge to restrict his primacy of the intellect to man's original state of righteousness before the

fall. The psychological conditions of choosing evil, as even secular philosophers have discovered, are exceedingly intricate. As
the Scripture says, the heart of man is deceitful above all things,
and it is exceedingly corrupt: who can know it? This raises a
most important point, the fact of sin, which so far has not been
brought into the argument.

Any discussion of man's mind and powers, to be at all Biblical,
must take into account the effects of sin. Calvin, Hodge and
Machen were keenly aware of this. They all knew that the en-
trance of sin into man's life altered his disposition as immediately created. In speaking of the intellectual approach to
Christianity, Machen says that

"there is nothing wrong with the method itself" (*ibid.* p. 130) ; "but
the trouble lies in the application of the method. . . . If you take
account of all the facts, you will be convinced of the truth of Christianity; but you cannot take account of all the facts if you ignore
the fact of sin."

In another place he explains his meaning a little more clearly:

"That does not mean that we finite creatures can find out God by
our own searching; but it does mean that God has made us capable
of receiving the information which he chooses to give . . . So our
reason is certainly insufficient to tell us about God, unless he reveals
himself; but it is capable (or would be capable if it were not clouded
by sin) of receiving revelation when once it is given" (*ibid.* p. 51) .

The effect of sin, though hardly mentioned before the last
two paragraphs, cannot be excluded as a factor in this discussion. There is some evidence that those who disparage the intellect do so because of a superficial view of sin. Man as a unitary
personality, man as a whole, is depraved. If any doctrine is
plainly taught in Scripture, it is the Calvinistic doctrine of total
depravity. Sin affects man in his every part. But those who make
religion an emotion and discount intellect deny or at least dilute

the terrible Biblical words of condemnation. They wish to reserve a part of man's nature pure and undefiled. Therefore, they make religion a matter of emotion because the emotions are supposed to be sinless, whereas the intellect is corrupt. Thus anti-intellectualism is combined with a denial of the unity of the person.

This is not to say that all fundamentalists deny the effect of sin on the emotions. And even when these views are entertained, they are not usually expressed in such pointed language. The summary of the last paragraph may be called an exaggeration. It is to be admitted also that frequently these implications are no more than semi-conscious. This would explain why sometimes an explicit statement of them draws forth a heated denial. Nonetheless there are instances where the emotions are given a privileged position. How else is the following material to be understood?

The Rev. John R. W. Stott of London has published a booklet entitled *Fundamentalism and Evangelism*. In a paragraph defending the emotions, he rather clearly equates the heart with the emotions, when he says, "Jesus told us to love the Lord our God with all our heart as well as with our mind" (p. 28); and in the next sentence he distinguishes between the mind, the heart, and the will. From page twenty to twenty-eight he repeatedly says that the mind is finite, fallen, hardened, blinded, and darkened. Now, this is perfectly true, and there are other truths that Mr. Stott asserts. But it is most significant, after all those condemnations of the intellect, to find that he says not one word against the emotions. So far as he expresses himself, we are at liberty to conclude that all the emotions are pure and holy. It would seem therefore that anti-intellectualism, at least as expressed by some fundamentalists, has a tendency to split the personality and to minimize the seriousness of sin.

But this is not Christianity. Christianity includes the primacy of the intellect and the sovereign claims of truth. There is no antithesis between the head and the heart, no depreciation of intellectual belief. Christianity cannot exist without the truth of certain definite historical propositions. To deny the truth of such propositions or to call them symbols of some mystic experience is not Christianity. On the contrary, by faith we *understand* that God created the universe; by faith we *assent* to the proposition that God is a rewarder of those that diligently seek him; by faith we *know* that Jesus rose from the dead.

The judgment of the Catholic Encyclopedia as quoted near the beginning of this section is ambiguous. If it meant to say that *some* "Non-Catholic writers have repudiated all idea of faith as intellectual assent," it states the unpleasant truth. If, however, it meant to insinuate that *all* "Non-Catholic writers have repudiated all idea of faith as intellectual assent," it is mistaken. For Reformed theologians will ever assert that if the creedal propositions are untrue, and if truth has no claim upon our assent, then Christianity would not be worth its hypocritical propagation.

Definition of Reason

Sufficient Biblical grounds have now been given to justify the intellectual character of faith. From this side of the question therefore antagonism with reason is no longer to be expected. What now remains is a definition of reason that will remove antagonism from the other side of the antithesis. The clarification of the nature of faith was undertaken in reference to the distortions of fundamentalism; the clarification of reason envisages the secular accusations that Christianity is unreasonable or irrational. For example, *An Introduction to Modern Philosophy*, by Alburey Castell, in introducing the Thomistic arguments, correctly distinguishes between natural theology and revealed theology. But frequently thereafter the author describes natural theology as rational theology, and the student receives the impression that revealed theology is irrational. Sometimes also the charge that Christianity is irrational comes from those that profess to be religious. They may even appeal to revelation. But, not to repeat the discussion of Neo-orthodoxy, in such cases religion and revelation are founded on common experience, so that supernatural revelation still appears irrational.

As an example the religious philosophy of the late Edgar Sheffield Brightman will serve. Reason, for Brightman,

"is the body of most general principles used by the mind in organizing experience . . . Revelation is not the body of most general principles used by the mind. Revelation must be tested by reasonableness, not reasonableness by revelation . . . it is not a criterion of truth, but presupposes a criterion by which it is judged."[5]

Again,

"reason—concrete and inclusively empirical, not merely abstract and formal—is the supreme source of religious insight."[6]

In opposition to this, Christianity should refuse to define reason as a body of general principles empirically obtained. Brightman's faith in a concrete empirical body of general principles is a misplaced faith. The history of rationalism and its outcome in irrationalism show that no such body of principles can be obtained. Indeed, it is significant that Brightman himself was unable to state these principles. In one place[7] he seems to try by offering a definition of reason in nine norms; but the norms he specifies, instead of being empirical, rather clearly resemble the so-called formal logic he elsewhere sets aside.[8] Brightman was therefore unable to apply his theory.

Since all attempts to obtain knowledge apart from revelation have failed, the Christian, in the next place, need only contradict Brightman's unsupported contention that experience cannot be judged by principles derived from revelation. The psychologists of today emphasize guilt and fear; the existentialists confront man with death. Cannot these experiences be understood in the light of information God has revealed? This revelation need not be tested, in fact, cannot be tested by reasonableness in Brightman's sense of the word, for Brightman's reasonableness does not exist.

Finally, since the accusation of unreasonableness fails because the philosophies that make it collapse into skepticism, the Christian now need only identify reason with that which Brightman called abstract and formal. Brightman's terms in this connection are a little unfortunate, and the next chapter will show that the modern theory of logical formalism is not to be adopted. Nonetheless reason may well be defined as logic. It should not be indentified with experience. When a Christian theologian is deducing consequences from Scriptural premises, he is reasoning—he is using his reason. To require him to test Scripture by sensation in order to avoid the charge of irrationality is itself irrational prejudice.

With this conception of reason there no longer remains any conflict between reason and faith. The futility of rationalism and the insanity of irrationalism are equally avoided. Truth becomes obtainable. And this, we believe, should constitute a strong recommendation for Christian revelation.

NOTES

1. Cf. the author's *Thales to Dewey*, pp. 275-278 (Houghton-Mifflin, 1957).

2. Spinoza, *Tractatus Theologico-Politicus*, chapter IV.

3. Anyone unconvinced by this brief account must read the first dozen pages of Part I of Berkeley's *Principles of Human Knowledge*.

4. This is argued in brilliant detail in *The Phenomenology of Mind*, chapters 1-3.

5. *Religious Values*, pp. 21, 22.

6. *A Philosophy of Religion*, p. 192.

7. *Nature and Values*, p. 106.

8. For a more complete discussion, cf. my *A Christian View of Men and Things*, pp. 253 and context.

3.

Inspiration and Language

The conclusion of the previous chapter was the thesis that revelation is needed as the basis of a rational world-view. In the study of religion and generally in modern philosophy attempts to establish truth without a word from God have resulted in a frustrated irrationalism.[1] Hence constructive thought must presuppose information that has been divinely given. This is to assume that the Bible is the word of God; and since God cannot lie, his word must be the truth. Obviously this raises the problem of verbal inspiration. The first part of this chapter will give some of the older background of this subject. More recently inspiration and revelation have been discussed from the standpoint of the possibilities of language. Is language a fit instrument for revelation? Such a question requires a two-fold discussion. First, there is the study of language, its nature, its origin, its possibilities, and its relation to inspiration. This is a topic of importance in its own right. Then, second, there is the question of method. Can it be successfully maintained that divine revelation, as the presupposition of all knowledge, offers a solution to the problems of language?

The Biblical Claims

The inspiration of the Scriptures, bearing as it does on the truth and authority of the Word of God, is of such obvious importance to Christianity that no elaborate justification is needed for discussing the subject. Indeed, it is even pardonable to begin with some very elementary material. Not only pardonable, but in fact indispensable. No discussion of inspiration can contribute much of value without taking into account the elementary Scriptural data. These data must be kept in mind. Yet, unfortunately, a number of these details have faded from our aging memories. More unfortunately the younger generation by and large has never learned the Scriptural data. In the last two or three centuries Christianity has suffered a slow but steady decline, and at present the theological standards of most seminaries are so low that the rich detail of Presbyterianism and Puritanism is never presented to the students. Therefore, first of all, some simple statements must be made about the doctrine of inspiration as it was commonly explained a hundred years ago.

It was in 1840 that Louis Gaussen published his famous little book *Theopneustia*. Gaussen was a Swiss theologian who, like J. Gresham Machen in this century, was deposed from the ministry and driven out of the church not because of unbelief, but because of his adherence to the truth of the Scriptures. And his book *Theopneustia* is a defense of inspiration. In it Gaussen amasses the astounding amount of material that the Scriptures have to say about themselves. And although that was a century ago, no one should approach the question of inspiration without a good knowledge of Gaussen's work, or at least without a good knowledge of what the Bible has to say about itself.

Gaussen opens his survey of the Scriptural data by quoting the well known verse, "All Scripture is given by inspiration of God." Here his pertinent observation is, "This statement admits of no exception; . . . it is all that is written; meaning thereby the thoughts after they have received the stamp of language." Then he proceeds to support this assertion with a tremendous number of references.

For example, Gaussen lists ten instances of phrases such as, "The mouth of the Lord hath spoken it," and "The Lord hath spoken." Only slightly different are other references which say, "I will open my mouth in the midst of them," and "The spirit of the Lord spake by me, and his word was in my tongue." Or, again, "The word of God came unto Shemaiah," "the word of God came unto Nathan," "the word of God came unto John," "the word that came to Jeremiah from the Lord." Beyond these there are the instances where it is said, "He put a word in Balaam's mouth;" "I will be with thy mouth;" "Thou, Lord, hast said by the mouth of thy servant David;" and "this Scripture must needs be fulfilled, which the Holy Ghost by the mouth of David spake before concerning Judas."

One should note well that the Spirit-given message is not merely the general idea of the passage, but rather the very words.

Deut. 18:18 "I will raise them up a prophet . . . and I will put *my words* in his mouth . . . and whosoever will not hearken unto *my words* which he shall speak in my name, I will require it of him."

Jer. 1:9 "Then Jehovah put forth his hand and touched my mouth; and Jehovah said unto me, Behold, I have put *my words* in thy mouth."

That the words themselves are inspired, may be seen also from the manner in which Jesus Christ used the Bible. Consider, for example, the Lord's reply to the Sadducees who denied the resurrection of the body. How does he refute them? By one sole word from an historical passage; by a single verb in the present tense, instead of the same verb in the past tense. "Ye greatly err," he said, "not knowing the Scriptures. Have ye not read that which was spoken unto you by God saying, I am the God of Abraham!" God on Mt. Sinai, four hundred years after the death of Abraham, said to Moses, not "I was," but "I am the God of Abraham." There is a resurrection, then, for God is not the God of a few handfuls of dust, the God of the dead: he is the God of the living. Those men therefore are still alive, and Christ has based the argument on a single word.

A few verses later the Lord asked the Pharisees about the divine nature of the expected Messiah. Here likewise to prove his point, he insists on the use of a single word in Psalm 110.

If the Messiah be the son of David, said Christ, "how doth
David by the Spirit call him Lord?" Here Christ emphasizes the
fact that David used this word through the guidance of the
Holy Spirit.

There is space for only one more reference to show that
Christ asserted the divine authority of the words of the prophets,
and his own words too. It is the statement of our Lord himself:

"If ye believed Moses, ye would believe me; for he wrote of me.
But if ye believe not his writings, how shall ye believe *my words*"
(John 5:46-47).

The effect of Gaussen's quotations and arguments is cumulative. Page follows page. Even to one who thinks he knows the
Bible fairly well, it is a surprise to see how frequently and how
emphatically the Bible speaks of itself. One ought to read all of
Gaussen's references and to note carefully the significance of
each. Only so can one see how pervasive the doctrine of inspiration is.

The last reference also takes us one step further into this
elementary material. Someone in ignorance might object that
even though God gave the prophets his words and made them
speak, the speaking has ceased these thousands of years, and we
have only reports of the speeches. The claim is thus made that
the Bible is not a revelation so much as it is the record of a
revelation. This question, concerning the relation of the spoken
word to the written word, was answered by Christ implicitly in
the previous references, but explicitly in this last one. Note
carefully, our Lord says, "Moses *wrote* of me [and] if ye believe
not his *writings*, how shall ye believe my words?"

When the words that God gave his prophets are written, they
become *The Writings*, i.e., the Scriptures. It is the Scriptures,
the Writings, that Jesus tells us to search for eternal life. In his
temptation, Jesus repels Satan by saying "It is written." Also in
John 6:45, 8:17, 12:14, 15:25, the phrase "It is written" settles
the points at issue.

Permit a final reference to one more exceptionally important passage. In John 10:34-35 Jesus is defending his claim to Deity. He quotes Psalm 82. Does he quote this Psalm because Psalm 82 is more inspired and more authoritative than any other passage in the Old Testament? Not at all. He says, "Is it not written in your law ... and the Scripture cannot be broken." Christ here has appealed to Psalm 82 because it is a part of the Scripture, and since all Scripture is given by inspiration of God, this passage is also inspired, for the Scripture cannot be broken.

Let it be repeated that the effect of this evidence is cumulative. One should have in mind the hundreds of instances in which the Bible claims plenary and verbal inspiration. This doctrine of inspiration is not something tenuously deduced from two or three isolated verses. On the contrary, it is the explicit, the repeated, the constant, the emphatic declaration of the Bible in all its parts.

Now, to conclude this survey of elementary detail, a pointed question must be put. If the prophets who spoke, if the authors who wrote, and if our Lord himself, are mistaken about verbal inspiration, if they are mistaken these hundreds of times, what assurance may anyone have with respect to the other things they said and wrote? Is there any reason to suppose that men who were so uniformly deceived as to the source of their message could have had any superior insight and accurate knowledge of man's relation to God? Still more pointedly: Can anyone profess a personal attachment to Jesus Christ and consistently contradict his assertion that the Scriptures cannot be broken?

The Dictation Objection

Since this elementary and abbreviated account of verbal inspiration has been based on a volume of a century ago, the next step, before bringing matters completely up-to-date, will be the examination of a century old objection.

The idea that God gave his words to the prophets seems to many liberals a mechanical and artificial theory of revelation. God, they tell us, is not to be pictured as a boss dictating words to his stenographer. And further, the writings of the prophets show clearly the freedom and spontaneity of personal individuality. Jeremiah's style is not that of Isaiah, nor does John write like Paul. The words are obviously the words of John and Jeremiah, not of a boss dictating to several stenographers. The stenographers of one boss will turn out letters of the same literary style; they do not correct his English. Now, therefore, if God dictated the words of the Bible, the personal differences could not be accounted for. From which it follows that the doctrine of verbal inspiration is untrue.

In answer to this objection, it is useful to note that the liberals rather uniformly misrepresent the doctrine they attack. This is true, not only of the doctrine of the verbal and plenary inspiration of the Bible, but of many other doctrines as well. Psychologically it is not surprising that some misunderstanding should occur. It is difficult to state accurately a position with which one strongly disagrees. Yet, when the misunderstanding has been publicly pointed out and still no correction is made, it begins to seem that misunderstanding has changed into misrepresentation. Accordingly the first and indispensable step in making a reply is to show clearly what does and what does not belong to the doctrine of the verbal inspiration. This has been done often enough before, but to leave the opponents with still less excuse, it will be repeated again here.

Now let us keep certain facts clearly in mind. In the first place, the differences in style—and they are so obvious that even a translation cannot obscure them—show decisively that the Bible was not dictated as a boss dictates to his stenographer. There have indeed been several theologians who have used the term *dictation*; and a very small number seem to have regarded the process as similar to modern office procedure. But others did not. Calvin, for instance, several times speaks of dictation, but his commentaries show that he was clearly aware of differences in literary style. Obviously he meant dictation in the more general sense of a command and an authoritative imposition. What is chiefly to the point is that the great majority of theologians who hold and have held to verbal inspiration, never accepted the mechanical dictation theory as described by modernists. B. B. Warfield, *The Inspiration and Authority of the Bible*, (p. 173 n. 9) writes,

"It ought to be unnecessary to protest again against the habit of representing the advocates of verbal inspiration as teaching that the mode of inspiration was by dictation."

And later (*ibid*. p. 421) he wrote,

"It is by no means to be imagined that it is meant to proclaim a mechanical theory of inspiration. The Reformed Churches have never held such a theory; though dishonest, careless, ignorant or over-eager controverters of its doctrine have often brought the charge. Even those special theologians in whose teeth such an accusation has been oftenest thrown (e.g., Gaussen) are explicit in teaching that the human element is never absent."

On a number of occasions and on a number of topics, it has been my experience that liberal theologians misunderstand, misrepresent, and even misquote the orthodox authors. Now, an occasional mistake should be overlooked; even a number of unrelated mistakes cannot be judged too harshly; but when the doctrine of verbal inspiration is so constantly misrepresented, one is tempted to suppose that the unbelievers found it easier to ridicule dictation than to understand and discuss verbal inspiration as it is actually taught by Reformed theologians.

How then, are the differences of style to be accounted for, and what does verbal inspiration mean? The answer to these questions, involving the relation between God and the prophets, takes us quickly away from the picture of a boss and a stenographer.

When God wished to make a revelation, at the time of the exodus or of the captivity, he did not suddenly look around, as if caught unprepared, and wonder what man he could use for the purpose. We cannot suppose that he advertised for help, and when Moses and Jeremiah applied, God constrained them to speak his words. And yet this derogatory view underlies the objection to verbal inspiration. The relation between God and the prophet is totally unlike that between a boss and a stenographer.

If we consider the omnipotence and wisdom of God, a very different representation emerges. The boss must take what he can get; he depends on the high school or business college to have taught her shorthand and typing. But God does not depend on any external agency. God is the creator. He made Moses. And when God wanted Moses to speak for him, he said, "Who hath made man's mouth? Have not I, the Lord?" Therefore verbal inspiration, like every other particular doctrine, must be understood in connection with the complete system of Christian doctrine. It may not be detached therefrom, and *a fortiori* it may not be framed in an alien view of God. In particular, verbal inspiration can be more clearly understood, and can only be properly understood in its relation to the Presbyterian, the Reformed, the Calvinistic doctrines of the divine decree, providence, and predestination. When the liberals surreptitiously deny predestination in picturing God as dictating to stenographers, they so misrepresent verbal inspiration that their objections do not apply to the Calvinistic viewpoint. The trouble is not, as the liberals think, that the boss controls the stenographer too completely; on the contrary, the analogy misses the mark because the boss hardly controls the stenographer at all.

Put it this way: God from all eternity decreed to lead the Jews out of slavery by the hand of Moses. To this end he so controlled history that Moses was born at a given date, placed in the water to save him from an early death, found and adopted by Pharaoh's daughter, given the best education possible, driven into the wilderness to learn patience, and in every event and circumstance so prepared that when the time came, Moses' mentality and literary style were the instruments precisely fitted to speak God's words.

It is quite otherwise with dictation. A boss has little control over a stenographer except as to the words she types for him. He did not control her education. He cannot trust her literary style. She may be totally uninterested in his business. They may have extremely little in common. But between Moses and God there was an inner union, an identity of purpose, a co-operation of will, such that the words Moses wrote were God's own words and Moses' own words at the same time.

Thus, when we recognize that God doeth his will in the army of heaven and among the inhabitants of the earth, when we understand that God worketh all things after the counsel of his own will, when we see God's pervading presence and providence in history and in the life of his servants, then we can realize that business office dictation does not do justice to the Scriptures. The Holy Spirit dwelt within these men and taught them what to write. God determined what the personality and style of each author was to be, and he determined it for the purpose of expressing his message, his words. The words of Scripture, therefore, are the very words of God.

CONTEMPORARY THEORIES

This brief and hasty survey of earlier discussions is intended merely as historical background for an examination of the contemporary state of affairs. Things have changed, and changed considerably. With the decline of Ritschlian liberalism and the rise of existentialism, neo-orthodoxy, and logical positivism, the opponents of verbal inspiration have shifted their attack. It is no longer whether the words of the Bible are the words of God or merely the words of fallible men. Today a more sweeping objection is made on the basis of a general theory of language. Philosophers have become interested in semantics; and some of their views would so alter the significance of words that with all the verbal inspiration imaginable, the Bible would be emptied of its Christian meaning. The philosophy of language as developed by scholars who are not particularly interested in any religion is not specifically directed against the inspiration of

the Bible; but, since a general theory of language includes
religious language and affects the total philosophy of religion,
it sweeps inspiration along with all the rest. The most prom-
inent, though not the most profound, result of this influence is
the idea that all religious language is metaphorical or symbolic.
No religious statement should ever be understood literally. In
the following pages, a few examples of this theme will be given,
accompanied by an admixture of criticism; and then the discussion will turn to the more profound implications of the general
theory of language.

Religious Language

As a first example, and particularly to show the present popularity of these ideas, two articles may be selected from the same
issue of *The Christian Scholar*, published by the Commission
on Christian Higher Education of the National Council of
Churches. In the issue of Sept. 1955, Geddes MacGregor has an
article entitled "The Nature of Religious Utterance," and
John A. Hutchinson writes on "The Religious Use of Language." Their common point of view rather than any minor
differences they may manifest is what concerns the present
argument.

MacGregor opens with Croce's assertion that "all language is
metaphorical, or none is"; and soon follows with Urban's rejection of literalism and his conclusion as to "the inevitably metaphorical and symbolic character of all language." MacGregor
does not wish to be held to the position of Croce and Urban
altogether, but he seems to accept the thesis that all religious
language is metaphorical or symbolic. If this be so, religious
utterances must be evaluated in a very different manner from
the usual analysis of logical propositions.

In support of his position MacGregor gives some examples,
and it will be our duty to determine whether or not these admitted cases require his conclusions. First, he refers to a college
choir whose Jewish, Unitarian, and Quaker members, majoring
in political science or anthropology, were singing a Medieval

hymn. Few if any of them understood the concepts of the hymn, and yet their words communicated the concepts to those persons in the audience who had the proper understanding. Similarly, a child does not understand marriage when he reads the last sentence of a fairy tale.

These examples, especially the second, are supposed to militate against a literal understanding of language because not even all adults have the same understanding of marriage. This word has "levels" of meaning; some words have many levels, others fewer. But if all words have several levels, there can be no literal meaning.

However, it does not seem that MacGregor's examples prove what he intended. Obviously, a child knows little about marriage, and no adult knows all. It is also true that many adults know only a few of the theorems that may be truly asserted of a triangle. But the ignorance of these theorems does not entail an ignorance of the definition of triangle nor of some of the simpler theorems. The same is true of marriage. Such an example therefore does not prove that there is no literal meaning whatever to these words.

Another illustration that MacGregor gives is that of a very ordinary preacher preaching a very ordinary sermon. Yet this dull sermon or a sentence of it becomes a vital message to someone in the congregation and his life is changed. Once again the words conveyed more meaning than the speaker intended, and hence, argues MacGregor, the meaning could not be literal. But why not? Could not the literal meaning of a sentence or two recall themes that had lain dormant in the hearer's mind? Could not even the literal meaning point out a new way of life? How can such an instance be made to show that all religious language is metaphorical or symbolic?

Finally, the author asserts that the theological proposition "God is omniscient" is never as satisfactory as the liturgical statement, "O my God, who knowest all things." For MacGregor religious utterance "is always in the second person singular."

Now, it seems to me, this last notion is obviously false. There are libraries full of religious books written in the third person. Systematic theologies, church histories, books on pastoral methods are all written in the third person, and they are religious books. Incidentally, the Bible is largely in the third person: "Who his own self bare our sins in his own body on the tree." Of course, the third person sentence and the second person sentence that MacGregor happened to choose, are not precisely equivalent. But the difference does not stem from the person of the verb. If the author had written the first sentence as "My God is omniscient," he would have had a third person sentence which is the exact equivalent of the second person phrase. It may not be a "satisfactory" mode of address, for it is not a mode of address at all; but this is not to say that it is not satisfactory for a creedal statement. Whatever may be the difference between second and third person verbs, it is not at all clear why second person verbs must be metaphorical rather than literal. If therefore one wishes to maintain that all religious language is metaphorical, it would be better to appeal to a general theory of language than to such examples as these.

The Hutchinson article in the same periodical develops the theory somewhat more clearly and more profoundly. The thesis is that "religion in all its range and variety consists of symbols." This would mean that Christ's death on the cross, Paul's activity in writing the Epistle to the Romans, and my reading it are nothing but symbols. Where MacGregor had hesitated, Hutchinson says expressly that "all language is metaphorical . . . Every common noun is a kind of dead metaphor. But religious terms or words are metaphorical in a further and distinctive sense." To support his view, Hutchinson sketches a religious epistemology which is based on images—a sort of mental idolatry—and which is assimilated to art and mythology. God always (note the always) speaks to man through images, and "religious experience is a process of being hit by such images."

This type of epistemology will be alluded to later on; but here I only wish to say that while Hutchinson may be describing his own religious experience, he is not describing mine. His sweeping generalization is simply not true to fact.[2]

One objection, however, Hutchinson feels obliged to answer. If myth is unavoidable in religion, some explanation is required as to the choice of myths. One person chooses Greek mythology; another Christian mythology. Doubtless such choices are often made unreflectively, but Hutchinson thinks that it is possible to make a rational choice of myths. The basis of such a choice is the adequacy of the myth to explain the facts of existence as we confront them in daily life and action.

It seems, however, that neither this nor any other attempt to justify a choice among myths can be successful. If myths were literal truths, one might be more adequate than another. The Greek myth of Zeus' method of producing rain might be considered more adequate or less adequate than the myth about the windows of heaven, attributed to the Hebrews. But if these stories are both mythological and symbolic, simply symbolic of the literal fact that it rains, it is hard to judge what adequacy requires. A literal statement from Aristophanes' *Clouds* might explain; but a myth explains nothing.

Furthermore, if all language is symbolic, the myth could not be a symbol of any literal truth; it would have to be a myth about a myth. For example, what could the cross be a symbol of? The cross, as it appears in printers ink or sculpture, is no doubt the symbol of Christ's crucifixion; but can the crucifixion itself be a symbol or metaphor of anything? The *prima facie* meaning of statements about the crucifixion is literal. And if someone says that religious language cannot be literal, there appears to be no rational method of determining what the crucifixion is symbolic of. Is it pessimistically symbolic of an inherently unjust universe or is it symbolic of the love of God? On what grounds could one decide, if nothing in the account can be taken literally?

But suppose now that someone decides without rational grounds. Suppose that the crucifixion, although it never occurred literally, were said to be symbolic of God's love. Then we must ask, is it a literal truth that God loves men, or is this symbolic too? Obviously this must be symbolic too, if all language is symbolic. And what is God's love symbolic of? No doubt it is symbolic of another symbol, which is itself symbolic of another. How could such a regress be of any value unless sometime, and the sooner the better, we come upon a symbol that symbolizes a non-symbolic meaning?

So long as the discussion concerns rain and the windows of heaven, it might appear that nothing important is involved. But when the crucifixion is swept in, and when terms such as ransom, justification, propitiation, expiation, and reconciliation are treated as metaphors and figures of speech,[3] the illusion of superficiality is dissolved. For from this sort of view it may be and has been concluded that divine revelation cannot be a communication of truth.

Doubtless the Christian reader is chiefly interested in a truthful revelation and in the literal meaning of Biblical statements. Yet it would be a mistake to suppose that educated Christians should not concern themselves with the several secular theories from which the religious implications derive. The preceding section on symbolism was given in connection with somewhat superficial articles in a periodical. These popular accounts are the mode in which more technical theories trickle down to the general populace. Therefore a more thorough-going examination of semantics or linguistics must be undertaken. This is all the more proper because most of the religious writers who make so much of myth and symbolism are conscious of their dependence on the more general theories of language. They may not be conscious of a still more general, a still more profound, and a much more radical theory of logic that lies behind the theory of language. This new logic as it appears in logical positivism and the philosophy of analysis will be taken into account at the end of this chapter. First, however, the discussion will continue with language.

Linguistics

To begin with, it may be well to indicate roughly the nature of the subject by asking some of the questions that need to be answered: What is a word? How can sound be meaningful? Does thought exist before and apart from language? How did language originate? Is language adequate for a knowledge of reality, or is its nature such that it automatically distorts the universe? Is all language symbolic and metaphorical, or are some sentences strictly literal? These and similar questions give a preliminary idea of the problem.

Let us choose as the starting point one phase of the origin of language. The Bible makes a brief mention of the diversification of tongues; but the origin of the previous single language is passed over in silence. Similarly, outside the Bible, no historical information is available on the first occurrence of speech. For this reason theories of the origin of language are speculative conclusions based on more general philosophic principles.

A theory common today holds that words originate in sense experience. All words are supposed to have had originally a physical reference. Words denoting relations are said to be primarily spatial. If a word is said to *stand for* an object, the relation 'standing for' is derived from positions in space; similarly a thought is *in* my mind as a chair is in a room; and what is worse, for logic, the *inclusion* of one class in another, e.g., all mammals are vertebrates, is also a spatial relationship.

If all words are primarily physical or sensuous, and if relations are basically spatial, either language cannot properly apply to spiritual and non-spatial subjects, or one must explain how the physical meaning can be changed into a spiritual meaning. How can sensory experience give rise to words for soul and God? Attempts have indeed been made to explain this extension of language, and these attempts should not be prejudged without examination. At the same time the physical origin of language is today frequently put in a form that makes this extension extremely difficult and in fact impossible.

Evolutionary theory is committed to tracing human language back to the cries and grunts of animals. Then by slow, gradual, and unspecified changes, these animal sounds eventually after many centuries become the words of human language. Inasmuch as the individual steps in this process have never been enumerated, it is hard to test the theory. It is all the harder since in the first place the exact status of animal sounds is not too clear. Parent birds give warning cries to their fledglings, and this can be construed as an example of the indicative function of language. But the cry probably does not indicate whether the danger is a hawk or a human being. Perhaps it may be said that the cry means, *Danger!* or, *Look out!*, and thus some plausibility may be gained for the theory by assimilating the cry to a word-sentence. But whatever the indicative function of such a cry may be, it must be one that is extremely vague. Nothing descriptive of the object is said. Note too the important fact that animal sounds are instinctive; they remain the same in all countries where the species is found; they also remain unchanged from generation to generation; whereas the words of language do not.

If none the less it is possible to find some connection between animal sounds and human speech, the theory under consideration has taken a form in which instead of animal sounds developing into meaningful speech, speech is reduced to the level of animals. Or, it may even be said, human language is reduced below the levels of cries and grunts, if these are supposed to bear some conscious meaning.

That is to say, evolutionary behaviorism not only makes language physical and sensory in its origin, but maintains it on the same level.

Leonard Bloomfield (*International Encyclopedia of Unified Science,* Vol. 1, Part 1, p. 227) speaks of responding to sounds "in a kind of trigger effect." Four pages later he says, "The scientific description of the universe . . . requires none of the mentalistic terms because the gaps which these terms are intended to bridge exist only so long as language is left out of account." He then offers the choice of behaviorism, mechanism, operationalism, or physicalism. In the continuation he further asserts, "Language bridges the gap between the individual nervous systems" (p. 233); and "Thinking is inner speech" (p. 235). Here, of course, 'inner' is spatial.

To avoid all mentalistic terms, naturalism equates the meaning of a word with the response of the organism; and the response is a physico-chemical reaction caused by the total environment. Not only the word but its meaning is a physical effect and in turn a physical cause. The word is not a sign of a concept, nor is the meaning a mental picture that resembles the object. Neither word nor meaning represents anything. The whole situation is exhausted in a chain of physico-chemical causes and effects in which a nervous system is one link. In animal behavior when a robin sees a worm, the 'sign' of the worm is a physical modification of the robin produced by light rays reflected by the worm.

Here one may wonder if the robin has a sign any more than the supermarket's electric eye has when we approach it. And if this is the case, could not an early form of language be found in the electric eye— particularly if the door squeaked a bit? The behaviorist would doubtless agree, but others have an uncomfortable feeling that there is a difference between physical causation and the interpretation of signs. It is a difference that cannot be expressed in the physical categories of space and motion. A mind is needed. Beyond any motion there must be intellection. In language the words or signs can occur, perhaps not apart from all causation, but they operate in defiance of the regularities of physical causation. What is the cause which causes us to use the word *worm*? We may say *worm* when we see one, and in this case it might be claimed that the light rays reflected from the worm produce the sound just as they make the robin chirp. But it is not light rays that produce the same sound when we choose the word *worm* for purposes of linguistic discussion. We call *worm* a noun and remark that it can be the subject of a verb. Are these remarks nothing but physical motions? Is the sound *worm* the chemical effect equally of light rays and of a linguistic discussion? Is the sound *noun* nothing but a physical effect of previous physics? Here the behaviorist explanation can be accepted only on blind faith. No, not even on blind faith, for faith is a mentalistic term. It must be accepted

on blind physics. It happens, however, that my physics cause me
to make other sounds, such as the sounds *mind* and *intellect*. In
particular the chemistry of my body produces the sounds. The
chemistry and physics of my larynx are as good as the chemistry
and physics of yours.

It is not the present purpose, however, to continue with a
general refutation of behaviorism or even to itemize all the
objections to its theory of language. At the moment the important point is that this theory of language is not arrived at by
an empirical study of language. No one has ever seen "language
bridging the gap between two nervous systems." No one has
ever isolated the causes which produce the word *worm* instead
of the word *noun*. In this respect behaviorism does not satisfy
its criterion of empirical verifiability. Instead of being based on
a study of words, the behavioristic theory of language is an
implication from the general position of naturalism. Though
naturalism is worthy of discussion, the present chapter will continue to be restricted as much as possible to questions of
language.

Eventually of course any theory of language will be based on
some more general world-view. References to and partial con-
firmation by linguistic phenomena must be appealed to, but it
seems improbable, indeed I wish to insist that it is impossible
for a purely phenomenological argument to place a theory of
language beyond all doubt. However some writers on language
and many of the theologians who discuss myth and symbols have
little to say about the more fundamental problems. What they
say often indicates clearly that they reject behaviorism. Sometimes they suggest an alternative philosophy. Therefore the next
step in the argument must be a few paragraphs on the symbolic
theory of language as detached from any behavioristic presuppositions.

One of the best and certainly one of the fullest accounts of the
philosophy of language is William Marshall Urban's *Language
and Reality*. The great length of his volume and the later modi-
fications of views given summarily on earlier pages make it im-

possible to do full justice to the author's precise position. The quotations must be taken as they are, apart from the complete context, simply as fairly faithful expressions of a widely held theory. Then too, since the original motivation of this chapter is the literal interpretation of Scripture, the details selected for consideration will have to do with the literal use of language. Unlike some of the writers already quoted, who hesitate to say that all language is mythological, Urban definitely holds that language is never to be literally understood.

"There are no strictly literal sentences" (p. 433). "Now strictly speaking, there is no such thing as literal truth in any absolute sense, for there is no such thing as absolute correspondence between expression and that which is expressed. . . . and any expression in language contains some symbolic element" (pp. 382-383).

Now, in the first place, it may be remarked, if there are no literal sentences at all, the meaning of statements in the Bible is vitiated no more than the meaning of statements in Caesar's *Gallic Wars*. 'David was King of Israel' and 'All Gaul is divided into three parts' are on the same level. They may both be called figurative, or symbolical, or metaphorical; but they are both historical in exactly the same sense. If all language is symbolic, the verbal inspiration of the Scriptures is in no more danger than the correct interpretation of any other text.

However, to call all language symbolic seems to empty of all significance the commonly recognized distinction between literal and figurative. Can one approve a theory of language that denies this distinction? What then has the reason for violating common usage?

Urban said, "there is no such thing as absolute correspondence between expression and that which is expressed." Accordingly, in the second place, one must ask whether there is absolute correspondence, and whether this is required for literal meaning. The notion of correspondence is vague. In one sense of the term a photo corresponds to or looks like its object; but no one supposes that a word corresponds to a thing in this way. Language is not a picture of reality. The letters c-a-t do not look like the purring animal. It is all the more true that words cannot possibly look like spiritual realities, if such there be, for these are not visible entities. But in a non-photographic sense a mathematical formula may be said to correspond to the motion of a freely falling body. Could not this be an absolute correspondence? Or, if the term *absolute* causes hesitation, could not such a formula be or be understood as a literal assertion? Further, if the sound *cat* is essentially an arbitrary sign of the animal, what more correspondence could be desired?

In criticizing the view that words are arbitrary or conventional signs of ideas and things, Urban several times appeals to an intuitive content in words. Primitive words are supposed to imitate, in some way or other, the things to which they refer. The word *ache* derived from the sound *ach*, is supposed to sound like a pain feels. While some people with lively imaginations think that this is plausible, examples taken, not from one's mother tongue, but from unknown languages will remove the plausibility. One of Urban's examples is *ouatou* and *ouatou-ou-ou*. He first gives the meaning in English and then asks if the word does not sound like the thing. If it did, that is, if there were an intuitive meaning in the sound, it should be fairly easy to guess the meaning of the word before the English translation is given. Now, among a million people someone might make a lucky guess; but the others would almost surely fail. Did you recognize all along that the two words mean *stream* and *ocean*?

On the other hand, if words are conventional signs, there can be absolute correspondence—if anyone wishes to call it that—by stipulation. This is seen most clearly in the terms that scientists deliberately coin. Volt and ohm 'correspond' completely to their referents. At any rate, when one says that the electric circuit in the house is one of 110 volts, the language is utterly literal. Aside from the technical terms of science, this is also true of many common sentences. The words *dog, chien,* and *Hund* have no intuitive content. They are mere signs. There-

fore when one says, 'the dog is black,' one ordinarily expects to
be taken literally. In such sentences there is no symbolic element. And this is true also of 'David wrote the Psalms.'

It must be admitted that Urban puts his finger on a serious
difficulty in the view that words are conventional signs. It is that
a first convention would be unintelligible. Communication
would be impossible. The Biblical Adam and Eve or the first
two evolutionary savages could not have talked to one another.
Adam would have selected a sound for tree, sun, or air, and Eve
would have had no idea what it referred to.

The difficulty of explaining communication has long been
recognized. The famous treatise of St. Augustine was preceded
by the keen insight of Gorgias. But the implausibility of intuitive content in words, the plausibility that they are mere signs,
plus the fact that even if some words had an intuitive content it
would not be of much help in solving the enigma of communication, are persuasive reasons for not following Urban.

There is another phenomenon also which, though it furnishes
no explanation of communication, effectively answers the objection to it. Even if some primitive words had an intuitive content,
the languages of today have virtually none. Must not Urban
himself admit that ninety-five percent of all words are now
conventional signs? Remember dog, chien, and Hund. But infants learn to speak, and parents communicate with them. Not
only so, but adults also have learned the little known languages
of remote tribes by living with them. These two miracles, the
infant and the missionary, will be better understood from
Augustine's viewpoint than on a naturalistic basis. But in any
case the "absolute correspondence" of arbitrary signs to referents remains, and literal sentences occur.

The attack on the possibility of literal sentences now continues by the alleged discovery of an ambiguity in the term
literal.

"The term literal is ambiguous . . . This may mean merely the
opposite of figurative, and the rendering of symbolic sentences into

literal sentences is equivalent to the expression of the figurative in non-figurative fashion. But literal also has another meaning, namely, primitive meaning. To interpret a symbol sentence literally would, then, be to interpret it according to the primary or original meaning of the words. If literal be taken in this second sense, then to say that expansion of a symbolic sentence is the substitution of a literal sentence is wholly false. For the symbolic meaning is precisely not the literal meaning. So interpreted the symbolic sentences, Napoleon is a wolf . . . are false" (*ibid.* p. 433) .

This quotation betrays a great confusion, though the last half of it is perfectly true. The source and explanation of the confusion may become apparent a little later as his argument for the necessity of symbolism is further developed; but the point of the confusion is obvious here. The quotation does not in fact give two meanings of the term literal. Literal in the sense of opposite to figurative does not differ from literal in the sense of primitive meaning. Urban has taken for ambiguity in the term literal two different procedures of interpreting figurative sentences. The example was, "Napoleon was a wolf." The literal, non-figurative, primitive meaning of the word *wolf* is of course a certain type of wild animal. To say that Napoleon had four legs and a shaggy coat is of course false. But while the predicate of the figurative sentence was not intended to be taken literally, the intended meaning can be stated in literal language: Napoleon was a wanton killer. And he is a wanton killer in the primitive and non-figurative sense of the words. Granted that the interpretation of a figurative sentence according to the primary and original meanings of the words results in a false or absurd misunderstanding of the intended meaning; yet it does not follow that the expansion of a symbol sentence by the substitution of a literal sentence is necessarily false, much less impossible. It is a question of which literal words are chosen. It is not a question of ambiguity in the term literal.

The source and motivation of this confusion lies in the view that "the symbol expresses adequately for our type of consciousness that which could not be fully expressed in 'literal' sentences" (p. 444). "It is not true that whatever is expressed symbolically can be better expressed literally. For there is no literal expression, but only another kind of symbol" (p. 500). "The symbolic consciousness, as we have seen, is a unique form of the cognitive consciousness" (p. 435). "Thus to expand the symbol tends to defeat its end as a symbol" (p. 434). Another contributing factor to the confusion above is the opinion that when the term literal is defined as primary meaning, "a literal sentence is one which refers to a sensuously observable entity . . . Applying this notion of literal . . . to the language of morals and religion . . . all such language is pronounced meaningless" (p. 436). In order therefore to preserve some meaning in religious language against the attacks of the logical positivists, Urban believes that he is forced to his view of symbolism.

It is cheerfully admitted that Urban wishes to oppose those who would deny all meaning to religious expressions. There is also a group that for convenience we may call the Anglican group, though not all are Anglicans. Antony Flew states that he is not a Christian at all. But most of them seem to be Anglicans: E. L. Mascall, Basil Mitchel, Austin Farrer, I. M. Crombie, Ian T. Ramsey, and others. These men have collaborated in the publication of a series of books that defend religious language from the charge of being meaningless, and they follow Urban at least in assigning a sensory origin to language, which origin then sets the problem of developing language from its sensory referents to its use in spiritual affairs. However, one may ask why the idea of primary meaning must be equated with a sensuously observable referent. On the principles of a naturalistic evolutionary theory, which none of these men ought to accept, the motions of magic and incantation may have been the primary sensuous meaning of terms like *spirit* and *God*. But unless those savages had some prior notion of a Being to be invoked, unless they had a "mentalistic" idea of something different from the ritual itself, it is difficult to understand why they would have gone through the motions. Or, conversely, if they went through certain motions only because of physical exuberance, it remains a mystery how the idea of God could have developed from such athletics.

If, on the contrary, the idea of God is an innate endowment by the Creator, and if the word *God* is an arbitrary sign of this spiritual referent, and if perchance magic incantations are degenerate forms of a pure original worship, then both the motions and the language are easily explained. It is much easier to see how in a degenerate religion a word of original spiritual import can have come to be transferred to a physical object, just as idols replace God, than it is to understand how words of sensuous reference only can come to take on purely spiritual meaning. This alternate view must now be considered.

THEISTIC LINGUISTICS

A theory of language, since it is only one part of philosophy, must, as was said above, depend on a more general world-view. In the case of the behaviorists this fundamental philosophy is consciously applied. In other cases the underlying principles may be but dimly apprehended, and may appear only as presuppositions to be discovered between the lines. It is even possible that some writers with less perspicacity explicitly deny what their theories implicitly assume. At any rate, every theory of language, and every other special theory, depends on some set of ultimate principles. Let us therefore choose Christian theism as our basis.

We shall suppose that God Omnipotent has created rational beings, beings who are not merely physical but who are essentially spiritual and intellectual, beings therefore who have the innate ability to think and speak. What then will be the implications relative to the problems of linguistics that can be drawn from this theistic presupposition?

For one thing this view places thought behind language and so contributes to the explanation of communication. Previous mention was made of Augustine's *De Magistro*. Christ is the

Logos or Reason that endows every mind with intellectual light. Christian theologians, even the poorer ones, have usually realized that in the moral sphere man is not born neutral. "Behold I was shapen in iniquity and in sin did my mother conceive me." Men are not born morally good or morally neutral, but they are born depraved. Intellectually also men do not come into the world with blank minds. Inherited depravity only emphasizes the presence of innate moral ideas. Those wicked Gentiles who did not want to retain God in their knowledge none the less failed to banish him, for they continued to know the judgment of God that those who commit such things are worthy of death. In addition to moral ideas Augustine teaches that the presence of Christ the Logos endows all men with certain speculative or philosophic ideas as well. Communication therefore becomes possible because all men have these same ideas. The situation is somewhat like that of cryptographers who can break any cipher. The symbols are at first unknown; but because the ideas expressed are common, the message can be understood. If language had no thought behind it, as the behaviorists claim, and if the symbols were just a random aggregate of marks, there would be no cipher to break.

It follows next that language cannot be assigned a solely sensory origin and a primitively physical reference. Theism of course need not deny that the names of animals and things refer to sensorily perceived physical objects; it need not deny that spatial relationships are well represented in language; it need not deny or distort any of our common gross experience. But it must assert that man's endowment with rationality, his innate ideas and *a priori* categories, his ability to think and speak were given to him by God for the essential purpose of receiving a verbal revelation, of approaching God in prayer, and of conversing with other men about God and spiritual realities. As a hymn says, "Thou didst ears and hands and voices, For thy praise design." For this reason a theistic theory of language would not labor under the burden of giving a precarious derivation or development of spiritual meaning from primitive physical reference. The spiritual meaning would be original. A dubious appeal to metaphor, symbolism, or analogy to explain this transition would be unnecessary.

This point requires some extended explanation, for it needs to be shown first that this theistic theory of language does not evade the problems by denying the usefulness of metaphor and analogy, and second that the Anglicans previously mentioned, with others who adopt the same outlook, fail to achieve their end of maintaining the meaningfulness of religious language, and that therefore in the third place, if their theories must be discarded, the view of the last few paragraphs is at least a better expedient.

First of all it is admitted that religious language contains analogies, metaphors, and figures of speech. Christ said, "I am the door." There are also the parables which, sometimes obscurely, point to similarities between sensory experience and religious principles. The Psalms most of all are poetic and pictorial. Thus the existence of metaphor and symbolism cannot be denied, nor shall it be argued that such language is in the least inappropriate. However, these literary embellishments with their aesthetic appeal and psychological impact are not to be construed as essentially different from figures of speech in books of history or even fiction. To do so is to create a pseudo-problem. Religious language is not essentially different from language on other subjects of interest. The position here maintained is not that religious language cannot utilize metaphor, but that the meaning of these metaphors, when one knows enough theology, can be stated, and less ambiguously, in strictly literal sentences.

Some writers, as we have seen, deny this. E. L. Mascall, who makes admirable criticisms of logical positivism, and who aims to defend the meaningfulness of religious language, makes his task impossible by accepting the admission of some Christian theologians that "there was something very peculiar about theological assertions which sharply differentiated them from the assertions of ordinary conversation," "unintelligible to the complete outsider" (*Words and Images*, pp. viii, 12). He also quotes

Farrer with approbation that "it is not necessary for us to get behind them [images] to a non-metaphorical understanding of facts. The images themselves illuminate us." And, "the metaphysician cannot point away from his analogically expressed thought about the natural mysteries to some non-analogical thought about them, which mean all that the analogical thoughts mean. He has not got any such non-analogical thought" (pp. 116, 117).

This is the theme I wish particularly to repudiate. The idea of a special and peculiar theological language essentially different from language used in other subjects is, I believe, completely untenable. Of course, physics uses technical terms such as proton and velocity, and in this sense we can speak of the language of physics, just as the language of baseball talks about curves, fouls, and umpires who should be killed. But these two "languages" are simply parts of one language—English, and the same rules of meaning apply in physics, baseball, and in "theological language" as well.

Theology versus Language

Sometimes the allegation that religious language can never be literal and must always be analogical is based on particular points of doctrine improperly understood. For example, I. M. Crombie[4] considers creation analagous to manufacture, but only analagous, not identical. In the case of ordinary facts, like the manufacture of a chair or table, we know their meaning when we understand a situation in which the facts would not be true. But the theist, asserts Crombie, claims that there is no situation which falls outside of divine creation. Therefore the meaning of creation is in doubt. We could never grasp the significance of statements about creation unless the rules of theological language differ essentially from those of ordinary language.

Here one might wonder what Crombie would have said if he had noted that no chair or table falls outside the category of manufacture. At any rate the theist can describe a situation, which of course he believes to be false, in which creation would not be true. If physical reality had existed from eternity, if the history of the world were not finite in time, then creation would never have occurred. In order for an assertion to be meaningful, it is not necessary that there exist situations in which it is true and other situations in which it is false. Such a criterion of meaning would prevent the assertion that water dropped into sulphuric acid produces a rise in temperature. Nor on such a theory could two and two always equal four. Meaningfulness does not depend on a statement's sometimes being false, nor does falsity imply that a statement is meaningless. What is meaningless can be neither true nor false.

Not only is Crombie's criterion of meaning doubtful, his notion of creation also appears to be ambiguous. "The theist," he says (p. 45), "does not pretend to know how the world began; he only claims to know that, however it began, God created it." Crombie's statement here does not do justice to the theist. Although the particular point to be criticized in this statement may seem relatively unimportant, in fact some will think that the criticism splits hairs, nevertheless the statement illustrates a tendency to confuse a question of theology with a question of language. In ordinary language the word *how* always refers to a process. How does one drive a car? How does one carve a turkey? How does one solve an equation? The answers to these questions all specify several steps in a process. Therefore it is inaccurate to say that "the theist does not pretend to know *how* the world began." He pretends to know that there was no *how*. Creation excludes process. Crombie's difficulty therefore does not lie in the usage of language, but in the theological content.

An even less convincing example of language difficulty is given by Flew and MacKinnon.[5] Their article argues that the first chapter of Genesis cannot be literal because the word *day* obviously does not mean twenty-four hours. But why should anyone suppose that the literal meaning of *day* is twenty-four hours? The word *day* more frequently refers to a period of twelve hours, more or less, distinguished from night. The one is as literal as the other. And even if the authors insist that *day* in the sense of a period of time, e.g., in my grandfather's day, is figurative, it is far from proving that such language cannot be expressed literally. These authors therefore are not convincing when a few pages later they insist, "I say *imaginative* deliberately; for writing in the New Testament is poetry rather than prose" (p. 175). Now, perhaps the word *day* is figurative in Genesis; but can anyone read Paul's epistle to the Romans and deny that it is prose? Such desperate expedients do not commend the theory.

Sometimes, however, the allegation that religious knowledge can never be literal, instead of being based on fairly evident misunderstandings, is founded on very difficult points of doctrine, points which constitute serious enigmas for a Christian theologian.

In the last book mentioned Flew has a chapter on *Divine Omnipotence and Human Freedom*. In the main it is a very well written attempt to show that the assertion of free will cannot solve the problem of evil, and as he goes through his argument he well enough lays bare the difficulties of the problem. There is, however, little connection with any theory of language. The whole is strictly theological. And if studied from the standpoint of theological content, its deficiencies are quickly seen. For, although the chapter contains some fine analysis of free will, so far as other views on the problem of evil are concerned it contents itself with a mere expression of distaste. For example, "All that we have to say in this paper is, of course, entirely beside the point for anyone who adopts any variant of the position that infinite creative power is its own sufficient justification" (p. 156). Such a solution Flew merely calls "uncomfortable." Or, at most he says, "All the bitter words which have ever been written against the wickedness of the God of predestinationism—especially when he is also thought of as filling hell with all but the elect—are amply justified" (p. 163). This is not argument; this is merely abuse; and it is unworthy of a scholar who wishes to look at things logically. Admittedly, the

existence of evil poses a major difficulty for the Christian. And
for this reason the last chapter of the present book will argue
through it in detail. Here the only point to be noted is that a
solution is not to be sought in rules of language but in the
concepts of theology.

The same is true of another matter. Again in the same volume
by Flew and MacIntyre, Bernard Williams gives an interesting
defense of Tertullian's famous paradox: it is certain because it
is impossible. Williams argues that religious language must
include at least one sentence about both God and the world. It
may be that God punishes men or that God became flesh; but
there could hardly be any religion unless God is related to the
world at least in one aspect. Unfortunately, however, God is
eternal and the world is temporal; "so when we come to a statement that is about both God and temporal events, it must be
unsatisfactory; for if it were not, we should have adequately
described the relation of temporal events to God in terms ap-
propriate only to the temporal events" (p. 203). Then Williams
makes an excellent point. If a religious person replies to this
argument that religious statements must be accepted by faith
and not by reason, Williams shows clearly that the reply is irrelevant. "If you do not know what it is that you are believing
on faith, how can you be sure that you are believing anything?
. . . To say that it is to be believed on faith and not by reason
does not face the difficulty, for the question was not how it
should be believed, but what was to be believed" (pp. 209, 211).
The authors under discussion do not seem to take this point
seriously enough. Unless religious language is meaningful,
literally true, and thoroughly intelligible, it is meaningless and
unintelligible, sound and fury signifying nothing. Williams'
point stands emphasis.

But to return to the relation between the immutable God and
the changing temporal events, perhaps it is Crombie who gets
to the bottom of the matter.

"We must acknowledge at once that in the ordinary sense we have no conception of the divine nature. We do not know God, and it would be absurd to claim that we know what kind of a being he is. Insofar as we use adjectives about him (omniscient, eternal, and so on) they do not enable us to conceive what it is like to be God. Omniscience is not infinite erudition, and what it is must be beyond our comprehension" (*op. cit.* p. 55) .

Crombie is clearly aware that all this is more than a question of language. Obviously it is necessary, if one wishes to defend theology against the charge of meaninglessness, to provide an epistemology that will permit man to have a knowledge of God. But the quotation just made would appear to make a knowledge of God impossible. Even revealed knowledge would be impossible, for we are said to have no conception of God or of what kind of a being he is. Omniscience is an attribute beyond our comprehension, and the adjectives we use have no ordinary sense. Yet the author wishes to allow some meaning to theological statements. To this end a special kind of language must be used. The assertion 'God loves us,' Crombie explains as a parable: "there is no literal resemblance between the truth which is expressed and the story which expresses it;" but there must be some "resemblance or analogy between, say, human and divine love" (p. 71). "Although we *believe in* the analogy, we do not *use* the analogy to give a sense to 'love' in the theological context. We postulate the analogy because we believe the image to be a faithful image . . . We do not understand the relationship in which God stands to the world, but we must also claim the right to name it 'creatorship' or 'sustaining'. The choice of the name is not aribtrary, although, since we do not understand the relation named, its use is in one sense equivocal" (pp. 72, 81).

This is highly unsatisfactory and falls completely within the scope of Williams' remark that "if you do not know what it is that you are believing . . , how can you be sure that you are believing anything?"

Trying to forestall criticism of his theory of parable or

analogy, Crombie remarks that his conclusions can be denied only if "(1) there can never be good grounds for committing a category-transgression, and (2) that there can be no 'meanings' which do not correspond to clear and distinct ideas" (p. 61).

One wonders how the mere statement of the only two conditions on which Crombie's theory can be denied is sufficient to dispose of the conditions. It seems so reasonable that one should avoid 'category-transgressions,' i.e., logical blunders, that one cannot be satisfied with simply brushing the principle out of sight. And while there may be some meaning embedded in the language of a man whose ideas are not clear and distinct, the meaning would surely prove to be an hallucination if it could be shown that the words could not be made to correspond to some clear or distinct ideas. Furthermore how can one construct a parable that relates a known object to something of which we have no concept at all? Meaningful analogies and honest comparisons can be made only if we know something about both terms. Unless a better defense of religious language and thought can be devised, the logical positivists will not be greatly embarrassed.

Literal Language

The theistic theory of language that was outlined a few pages back is here offered as a better solution to the whole matter. How it will apply to logical positivism will be seen a little later, but how it applies to the theory of metaphors and parables should already be clear. First of all, it provides for a knowledge of God without which speech would be vain sound. The Logos is the rational light that lighteth every man. Since man was created in the image of God, he has an innate idea of God. It is not necessary, indeed it is not possible for a blank mind to abstract a concept of God from sensory experience nor to lift sensory language by its bootstraps to a spiritual level. The theories of empiricism, of Aristotle, of Aquinas, of Locke, are to be rejected.

The positing of innate ideas or *a priori* equipment does not entail the absurdity of infants' discoursing learnedly on God and logic. To all appearances their minds are blank, but the blankness is similar to that of a paper with a message written in invisible ink. When the heat of experience is applied, the message becomes visible. Whatever else be added, the important words refer to non-sensuous realities.

The impossibility of converting sensory language to spiritual use by parable and metaphor arises from the necessity of knowing both items of comparison before a comparison can be made. The metaphor or the parable has meaning only if there is some similarity that can be stated in non-metaphorical, literal language. When Crombie said that "we postulate the analogy because we believe the image to be a faithful image," he contradicts his previous statement that "we do not know God, and it would be absurd to claim that we know what kind of a being he is." It seems obvious that if we have no knowledge of God there would be no basis for choosing the parable 'God loves us' rather than the parable 'God hates us.'

The theory of metaphor, parable, or symbolism, as it holds that literal language is impossible, naturally denies that the truths expressed in metaphor can be expressed literally. Sometimes authors try to show that poetry and symbolism lose value when attempts are made to state their meaning in prose, and this failure in translation is taken as evidence for the general theory of symbolism.

If, on the other hand, religious language can be literal, not only may symbolism be translated into ordinary prose, but the symbols must be regarded as less adequate, though perhaps more literarily beautiful, expressions of the truth than the literal statements are.

Opposing any such suggestion, Urban, whose great work was quoted earlier, writes,

"In Whitehead's words, the symbol is merely a surrogate for something else, and what we want is that something—not the substitute. In other words, the ideal would be to dispense with symbolism or to have wholly non-symbolic truth. This, it seems to me, is a fundamentally mistaken notion. In the first place, such an ideal is really impossible in view of the very nature of language and expression. If there were such a thing as wholly non-symbolic truth, it could not be expressed" (*op. cit.* pp. 445-446).

Yet this that Urban considers "a fundamentally mistaken notion" seems to others besides Whitehead to be fundamentally correct. Some hints have already been given that such an ideal is not really impossible. One further example will be given. It will be used as a basis for a *reductio ad absurdum* of Urban's view, and it will be chosen from the Bible to bring the whole discussion closer to the question of verbal inspiration than it may have seemed to be in the last several paragraphs. Let us take the words of John the Baptist, "Behold, the Lamb of God." The lamb is a symbol.

A symbol is a sign, but not all signs are symbols. The plus and minus signs of arithmetic, even though they may sometimes be called mathematical symbols, are just arbitrary conventional signs. Marks of other shapes could have served as well. Crombie above, it will be remembered, tried to maintain that his words, names, and metaphors were not arbitrary; and in this example obviously an elephant as a symbol of Christ could not have served as well; and a fish was later used only because of an acrostic. John the Baptist's choice of a lamb was not arbitrary; it was rooted in the Mosaic ritual. An arbitrary sign, whether a word or a mathematical figure, merely designates the concept. When we are studying mathematics or reading a newspaper, we do not normally think of the shape of the signs, but rather give exclusive attention to the thing signified. In the case of the symbol, however, some of our attention is fixed on the symbol. If the Baptist had said, Jesus is Lord, no one would have given thought to the sound as such; and there is nothing in the situation except the sound and the meaning. But when he said, "Behold the Lamb," the situation included not only Jesus and the sound of the words, but also the lambs that the word Lamb summarized. To understand the Baptist's message about Christ therefore, it was necessary to think how literal lambs could symbolize Christ. This is not the case with a designatory sign.

John the Baptist expected his auditors to remember the sacrifices in which the worshipping sinner had placed his hands on the head of the lamb, killed the lamb, sprinkled the blood round about the altar, and burnt the lamb on the altar. Because of these reminiscences the Baptist's language was vivid. He pictured the ritual of the ages. One word summarized an entire religious system.

But is this symbol adequate? Does it express what cannot otherwise be expressed?

Undoubtedly this symbolism was adequate to attract the attention of the auditors. In doing so, it functioned more effectively than a literal lengthy explanation. Symbolism and the more ordinary figurative expressions have their use; and unless they were better adapted to their aim than other language, they would cease to be used.

Yet, if the purpose is insight and understanding, symbolic language must be recognized as seriously inadequate. If a missionary should repeat John's words to people who had never heard of the Jews, the meaning would not be conveyed. Even if one knew that the Jews killed lambs and went through certain motions, one could hardly guess what John meant. First of all literal language is necessary to explain the significance of the Jewish sacrifices. The death of the lamb represented the penalty of sin previously incurred by the now repentant Jew. But though the man had incurred the penalty, the penalty was discharged by a substitute. And God was satisfied. Furthermore, the visible sacrifice was itself symbolic of a greater sacrifice. There was some future event prophesied in which one whose visage was so marred more than any man would be led as a lamb to the slaughter, by whose stripes we are healed. Then centuries later, John the Baptist announced, "Behold the Lamb of God that taketh away the sin of the world." The lamb is a symbol of the vicarious satisfaction of justice.

Without such a background of literal meaning, one could hardly guess the point of the symbol. One would not know what the symbol symbolized. The symbol is merely a surrogate for something else, and what we want is the real thing and not the symbol. To be sure, the lamb is not simply an arbitrary sign, as the swastika was for the Nazis; but unless some literal information was forthcoming, John's symbolic sentence could not have been understood. With this information, it can be. And these remarks return us to the analysis of John A. Hutchinson's article on *The Nature of Religious Utterance,* near the beginning of this chapter. The *reductio ad absurdum* then is complete.

On a theistic world-view therefore, a view which holds that God created man and revealed himself to him in words, language is adequate for theology. Linguistics, unless controlled by naturalistic, atheistic presuppositions, can therefore offer no objection to the doctrine of verbal inspiration. The Scriptures contain metaphors, figures of speech, and symbolism, for the Scriptures are addressed to men in all situations—situations in which their attention needs to be aroused and their memory facilitated, as well as situations in which plain information must be conveyed. But since symbolic language and metaphor depend on literal meaning, the most intelligible and understandable expressions are to be found in the literal theological statements, such as those in Romans. And outside the Bible the most accurate and satisfactory expressions of Christianity are the carefully worded creedal statements of the Westminster Confession.

LOGICAL POSITIVISM

The majority of the authors so far quoted have been trying to defend religious language from the accusation of the logical positivists that religion and metaphysics is nonsense. These authors recognize that logical positivism is an enemy of all religion, they wish to escape its influence, and they have at times made keen criticisms of it. If their alternate theory has failed, it is only because they have not sufficiently stressed the literal concepts of non-arbitrary logic without which no theory can be maintained and with which logical positivism is reduced to ruins.

Though the Anglican group does not stress logic sufficiently, there are others who stress it even less, and who therefore show a greater, even if unconscious, affiliation with the logical positivists. Emil Brunner is a good example. One of his main points is that God "does not communicate something to me, but himself." That is to say, revelation is not the impartation of truth. "All words have only an instrumental value. Neither the spoken words nor their conceptual content are the Word itself." And, "God can . . . speak his Word to a man even through false doctrine."[6] Not only does Brunner empty revelation of all conceptual content, he also accepts or rejects inferences by subjective preferences. Jewett (p. 104) translates *Die christliche Lehre von Gott:*

"The purely rational element of thought in logic has the tendency to proceed from any given point in a straight line. Faith, however, constantly bridles this straight line development . . . Theological thinking is a rational movement of thought, the logical consequences of which are constantly, at every point, through faith, turned back, curtailed, or destroyed . . . Only by the constant breaking of systematic unity and logical consistency . . . does thought arise which may be designated as believing thought."

Thus, as Jewett goes on to show, Brunner accepts valid implications when it suits his purpose to refute Schleiermacher; but when he finds himself unable to refute the predestinationism of Calvin, he decides that now he will have his faith bridle logic and will pay no attention to valid implications. But if logical consistency can in this way be used in one case and discarded in another, what is to prevent one from selecting a few ideas from Buddhism, a concept or two from Islam, and a bit of nonsense from Christian Science too? After all, revelation is not a communication of truth, and the conceptual content of the words is not the real thing. There is therefore no law against contradicting oneself.

This repudiation of logic indicates that a fitting conclusion to this chapter can be provided by a short discussion of the law of contradiction. Now, the most vigorous opponents of immutable logic are today the logical positivists, and to them we shall now turn.

Logical positivism or the philosophy of analysis as it is sometimes called not only repudiates divine revelation but all non-empirical metaphysics as well. In particular it denies any innate or *a priori* forms of the mind, traditionally regarded as necessarily true. Logic and mathematics are explained as linguistic conventions that have been arbitrarily selected; or if not altogether arbitrarily, they have been selected as useful tools to do a job. Past history exemplifies different selections. The logic of Whitehead and Russell is one, and the logic of Aristotle is another. To quote A. J. Ayer,

"It is perfectly conceivable that we should have employed different linguistic conventions from those which we actually do employ."

John Dewey in his *Logic* (pp. 82, 101, 328) objects to the statement of H. W. Joseph that "It is more in respect of the problems to be answered, than of the logical character of the reasoning . . . that Aristotle's views are antiquated." Dewey holds that logical forms arise from subject matter, and when the subject matter changes sufficiently, logic changes too. He compares logic with legal concepts. The concepts arise out of social conditions and change with them. The laws of one age are not those of another. Similarly, we are led to believe, the laws of logic are not fixed, but change with changing conditions.

Positivistic, humanistic, or atheistic as this philosophy is, it apparently attracts Biblical translators and even teachers in American Bible schools. Recently an instructor in one of the well respected Bible colleges published an article in which, along with what seemed to be a mechanistic theory of sensation, he rejected Aristotelian logic as an unwarranted, unnatural verbalization and accepted at least some of Dewey's instrumentalism. This sort of thing is seen also, though perhaps in a less conscious form and to varying degrees, in the pietistic deprecation of a so-called human logic as opposed to some unknowable divine logic.

In defense of so-called human logic, in defense of the literal meaning of words, and therefore in defense of verbal inspiration, I wish to challenge the opposing viewpoint to face the argument and answer unambiguously. I wish to challenge them to state their own theory without making use of the law of contradiction.

If logical principles are arbitrary, and if it is conceivable to employ different linguistic conventions, these writers should be able to invent and to abide by some different convention. Now, the Aristotelian logic and in particular the law of contradiction requires that a given word must not only mean something, it must also not mean something. The term dog must mean dog, but also it must not mean mountain; and mountain must not mean metaphor. Each term must refer to something definite and at the same time there must be some objects to which it does not refer. The term metaphorical cannot mean literal, nor can it mean canine or mountainous. Suppose the word mountain meant metaphor, and dog, and Bible, and the United States. Clearly, if a word meant everything, it would mean nothing. If, now, the law of contradiction is an arbitrary convention, and if our linguistic theorists choose some other convention, I challenge them to write a book in conformity with their principles. As a matter of fact it will not be hard for them to do so. Nothing more is necessary than to write the word metaphor sixty thousand times. Metaphor, metaphor, metaphor, metaphor.

This means the dog ran up the mountain, for the word metaphor means dog, ran, and mountain. Unfortunately the sentence "metaphor metaphor metaphor" also means, Next Christmas is Thanksgiving, for the word metaphor has these meanings as well.

The point should be clear. One cannot write a book or speak

a sentence that means anything without using the law of contradiction. Logic is an innate necessity, not an arbitrary convention that may be discarded at will. Whether it be the atheistic philosophy of A. J. Ayer or the pietistic depreciation of our fallible human logic, such theories make verbal inspiration impossible. But, fortunately, these theories make themselves impossible as well. They are self-refuting because they cannot be stated except by virtue of the law they repudiate.

I conclude therefore that literal language, innate logic, and verbal inspiration have nothing academic to fear from such theories as these.

NOTES

1. Cf. the author's *Thales to Dewey*, chapter 11, (Houghton Mifflin, 1958).

2. A further discussion of images will be found in my *Thales to Dewey*, p. 382.

3. John Mackintosh Shaw, *Christian Doctrine*, p. 207.

4. *The Possibility of Theological Statements*, chapter two in *Faith and Logic*, edited by Basil Mitchell, pp. 43, 45.

5. *Creation*, Flew and MacKinnon, in *New Essays in Philosophical Theology*, Flew and MacIntyre, p. 170 ff.

6. *Divine Human Encounter*, pp. 85, 110, 117. See also the definitive monograph *Emil Brunner's Concept of Revelation* by Paul King Jewett.

4.

Revelation and Morality

From antiquity to the present, questions of morality, of good and evil, of right and wrong, of value, of the purpose of human life have been frequently and carefully discussed. Plato and Aristotle, Spinoza and Kant, Butler, Bentham, and Sidgwick are a few of the better known authors. And like these philosophers every thinking person must reflect on the principles or maxims that guide his conduct. Which of two incompatible lines of action is it right to follow? Which of two incompatible principles ought to be acknowledged? If action is to be based on principle, how does one justify the principle? These questions, which demanded the attention of Plato, are no less demanding today.

Ethical Disagreement

If the people of the United States were asked to give examples of moral principles, most of the answers would include the sixth, the seventh, and the eighth of the Ten Commandments. Thou shalt not kill, thou shalt not commit adultery, and thou shalt not steal have usually been regarded as important moral laws. An orthodox Christian, or for that matter an orthodox Jew, can sincerely and consistently inculcate these laws because he believes them to be the laws of God. They are right because God has commanded them. And they are laws because God imposes penalties for their transgression. Thus moral convictions and moral education, based on law and right, can be consistently grounded on Biblical revelation.

On the other hand, contemporary American humanism like pagan antiquity neither has this ground for morality nor does it unexceptionally recognize these laws. Professor Edwin A. Burtt, a humanist himself, in both editions of his *Types of Religious Philosophy*, reports that the more radical humanists regard "sex as an essentially harmless pleasure which should be regulated only by personal taste and preference." Similarly, with reference to the other two commandments, the political radicalism of many naturalists in attacking the right of private property has included plans of taxation and other economic proposals that a conservative would call legalized theft. Nor is it difficult to identify godless governments which make use of torture and murder. Thus at least some humanists repudiate, not merely the basis of the Ten Commandments, but their content as well.

No doubt other humanists disapprove of the brutality and murder inherent in Marxism. Some may even have a kind word for private property. And some of course would not advocate adultery. But the problem that naturalism must face is this: Can an empirical philosophy, a philosophy that repudiates revelation, an instrumentalist or descriptive philosophy—can such a philosophy provide a justification for any of the Ten Commandments? Are not those humanists who still oppose murder and theft living on the Christian capital inherited from their Puritan ancestors? Or, rather, the more important question is this: Can humanism, having rejected revelation, provide a logical ground for any moral laws whatever? Can naturalism furnish a rational basis for any of the decisions of life? Or, are all choices, like Burtt's choice of sex, merely matters of personal taste and unreasoning preference?

The following argument in answer to these questions is designed to lead to the conclusion that a rational life is impossible without being based upon a divine revelation. The method of arriving at this conclusion will be to analyze the implications of non-revelational ethics. Some detailed arguments to this effect I have given elsewhere.[1] Here this material will be briefly summarized, and to it some additional analyses will be added.

UTILITARIANISM

According to the principle of utility as popularly expounded in the nineteenth century the choice between two lines of action should depend upon a calculation of the amounts, durations, and intensities of the pleasures and pains that each action would produce. That line of action is right and to be chosen whose total of pleasure is the greater. Since, however, the action of any one person affects others, at least to some degree, the calculation must include the pleasures and pains of all the persons affected; and it is this total that indicates what ought to be done.

Nor is this calculation to be restricted to immediate and obvious consequences. For example a man in making his will may bequeath a good sum to a charitable institution. But about the time he dies, new directors are elected who are inefficient or even corrupt. Their squandering of his legacy seems to produce less pleasure for the public than some other provision might have done. Therefore one is tempted to say that the bequest, on utilitarian principles, is immoral. This need not be so. For in addition to these consequences one must also calculate the effect of the donor's beneficent example in stimulating philanthropy among other men of wealth, and also indeed in strengthening his own character for the remainder of his life. These consequences, plus a few others that might be imagined, could possibly overbalance a slight degree of corruption so that the sum total of pleasure produced would justify the act.

The consequences therefore by which an act is determined to be right or wrong include all the consequences and all the people affected. Pains are to be balanced off against pleasures. Thus Utilitarianism can in short be said to aim at the greatest good of the greatest number, i.e., the greatest total of pleasure.

The Greatest Good of the Greatest Number

Some surprising implications may be drawn from the principle of the greatest good of the greatest number. In 1940 the population of Germany was perhaps ninety million of whom six million were Jews. Hitler massacred five million of them. Let us say this caused five million units of pain. But as the Germans were largely anti-semitic, the massacre and the seizure of Jewish property gave each German a unit of pleasure. Suppose even that the quick death of the gas chamber caused each Jew two units of pain. This still results in a surplus of pleasure over pain. Must not Utilitarianism conclude therefore that the massacre of the Jews was right? At any rate this is approximately the theory by which the communists have justified their massacres of Ukrainians, Hungarians, and an estimated sixteen million Chinese. When one thinks of all the good that communism will do for all future generations, a few million murders is insignificant.

The deliberate infliction of pain by massacre may be more shocking to the conscience of the free West than lesser injustices are; but whether massacre or unjust taxation, is it not the principle that the majority rules? In the United States the very wealthy are heavily taxed. The poorer majority believe they can give themselves more pleasure by inflicting pain on the minority. The defense offered is the greatest good of the greatest number. But does not this defense apply to massacre with the same force that it applies to the graduated income tax?

All non-communistic utilitarians deprecate murder. They ordinarily try to avoid lesser injustices also, though they may argue that the graduated income tax is not unjust. But the problem becomes acute when a member of the minority decides to oppose the will of the majority. The Latvians, the Hungarians, and the Tibetans resisted communism. That is, they opposed the greatest good of the greatest number—just as a former governor of Utah resisted the income tax and thereby tried to harm the majority. But it is wrong to oppose the greatest good of the greatest number. Therefore the minority should cooperate in inflicting pain on itself so that the greatest total of pleasure may be achieved.

Originally Utilitarianism took its start from the theory of Psychological Hedonism. Bentham assumed as a scientific fact that all men are completely dominated by two sovereign masters: pleasure and pain. The one is man's sole motive and the other cannot possibly be desired. Whether this is a scientific fact or not, it has at least a degree of plausibility. The next step in Utilitarianism was to advance from Psychological to Ethical Hedonism. The good is pleasure; my good is my pleasure; and it would be as immoral as it is foolish to cause myself harm. This also is at least plausible.

But Utilitarianism is not individualistic Hedonism. Bentham aimed at the sum total of pleasure of the whole human race. Sidgwick after him denied that "my good is my pleasure." Only the greatest good of the greatest number could qualify as the criterion of a moral action. If a given line of action results in harm to me but produces a greater total of pleasure to mankind, then it is immoral for me to seek my own good. In this case I must seek my own harm. And this is not plausible. Certainly it is not plausible that the Latvians, Hungarians, and Tibetans should cooperate in their own destruction. Here then is the problem of the conflict between the good of an individual and the sum total of pleasure for the human race.

Utilitarians have tried to avoid this conflict in two ways. First, Sidgwick assumed, presupposed, or broadly hinted that ultimately the pleasures of all people harmonize. The seeming conflict depends on a mistaken calculation. In reality my good is compatible and ultimately identical with the good of everyone else. No real conflict is possible. The pleasure of inflicting pain on any one always entails future pains that cancel out the pleasure. Therefore whether a person seeks his own greatest pleasure or whether he seeks the greatest pleasure of the whole race, he will do precisely the same thing. Every action that promotes the one, promotes the other also.

Such a view successfully avoids the justification of massacre; but unfortunately it is a view that Utilitarianism cannot logically accept. Utilitarianism makes a point of calculation and scientific observation. It attempts to be a descriptive theory. But it is not an observed nor an observable fact that the pleasures of all people harmonize. One might believe it on faith, but not on experience. Even if the communistic calculations that justify massacre are mistaken, there is no evidence that the pleasures of all people have harmonized in the past and obviously there is as yet no evidence at all about the future. In fact, the preponderance of evidence is against it. The conflict of wars, the conflict of religions, the continual cross purposes of individuals all seem to show that if one person gets what is good for him, another person cannot. Hence a theory that repudiates faith or revelation and is based on observation cannot logically object to massacres. At least it cannot object to my seeking my own good at the expense of others.

Sidgwick indeed argued that if we may assume "such a Being as God by the consensus of theologians is supposed to be," we may establish morality on a utilitarian basis. But he hesitated to assert the existence of God on the basis of ethical data. In this he was wise. If it were possible to show empirically that all pleasures harmonize, perhaps the existence of God could be inferred; but in the absence of such evidence, the inference remains ungrounded. In the end Sidgwick cautiously confesses to a sort of skepticism.

What makes a utilitarian appeal to God still more incongruous is that not any kind of God will do. The conflict between individual and public good cannot be resolved by Aristotle's First Mover or by Hegel's Absolute Spirit. On the contrary it must be a Being such as God "by the consensus of theologians is supposed to be." Having been written in nineteenth century England, this phrase designates the Christian God. That is to say, if an appeal to God is to remove the conflict between private and public good, and if a massacre is to produce pain for its perpetrator, then the God appealed to must punish Stalin in a future life and must reward his now dead victims to even things up. Stalin certainly did not suffer for his crimes in this life. He seems to have been one of the most successful men who has ever lived. And obviously his victims did not get their equal share of pleasure. Only if God punishes Stalin in hell can it be maintained that God harmonizes all pleasures. But a utilitarian appeal to heaven, hell, and a future life is an illegitimate appeal to Christian principles. Bentham rather explicitly restricted his sanctions to this life. In general, Utilitarianism is a this-worldly theory. Therefore the appeal to God, if made at all, is illegitimate, and the conflict remains an insoluble difficulty.

There is, however, a second way in which Utilitarianism can avoid the justification of massacre. The suggestion is also found in Sidgwick; but it is more interesting to note that after sixty years during which Utilitarianism has been largely neglected by writers on ethics, a contemporary now returns to this second idea. The greatest good of the greatest number is by itself an incorrect principle. The criterion by which to distinguish a good act from an evil act is not the mere total of pleasure, but the equality of its distribution. Massacre may, arguably, produce a greater total of pleasure; but the summum bonum is the equal distribution of pleasure. Every person in the world should have one unit of pleasure before anyone has two. Or, if I may say so, no American should have a college education before every Chinese has a bathtub.

Aside from the illustration provided in the last sentence, such is the contention of the recent volume, *Ethical Value,* by Professor George F. Harouni. His main point, at least for the present purpose, is that the equal distribution of good—which he prefers to identify as satisfaction rather than pleasure—is a criterion of value independent of the amount of happiness achieved. When he comes to consider the conflict between individual and public good, or, as he phrases it, the relation between utility and justice, he finds the problem insoluble except on one premise. Dismissing several attempted solutions he concludes, "the only alternative open to me, then, is *to stuff into my definition of 'right' all that is required*" (italics, his). That is to say, Professor Harouni defines right or good as the equal distribution of satisfactions. This really assumes the point at issue. For example, he refuses to discuss Kant's view that only a good will can be good without qualification, on the ground that it is not an analysis of the meaning of good. This refusal is unsatisfactory, for neither Kant's view nor that of Egoistic Hedonism can be refuted by simply defining them out of existence.

To enforce the point that a definition does not solve the problem under discussion, a few remarks on equality may be added.

First, there is the unanswered question of why equality of distribution should be chosen rather than the greater total. A reason rather than a definition is called for. Second, equality is not a rational criterion. Surely it is not rational in Kant's sense of the term. Its denial does not produce a logical contradiction. Or, if this is not what is meant by 'rational,' we can only ask, What is? Is it meant merely that equality is plausible? But, third, Harouni's criterion is not plausible. It implies that I am under obligation to harm myself, at least to the extent of not enjoying pleasures I might achieve, until all other people have as much satisfaction as I now have. Does this mean that I ought to distribute my philosophical library to the Tibetans and Nepalese? If not, what does it mean? These three points are honest material questions and cannot be set aside simply by deciding to define good as the equal distribution of satisfaction.

Calculation

But perhaps the most crushing objection is that the calculation required under all these forms of Utilitarianism is impossible. It is impossible if we consider only one's individual good and all the more so if we try to total in the whole human race. Without calculation Westerners have a strong suspicion that murder causes a surplus of pain over pleasure, yet in less violent and more ordinary matters what is there to rely on but pure guesswork? Should I buy stock on the New York Exchange? There is something more than guesswork by which we can reasonably conclude that one stock will be more profitable financially than another. But will the money gained give me more pleasure than another course of action. Perhaps I should buy a new car instead. Or should I invest my money at Las Vegas and Reno? How will each of these affect my grandchildren? Is it better for me, a young man, to become a physician, a veterinarian, or an engineer? Should I major in English, History, or Geology? These are perfectly serious questions that many people have had to ask themselves. But how could anyone possibly estimate the amounts, the durations, and the intensities of the pleasures to be caused by each of these decisions, not only the pleasures he himself will experience, but the pleasures of all others who will be affected by his action? Is not utilitarian calculation impossible?

Utilitarianism holds that the goodness or moral character of an act depends on its tendency to produce pleasurable consequences for the human race as a whole. Surely it must be admitted that the impossibility of deciding which of two actions conduces to the good is a legitimate point of criticism, for a theory of ethics that gives no specific guidance in the actual circumstances of life can hardly be called a theory of ethics at all.

The Good

Yet there is another and still more important point of criticism. An acceptable theory of ethics ought at least to identify the end of action, even if it cannot indicate the effective means thereto. Now, Utilitarianism has just shown itself unable to do the latter; can it then do the former? Is the good at which we should aim personal pleasure, the greatest sum total of pleasure for everyone, the equal distribution of pleasure, or something altogether different from pleasure? Is it possible to know what the good is? Again, a theory of ethics that failed to identify the aim of life is even more obviously no theory of ethics at all.

For the purpose of considering this point, the language and the discussions of the twentieth century are clearer than those of the nineteenth. Though it is true that Utilitarianism made pleasure the goal of all our activity and gave some reasons therefor, the ambiguity of the term pleasure has been noted by nearly every anti-hedonistic writer from Plato on. So great are the contrasts among pleasures that John Stuart Mill was forced to abandon the basic hedonism that made these differences im-material. The problem has been examined more explicitly in recent years, and the term value has been substituted for pleas-ure. Such a substitution, whether it be the term *value* or *satis-faction,* can hardly alter the nature of the problem; the diffi-culties remain the same; but perhaps it will seem more up to date to use twentieth century language.

First, however, let us state the questions once more. Is it possible for a descriptive theory of ethics, an empirical theory of ethics, a theory that makes no use of revelation, to give us a rational program for life? How do the naturalists and humanists, or even those who try to base a religion on experience, arrive at their conclusions respecting the good?

Values in Experience

The usual method in recent literature is to claim that values can be found in experience. The late Edgar Sheffield Brightman is a good example of those who try to base a religion on values found in experience. He defined value as "whatever is actually liked, prized, esteemed, desired, approved, or enjoyed by anyone at any time . . . Good," he says, "is synonymous with value." Burtt, on the other hand, speaking for the humanists, finds in experience the values of friendship, art, and science. Dewey also finds that art is of value, though he often uses the more commonplace arrangements of heating, lighting, and speedy communication as instances of values. But whatever the par-ticular items are, the fact that they are values is supposed to be a discovery of experience.

Brightman's definition of value is particularly broad. If we are to call valuable anything that anyone has ever liked or enjoyed, then we should have to list not only friendship, art, and science, but also whiskey, gambling, and crime. Nor are these last three to be added merely as the hostile criticism of an unfriendly opponent. On the contrary, Gardner Williams of the University of Toledo, in his volume, *Humanistic Ethics* (page 6), says, "Selfish ambition, or the will to power, when successful, is intrinsically good because it is intrinsically satisfactory." Thus murder is a value because it has been discovered as a value in experience. Successful murder and ambition have been conspicuously exemplified in the dictator Stalin. Let it be admitted that you and I do not have the skill and the determination to emulate him; our efforts to dominate a nation would soon fail and we would come to grief; but can empirical theories consistently disapprove of such an eminent success as Stalin? Is not murder as truly a value as art, or prayer, or modern heating systems?

It happens that most of the humanists, and of course the religionists like Brightman, want to produce a theory that would condemn murder and brutality. How they proceed, we must examine with care. But much more important than condemning brutality is the necessity of avoiding the chaos of subjectivity implicit in the definition of value as anything anyone likes or enjoys. Strange as it may seem, there would be less logical objection to a theory that definitely recommended murder than to a theory that made all desires equally legitimate. If dictatorship and domination is the goal of life, then at least there is a norm of conduct that applies to all mankind. It may not be the norm you or I now accept, but it is a definite norm. And that makes it a theory of ethics. But if all we can say is that murder is right for Stalin, and prayer is right for Brightman, and guzzling booze is right for the alcoholic, then we have no ethics at all because we have no theory at all. In such a case there is no universal norm.

It is essential therefore that those who begin with values as enjoyments found in anyone's experience must somehow show that certain values are values for all men. Brightman in his way and Dewey in his both try to avoid the chaos of subjectivism. A previous footnote gave a reference to Brightman's theory of value, and the arguments will not be reproduced here. But since Dewey has so widely influenced the American scene, it seems wise to summarize the criticism contained in the monograph mentioned in the same footnote.

DEWEY AND INSTRUMENTALISM

For Dewey and Instrumentalism the difficulties of ethics are important not merely in themselves alone, not merely for a theory of ethics by itself, but much more for the entire scope of that type of philosophy. If there is any crucial point at which humanism is obligated to present a convincing and indeed an unanswerable argument, it is with respect to the field of ethics. Of course the reason is not that ethics, unlike symbolic logic, is immediately important to the everyday life of an individual whether he is a philosopher or not. Nor is the reason merely that ethics is essential to a comprehensive system of philosophy. This would be true for Aristotle and Hegel as well as for Dewey. But rather, Instrumentalism must stake its claim on ethics because it makes an activistic practical interest the foundation of its system. This is the school that has inveighed most vehemently against ivory towers and the detachment of empyrean contemplation. Eternity and otherworldliness are called delusions. Thinking concerns this world, and ideas are plans of overt action. Ethical principles are absolutely basic in humanistic pragmatism.

This is not true of Christianity. Admittedly Christianity with its message of salvation from sin lays great stress on a hunger and thirst after righteousness. Particularly in the Calvinistic tradition the Ten Commandments have been emphasized. But ethics is not the foundation of the Christian system. Christianity is based on theology, and ethics is a derivative subject. What is right and what is wrong is determined by God's commands. But with the instrumentalists ethics is the basic subject.

That Instrumentalism recognizes its need of ethics could be documented many times over. Nearly any one of Dewey's books would furnish apposite quotations. Here only one will be used, a quotation from his *Quest for Certainty* (p. 252).

"The effective condition of the integration of all divided purposes and conflicts of belief is the realization that intelligent action is the sole ultimate resource of mankind in every field whatsoever."

A second reading of this quotation shows its universal application. Not some only, but all divided purposes are to be integrated; not some subjects only, but every field whatsoever is covered. Intelligent action is man's sole ultimate resource; there is no other at all. There is no God from whom man can obtain comfort, encouragement, and strength, much less wisdom, instruction, and intervention. Man has only himself.

It is this atheism that throws into relief the desperate need of an irrefragable theory of ethics. If humanism fails to save man from the plight of his conflicts in every field whatsoever, humanism fails indeed. It may have an admirable theory of science, it may devise effective aids in education, it may stimulate professors to take part in politics; but since science and politics are only means to chosen ends and ideals, if humanism cannot rationally justify one ideal as against another, if its theory of ethics cannot give clear cut guidance in the perplexities of life, it will have failed in its main endeavor and must be abandoned.

The main topic of the present discussion is the identification of ideals, norms, or values. Something along the way will have to be said about the means to the achievement of these values, but the main interest is in the end to be attained. In the language of the Shorter Catechism we are asking, What is the chief end of man? Let us not prejudge the matter, however. Dewey would hesitate at the idea of one single chief end. He prefers to speak in the plural. Let us then do likewise. Our aim is to identify norms, ideals, or values.

Changing Morality

First of all it must be noted that whatever ideals or standards Dewey may propose, they are not to be regarded as fixed and final norms for all human beings.

"We institute standards of justice, truth, esthetic quality, etc. . . exactly as we set up a platinum bar as a standard measurer of lengths. The standard is just as much subject to modification and revision in the one case as in the other on the basis of the consequences of its operational application . . . The superiority of one conception of justice to another is of the same order as the superiority of the metric system . . . although not of the same quality" (*Logic, The Theory of Inquiry,* p. 216) .

This comparison between a standard of justice and a standard of measurement is not an adequate illustration for Dewey's purposes. In measuring lines the result is the same whether one uses inches or centimeters. When two weights are compared, grams and ounces will uniformly agree on which is the heavier. But in morality Dewey will have an act to be commendable on one standard and evil on another. For Dewey's purposes, then, another illustration is better.

Moral standards, he says, are like language in that both are the result of custom. Theories of absolute ethics argue that ideal standards antecede customs and judge of their rightness or wrongness; any alleged ideals that are merely the result of custom could not be its judge. That this absolutism is at best unnecessary is seen in the case of language. There were no antecedent principles of grammar. Language evolved from unintelligent babblings and instinctive gestures. Then came the rules of grammar and the apparatus of literacy. This, however, is not the end, for the language and its grammar change to meet new situations and new needs. Words change their forms and meanings, new expressions are invented, and the old rules become archaic. Nevertheless the rules of language, though merely the unforeseen and unintended results of custom, exercise their authority over us. Grammar and morals are both a part of life. No one can escape them, even if he wants to. Man's choice is simply between adopting more or less significant customs.

This analogy between the rules of grammar and the principles of morality carries important implications. Most obvious is the fact that different nations use different languages. Of course, if we wish to speak French, we must conform to its customs sufficiently to be understood. And if we are born French, we do not have much choice at first. Eventually, however, it may become possible to emigrate to the United States. This involves a decision to speak English rather than French. The opportunity to disapprove of the moral customs of a nation, and against social pressure to live a different kind of life, is more readily available than emigration. The Christian martyrs of the early centuries and of the Reformation had decided against prevailing custom. Does not this require a moral norm superior to the customs that are condemned?

Dewey's analogy with language tends to minimize the importance of this question. After all, it is of no great moment whether a person speaks French, German, or English, nor whether he breaks a few rules of grammar in doing so. But Christian missionaries report that in certain sections of Africa social customs are such that girls scarcely reach their teens before they have been raped a half a dozen times. And it was only last century that there were cannibal tribes on several Pacific islands. Even today as independence is granted to the Congo, cannibalism, as well as tribal warfare, is reviving. Missionaries have opposed these "moral standards," these products of custom, these results of instinctive gestures. They preach that divinely revealed, fixed, and universal standards condemn such actions. Now, if this is not true, and if ethics is analogous to language, can there be any justification for imposing the customs of one society upon another society? Does not the condemnation of one set of customs require a norm that is more than the effect of another set of customs?

Dewey has an interesting and perhaps a disturbing answer to this question. In the first place he asserts that the proponents of fixed standards, such as Christian missionaries, are self-deceived. They have in fact no absolute norm. Their moral ideas are merely the results of the customs of their own group. Custom therefore is still the source of all morality. Now, in the second place, the opposition of one custom to a wider custom is a form of class warfare, indeed "the most serious form of class warfare." Class warfare is not overscrupulous. Each side treats its opponent as a willful violator of absolute moral principles. Thus we have the present conflict between the bourgeoisie and the proletariat. Hence the notion of fixed moral standards results in a war that can be ended only by force.

Thus by this twofold answer Dewey consistently explains how, even if morals are nothing more than custom, moral conflicts between societies can as a matter of fact occur. But in doing so does he not imply that cannibalism is as good in its place as Christian morality is in its place? Does not the tone of his remarks suggest that rape remains commendable in Africa and that Christian missionaries are despicable imperialists? The difference in moral standards therefore is not the difference between inches and centimeters, which always give the same result; it is a difference such that no ideal or norm applies everywhere, to everybody, and all the time.

Values in Experience

The denial of fixed and universal standards is of major importance; but there is also a lesser problem that Dewey must face. Even if the values of Africa and of Christendom differ, how can the people in either society identify their values in the flux of experience? Can Dewey's methods, when applied in the United States, distinctly conclude that one particular type of action is good and valuable, and another type is not?

John Dewey believed that he had seen the problem clearly and that he had discovered the key to its solution. The deepest problem of modern life, so he held, is the integration of man's beliefs about the physical world with his beliefs about human values. In the Middle Ages science and religion were harmonious because they were both developed against a single philosophical background. All problems were solved on Thomistic principles. Today, however, medieval science has disappeared, but common beliefs about value still retain some medieval flavor. Since, now, modern conduct is mainly motivated by modern science, the result is that the conduct of modern man conflicts with his beliefs about values. Because of two reactions to this conflict, two disadvantages arise. Some men with a strong emotional attachment to the antiquated theory of value disparage and retard science, at least by dissipating their energies in unfruitful endeavors. The other type accepts science wholeheartedly, but because the values they have been taught cannot be scientifically established, they repudiate value altogether. Therefore the important problem for a philosophy that does not wish to be isolated from modern life is to harmonize modern theory and practice.

The solution of this problem is to be found in a more thorough exploitation of scientific method. As science detached problem after problem from the medieval syntheses, its successes accumulated until now in the twentieth century there is reason to suppose that all the problems of humanity are amenable to the same method. Beliefs about values, about ethics and sociology, are today in much the same state as were beliefs about physics in the prescientific era. What is needed is the application of scientific techniques. Only two attitudes block the acceptance of this view. With some there is a basic distrust of the capacity of experience to develop standards, ideals, or norms for life. This first attitude depends on eternal values and appeals to a Supreme Being. No hope can be expected from such a theistic view. Secular interests now dominate men's minds; the sense of transcendental values has become enfeebled; the authority of the church has diminished; men may profess the old religion, but they act secularly. This divergence between what men do and what they say is the outward evidence of the conflict in modern thought. To solve the problem and remove the conflict men's thoughts should be made to conform to what they do. To invent an example Dewey does not use: men play golf on Sunday and believe in the existence of God; while continuing to play golf, they should be taught to repudiate belief in God, rather than to change their conduct and go to church.

The second attitude which blocks acceptance of the scientific method is the enjoyment of pleasures, goods, or values irrespective of the method used to produce this enjoyment. Such a view supposes that "to be enjoyed and to be a value are two names for one and the same fact." This attitude or theory of value is superior to the theistic view in that the values are concrete experiences of desire and satisfaction here and now. Its failure arises from the fact that these enjoyments are casual and unregulated by intelligence. Escape from transcendental absolutism is not to be had in casual enjoyments, but in defining value by enjoyments which are the consequences of intelligent action.

"Without the intervention of thought, enjoyments are not values but problematic goods, becoming values when they reissue in a changed form from intelligent behavior" (*Quest for Certainty*, p. 259).

Enjoyments therefore are fugitive and precarious so that there is needed a method of discriminating among them on the basis of their conditions and consequences. Goods are just goods, with certain intrinsic qualities; of them as goods there is nothing to be said: they are simply what they are. Whatever can be said of them pertains to their causes and effects. The reason for enjoying an object is often that it is a means to or a result of something else; the reason concerns the cause of the enjoyment and has nothing to do with its intrinsic qualities.

Before continuing the summary, one should stop to note a confusing factor in the lines above. True it is that things are *often* enjoyed, or at least chosen, because they are causes of something else. Such goods, by some authors, are called instrumental as opposed to intrinsic goods; and they range from taking a cab to the airport to visiting the dentist. But Dewey's argument really requires that this be the case, not just "often," but *always*. Let us stop and ask whether all goods are instrumental, or whether some are intrinsic. Is it true that the reason for enjoying something has nothing to do with its intrinsic qualities?

This question should be kept in mind as the summary proceeds.

A genuine good therefore, Dewey continues, differs from a spurious good because of reflection on consequences. All criticism concerns consequences because no properties carry adequate credentials on their face.

In this connection two points should be raised. The first, mentioned a few lines above, concerns the antecedents of which the value in question is a consequence. This point has to do with the enjoyment of casual pleasures irrespective of the method used to produce them. The second and perhaps more important point touches on the consequences which the enjoyment itself produces.

To invent an example, suppose that a man applies for a job, does his work, and is paid; in such a case the money is not a spurious good but a real value because it was earned by intelligent action. Had the man found the same amount of money on the sidewalk, it would not have been a real value. So Dewey contends. To most people, however, money found is just as valuable as money earned. In fact, although the purchasing powers of a dollar earned and of a dollar found are the same, the work of earning may be so lengthy and laborious that the sum of a life's values are diminished by intelligent foresight and increased by a lucky find. The workman's time and strength might well be so exhausted that what the dollar buys could barely be enjoyed. Thus one might say, in sharp contrast with Dewey, that the casual, unearned enjoyment is the greater value.

Of course, if Dewey meant merely that it is not wise to depend for one's living on finding money in the street, his argument would be sound enough, but it would be trivial. A theist of the most pronounced supernatural views, as well as the Epicurean who tries to avoid trouble by dozing in the sun, would agree that a certain amount of planning and work are necessary for most of our ordinary satisfactions. This triviality cannot be the basis of Dewey's antagonism to theists and Epicureans. His expressions and emphasis seem to say that unexpected enjoyments are simply of no value. They are spurious.

This view, which seems so odd to common sense, apparently depends on the thesis that the value of an object depends on its being a result of and a means to something else, and in particular does not depend on its intrinsic enjoyable quality. Nothing is valuable in itself. Enough has been said now of the antecedents of the enjoyment; the second point concerns the consequences of the enjoyed value.

On this point too the criticism, continuing to press the issue of intrinsic value, will be much the same. It may be granted that we assign value to money because of the possible consequences, namely, the things we can buy with it; in this sense a bill or a check, being only a piece of paper, does not carry value credentials on its face. But is this to say that nothing does? Is there nothing valuable for itself alone? Are all values merely instrumental? Is there no final end whatever?

For purposes of illustration a game of chess will do. Is the pleasure of chess dependent for its value on the consequences? Of course, chess may be used to cement friendships, and no doubt other consequences could be ingeniously listed. But ordinarily the reason for playing chess is not at all that the game is a means to or a result of something else. On the contrary it has all to do with its intrinsic value-quality. If the credentials on its face were not adequate, chess would not be chosen.

Dewey, in strange company with Aristotle, might spurn this illustration of chess. Playing games is not a sufficiently serious activity to be commensurate with major human endeavors. Besides, as Aristotle said, recreation is for the sake of work: we play in order to work, we do not work in order to play. Although such sentiments fit the Aristotelian viewpoint very well, it is not so clear that Dewey can use them with much consistency. If nothing is intrinsically valuable, how could one insist that play is a means to work rather than the reverse? If nothing carries its own credentials, how could one distinguish between the serious and the trivial? Aristotle made recreation a means to an intrinsically valuable activity, an activity that is chosen for its own sake and not as a means to anything else. But if, as Dewey says, there is no final cause and if everything is chosen merely as a means to something else, and never because of its intrinsic qualities, does it make any difference what we choose?

Young men and women in large numbers choose to go to college. On Dewey's theory, only too well accepted by the students, the reason cannot be any intrinsic value in knowledge. To give such a reason would be to flee from reality and take refuge in the discredited Aristotelian ivory-tower. For the young man college is a means of getting a better job; for the young woman it is a means of getting a better man. But neither the family that marriage brings nor the food that the job supplies is to be chosen for any intrinsic quality. These too are merely means to something else. College is the means to a job; a job is the means to marriage; marriage is the means to a family; a family, along with the job, is the means of sending a son to college. But chess is the means of restricting social contacts to a small number; restricting social contacts is the means of avoiding marriage; single blessedness saves the money one would spend on a son's tuition; and this money is the means for purchasing a more handsome set of chess men. But why follow one causal series rather than the other? All activities are valueless means to other valueless means. The means have no end, and choice has become irrational. Or, at least, choices are based on nothing else than personal preference.

Here it would seem that another humanist sees more clearly than John Dewey. Gardner Williams writes,

"It does not matter, from an individual's point of view, how he is satisfied, so long as, in the long run, he is satisfied."[2]

In this context the *how* would seem to include, not only the identification of the object that gives satisfaction, but also the means by which the object was obtained. In this case the object would be equally valuable or satisfying, whether it was obtained by intelligent foresight and attention to the means of production, or whether it was obtained by pure luck.

To these last assertions Dewey would probably reply with some expressions of disgust. Such opinions he would repudiate, not merely as a lack of enthusiasm for scientific method, but also as an avoidance of responsibility for reconstructing economic, political, and religious institutions. In a number of places Dewey bases his rejection of opposing theories on sociological preferences. Epistemology, for example, wastes time that could profitably be spent in remedying social evils. Thought should not be employed for any private good; if it aims at some special result, it is not sincere. Strange to say, in this context he even speaks of "something worth while for itself," though on the next page he adds with more consistency that "there is no particular end set up in advance so as to shut in the activities of observation, forming of ideas, and application." Instead of

"emotional satisfaction and private comfort . . . the satisfaction in question means a satisfaction of the needs and conditions of the problem out of which the idea, the purpose and method of action arises . . . So repulsive is a conception of truth which makes it a mere tool of private ambition and aggrandizement that the wonder is that critics have attributed such a notion to sane men" (*Reconstruction in Philosophy*, pp. 124, 126, 157).

But is Dewey's disgust a sufficient reply to the objections? On what grounds can he construct a theory of sociology that would eliminate epistemology as a waste of time? Can he distinguish a social evil from a social value? By what logical argument can Dewey recommend college rather than chess? Has he any reason for being disgusted at private good? He cannot rightly claim that critics have mistakenly attributed crazy notions to sane men. Professor Williams is a sane man; so were the Sophists and the Epicureans. And many other men will refuse to relinquish particular ends, private comfort, and intrinsic goods merely because Dewey finds them repulsive.

Security and Scientific Ethics

Behind Dewey's disgust and behind the insistence that the

methods of science will solve ethical problems lies a contrast that Dewey was fond of emphasizing. It is the contrast between certainty and security. Religionists, mystics, and deluded Platonists seek for certainty and sometimes claim that they have actually come into possession of absolute truth. But the instrumentalist theory of science and F.C.S. Shiller's keen criticism of Plato show that fixed truth cannot be had. The traditional desire for certainty should therefore be abandoned. In its place modern science has provided something much better—security. Chemistry improves the food supply of civilized peoples. Physics allows for the invention of telephones, radio, and jet planes. If, now, we scientifically study the means and conditions by which ends or values can be made more secure, we have in Dewey's opinion solved the problems of ethics.

But what is the problem of ethics? Is it indeed the problem of security? Is it not rather the choice of what to secure? Dewey has indicated some rather definite political choices. He opposes laissez faire, liberty, and individualism and advocates some type of collectivism. Yet we are forced to ask whether the scientific method of his theory compels us to choose the one rather than the other. Science furnishes means to whatever a man may choose. But can it furnish any reason for choosing this in preference to that? The main question therefore is not how to secure values but how to select them. To substitute security for certainty under these conditions must be an act of philosophic and existential desperation.

However, security, reflection on conditions and consequences, and the disparagement of intrinsic qualities, are a consistent application of the parallelism of ethics with science. Science turned its back on the immediately perceived wetness of water in order to form a conception, H_2O, that could produce more secure and more significant experiences of the wetness. Things enjoyed should be treated similarly; they are possibilities of values to be achieved. To say that something is enjoyed is equivalent to saying water is wet. This may be a fact but it is not a value. A value is something satisfactory, and the satisfactory is that which *will do*, i.e., a prediction concerning the future, not a statement about the present. A statement about the present, such as, this experience is satisfying, only raises a problem. Granted that we enjoy it, how is the enjoyment to be rated? Is it a value or not? Is it something *to be* enjoyed? To say that it is a value means that it will continue to satisfy. It *will* do. A statement of present fact makes no claim on action, but a judgment about what is *to be* desired looks to the future and possesses *de jure* and not merely *de facto* quality.

In the light of previous ethical speculation the distinction between a merely *de facto* quality and a *de jure* quality would seem to be an important one. Is it possible to see that one enjoyment will not do and that another will do? How can we distinguish the value that will continue to satisfy in the future from the one that will not? And how can this distinction be made without private comforts and final ends?

Dewey notes that although values must be connected inherently with likings, preferences, or desires, they are not to be connected with any random preference, but only with those rationally approved after examination. The conflict between thoughtless, sporadic wishes and plans reflectively chosen for long term purposes is a common one. About the first people usually say, I would *like* to do or have this; but about the second they assert, with regret or determination, I *ought* to do that. Dewey must take into account the 'ought' of traditional morality, and the distinction between *de jure* and *de facto* is to the point. The question is whether instrumentalism can justify such a distinction. What sort of examination will reveal that one liking is to be approved and another rejected? And inasmuch as Dewey criticizes the rationalistic theory on the score that it affords no guidance, one naturally expects that Dewey will provide the guidance.

What sort of examination Dewey has in mind is clear enough —at least it is easy to quote the sentences by which Dewey believes he has met the requirements. In fact he puts one of them in italics: "Judgments about values are judgments about the conditions and the results of experienced objects; judgments about that which should regulate the formation of our desires, affections, and enjoyments." When duties or values conflict, dogmatism attempts to construct a scale of values. But this, says Dewey, is a confession of inability to judge the concrete. The alternate to a hierarchical scheme is judgment by means of the relations in which values occur. One must examine their causes, conditions, and consequences, their interactions and connections; the more we ascertain of these details, the more we know the objects in question, and the better we can judge its value. He states,

> "Enjoyments that issue from conduct directed by insight into relations have a meaning and a validity due to the way in which they are experienced. Such enjoyments are not to be repented of; they generate no after taste of bitterness."

Dewey's argument here depends on three related assumptions: that casual enjoyments are not values, that values are means to ends, and that enjoyments chosen in the light of their relations are not to be repented of. He gives an example. Heating and lighting, speed of transportation and communication, have been attained, not by lauding their desirability, but by studying their conditions. "Knowledge of relations having been obtained, ability to produce followed, and enjoyment ensued as a matter of course."

If this example is intended to show how scientific method can produce ideals, it is not convincing. Scientific method undoubtedly secures speed of transportation, but enjoyment and satisfaction do not follow as a matter of course. Speed of transportation and communication help to make war more horrible. Knowledge of relations and ability to produce can be directed toward painful ends as easily as toward pleasurable ends. In both cases the means are valuable for the production of the ends; and in both cases the agent may have an exhaustive knowledge of causes, conditions, consequences, interactions, and connections; but where is it shown that scientific procedure can distinguish between a good end and an evil end? In other words, must there not be a value, a good, an end, whose intrinsic goodness can motivate a choice before our knowledge of means, conditions, and circumstances will lead us to secure it? Can science possibly justify ideals?

Evil Ideals

It is in this line of thought that the distinction between *de facto* and *de jure* quality becomes clearly necessary. Dewey agrees that there are wrong ideals. Without aesthetic enjoyment mankind might become a race of economic monsters, capable of using leisure only in ostentatious display and extravagant dissipation. Apparently no amount of knowledge of interactions and relations will make economic monsters a value. But why not? The peace settlement of World War I was made with the most realistic attention to concrete details of economic advantage, and Dewey never tires of insisting on concrete details; the aims too were broadly social and were not limited to private comfort; but at Versailles, according to Dewey, it was attention to economic advantage distributed in proportion to physical power to create future disturbances. And presumably this was bad. The evil of such a situation does not arise from the absence of ideals; much less, it must also be said, from an ignorance of details; but rather the greatest evils arise from the wrong ideals. How then can further attention to realistic detail identify valuable ideals? Dewey berates shortsightedness and insists that one should not sacrifice the future to immediate pleasure. But will far sightedness solve the problem if it cannot see far enough to pass beyond valuable means to an intrinsically valuable end?

That the methods of science cannot be applied in the determination of ethical principles can best be appreciated if one keeps clearly in mind the specific results Dewey thinks he has obtained by his methods. And to make the discussion still more concrete, the ideals mentioned by one of Dewey's whole-hearted and influential disciples—Professor William Heard Kilpatrick —will be added to the list. In every case the question must be:

Does scientific method show whether this ideal is good or evil?

For one thing, Dewey repudiates the aims of private, one-sided advantage: "a personal end is repulsive." An instrumentalist theory of truth, he complains, has too often been thought of in terms of satisfying some purely personal need. This is a mistake. The satisfaction that Instrumentalism provides, Dewey explains, is "a satisfaction of the needs and conditions of the problem out of which the idea, the purpose and method of action, arises. It includes public and objective conditions."

Superficially at least this much may be admitted. Whether I am developing new vaccines or investing in the stock market, there is plenty of stubborn objectivity to be taken into account. And in this sense the problem has "needs and conditions" which must be satisfied. But what shall be said of the prior choice between developing vaccines and investing in the stock market? The former presumably is not privately or personally motivated (though of course it may be), and the latter is as good an example as any of purely personal satisfaction. But what procedure of science—either biological science or economic science, not to mention physics and chemistry—demonstrates empirically that a purely private end is repulsive? Certainly there is here an unbridged gap between Dewey's premises and his conclusion; and it would seem that the gap is unbridgeable. Egoism is not so easily refuted.

If a broad rejection of personal aims is too vague, Dewey also has more specific ideals. He mentions health, wealth, friendship, industry, temperance, courtesy, learning, and initiative, (*Reconstruction in Philosophy*, pp. 166-169), as well as lighting, heating, and transportation. These specifications are indeed sufficiently definite; and as they are typical, they go a long way toward rescuing ethics from the bog of eternal values, if not from the rigidity of fixed truths.

Kilpatrick is similarly specific. Bodily health and vigor is a good that no modern-minded man would deny. A well-adjusted personality, satisfying personal relationships, meaningful work as opposed to a life of leisure, music, an adequate social life process, and a non-supernatural religion are examples of Kilpatrick's twelve constituents of the good life. Morality is whatever advances this good life.[3]

Further specific ideals can be inferred from his deprecation of ancient Sparta's military system and his praise of Periclean Athens (pp. 286-289). He is also explicitly opposed to racial discrimination (p. 340); he holds that laissez-faire is an evil (p. 405), as is also the old-fashioned Americanism that believed in the government's duty to protect private property and to maintain inalienable rights (pp. 403, 54-55).

Most emphatically he is opposed to religious liberty. Not only would he prevent religious groups from maintaining schools and colleges (p. 254); he believes it is "undemocratic" to allow parents to teach the doctrines of their religion to their own children. Apparently the government, as in Russia, should invade the home and enforce belief in humanistic secularism.

Two questions, however: Was it the scientific method that selected these ideals, and was it laboratory procedure that proved their desirability? Or, are these ideals the evil ideals of secular bigotry?

Murder

Dewey, as was said before, admits that some aims are evil. In one of his books he asserts that no honest person can convince himself that murder would have beneficial consequences, and he also adds that a normal person will immediately resent an act of wanton cruelty. There are, none the less, a large number of people, presumably abnormal, who enjoy bull fights. But Dewey stakes his claim on normal people, who are fair-minded.

Philosophically this begs the question. The members of the S.P.C.A. regard bull fight fans as a low breed of humanity. In return the latter believe that the former just do not have a normal sense of fun. On what basis then is this disagreement to be resolved? Must not one first define the right and good and only on this basis decide who is normal and fair-minded? Or can we simply say that these honorific designations are to be applied to the preferences of the majority? The plausibility that a normal person resents wanton cruelty and condemns murder lies in the fact that the statement is true in the United States, at the present time, because of our Christian heritage. But it is not true in communistic countries. There murder and massacre are definitely accepted as having very beneficial consequences. Now, if Dewey and Kilpatrick succeed in destroying Christianity by prohibiting parents to give their children religious instruction, could anyone be sure that massacre would be still thought wrong?

One difficulty here is that Dewey assumes a universal moral agreement, whether on murder or on bull fights, where none or little exists; and the reader is expected to accept the assumption without question. Dewey's statement about murder and wanton cruelty is not only factually untrue, but it also begs the question because he has nowhere produced scientific evidence that murder never has beneficial results. Nor can his own principles consist with such a fixed moral norm as this would be, if it could be proved. Dewey's insistence on the tentativeness of all practical hypotheses requires him to admit that wanton cruelty may some day be the most efficient means to a social goal.

This emphasis on the disagreement about murder, the disagreement between Spanish bull fighters and Puritans, between Christian parents and Kilpatrick, between any two incompatible ideals underscores the most serious flaw in Dewey's philosophy. To resolve such disagreements, Dewey must promise that science will decide between the aims of parents versus the aims of secular educators. In general, Dewey's assumption is that science can produce well nigh universal moral agreement. Or, at the very least, science can determine values. But Dewey has failed the test at its easiest point. Was not murder the clearest example of evil—an example that every fair-minded person would agree to? Yet Dewey has not succeeded in showing how this moral judgment can be justified by scientific procedure. Indeed, for all his insistence that science can solve all problems and that values can only arise through relating means to proximate ends, Dewey, so far as I know, has not given a single instance of thus discovering a value. He seems to admit as much.[4] But is it unreasonable to ask for just one instance?

Is Life Worth Living?

One critic of Dewey remarked that however much Instrumentalism asserts universal flux, the system has one eternal, fixed, unchangeable absolute: the value of inquiry, the importance of solving problems. Behind this fixed truth is the more general principle that life is worth living. Surely this point ought not to be evaded and passed over in silence. It has been a matter of disagreement. It marks out an indeterminate situation. It should be a subject of inquiry, requiring a solution in terms of some idea that is a plan of action. Nor is it an artificial problem. Many men face it under various forms.

In the twentieth century the form in which death becomes a live option for many materializes under totalitarian oppression. Thousands have risked death by fleeing through the iron curtain of barbed wire and machine gun bullets. Other thousands met death in the Hungarian bid for freedom. All of these would doubtless have preferred to live, but by risking death they showed that they thought that life was not worth living under communism. There is also a smaller number who have committed suicide. Then too there are others who have committed suicide without having been driven to it by such oppression. Several of the Stoics decided that it was better to die than live. In the United States also the suicide rate has risen sharply during the last fifty years. The value of life therefore is not an artificial problem, and Instrumentalism is obliged to defend its optimistic or at least melioristic attitude. Christianity with its revelational basis asserts that suicide is immoral; but what can be said by an empirical, descriptive philosophy?

This question of suicide is not to be understood as just one detail among many. It is not as though we had canvassed the merits of stealing, lying, adultery, murder, and, oh yes, there is one more, suicide. On the contrary, the mention of suicide is intended to bring to the fore the absolutely indispensable pre-requisite of all other ethical decisions. Theft versus honesty and cruelty versus kindness are possible choices only if we have previously decided to continue living. On what basis therefore can it be shown that life is worth the time and trouble?

The value of life, and therefore the manner of living it, when suicide is ruled out, is not the matter of exuberant agreement that Dewey seems to assume. All that Dewey takes so whole-heartedly for granted has been vigorously denied and attacked by thinkers of world renown and by significant portions of the human race. Buddhism, for instance, holds that pain is a neces-sary element in the universal process; desire is the cause of pain; and suppression of desire, completed in the unconsciousness of Nirvana, is the only remedy for pain. A Buddhist would prob-ably say that these principles are such obvious conclusions from an observation of the world that only the willfully blind can fail to see them.

In the Western world this view was adopted by Arthur Schopenhauer. True, neither the Buddhists nor Schopenhauer believed that suicide is the proper solution. Nevertheless it should be clearly kept in mind that the type of life that follows from a pessimistic principle must be vastly different from that based on a confident meliorism.

Hence a first conclusion is inescapable. Those moralists who have proceeded as if all men agree on what is desirable must be judged to have failed. They must be forced to open their eyes and face the basic problems. Not only must they be forced to explain why, instead of brutality and totalitarianism, they prefer certain elements salvaged from Christian morality; but they must also be forced to justify life itself. This they have not done and therefore their systems are failures.

Concluding Criticism

To return to Dewey's main thesis that science can solve the problem of morality, the criticism that has controlled the argu-ment all along is twofold. First, scientific method does not justify the ideals of Dewey and Kilpatrick; and, second, scientific method cannot justify any ideal.

Though the first point is of lesser logical importance, it is not without *ad hominem* value, and, in addition, it may perhaps find more ready acceptance. For scientists as well as the average citizen can see clearly that there is nothing in laboratory methods that demands as an ideal the governmental suppression of religion.

True, there is a "scientism," adopted by the communists, that holds religion to be an opiate. This atheism would limit all aims and ideals to this world; there is no supernatural realm, no life after death, no future world. And since this is an absolute fixed truth, commissars are justified in preventing parents from teaching religion to their children. But the argument that leads from a description of laboratory methods to the conclusion that secularism is desirable does not exist.

Even if it could be shown, as indeed it cannot, that laboratory methods validly imply secularistic totalitarianism, the latter would not thereby become ideal. In such a case many people would choose more freedom and less science. The physical discomforts of a pre-scientific society are minor in comparison with the spiritual torture of an inquisitorial bureaucracy.

The gap between the premises of scientific method and the ideals which Dewey and Kilpatrick offer as conclusions is no less real, if a trifle less evident, in the case of health and transportation than in the case of religious liberty. Good health and speedy transportation have not been made desirable by any increase of scientific technique. They were not in the first place chosen as ideal because of any incipient scientific knowledge. Obviously science has done wonders in medicine and has increased the speed of transportation beyond the imagination even of Jules Verne; but science neither causes men to desire them nor causes them to be desirable. On the contrary, it is because men chose them as ideals that scientists began to look for means of securing them.

Indeed, the more science is stressed as instrumental, the more evident it should be that it cannot establish ends or ideals.

This is the second part of the concluding criticism. Scientific method can produce no ideals whatever. Science is instrumental. If a group of educators wish to extinguish religious liberty, a scientific attention to the details and relationships of psychology, sociology, and politics will help them to their end. The same scientific technique can be used for the opposite purpose. The techniques of medicine can cure diseases that were usually fatal a century ago; but this same technical knowledge can just as easily be used to produce these diseases. In fact, cancer research at present is largely interested in producing cancer. But no instrumental technique, whether medical or political, can furnish any basis for deciding how to use it.

Therefore the contemporary humanist attempt to solve the problems of ethics by the application of scientific methods must, fortunately, be adjudged a failure.

Since too this criticism engulfs previous secular theories, such as Utilitarianism, it seems to follow that a more sympathetic consideration ought to be given to divine revelation than is customary in the universities of our land. To a discussion of Christian ethics therefore, we now turn.

CHRISTIAN ETHICS

At the end of the first chapter it was said that solutions or conclusions can be based only upon definite premises. Scattered observations, mystical insights, and poorly defined generalizations make no logical appeal. The present volume therefore is based upon the truth of the Bible; and because of faulty interpretations and inconsistent formulations, the sense of the Bible is determined by the Westminster Confession. No apology is offered for this procedure; it seems only honest to state the premises of the argument.

The Divine Legislator

It will of course be universally admitted that the Bible presents God as the moral governor and judge of the world. The Bible contains commands, precepts, laws; warnings, assurances, exhortations; the threat of punishment and the promise of heaven. For the present purpose, however, it is another of God's prerogatives that needs emphasis. Not only is God the governor and judge; prior to this he is the legislator. It is his will that establishes the distinction between good and evil, right and wrong; it is his will that sets the norms of righteous conduct. For those unfamiliar with the history of the subject, this thought must be somewhat developed.

In Plato's *Euthyphro* Socrates asks the young man what is pious or right. After the usual confusion between example and definition is cleared up, Socrates elicits the answer that piety is that which is dear to the gods. Greek polytheism must worry with the possibility that the gods may disagree; but this part of the dialogue is not needed here. What is of permanent importance is Socrates' next question: Is an act holy and pious because it is dear to the gods, or is an act dear to the gods because it is holy?

At this point Plato's treatment of the difficulty becomes extremely instructive. Utilizing the inductive method common to the early dialogues, Socrates continues: we speak of being carried and of carrying, of being led and of leading, of being seen and of seeing; then too we conceive of being loved and of loving. Now, tell me, says Socrates, is a thing which is carried a carried thing because someone carries it, or does someone carry it because it is a carried thing? Again, is a thing which is seen a seen thing because someone sees it, or does someone see it because it is a seen thing? The answers of course are obvious. Similarly a thing is loved or beloved because someone loves it; it is not loved because it is beloved.

Here it may be better to quote exactly. "What then shall we say about the pious, Euthyphro? You admit that it is a thing loved by all the gods, do you not?—Yes.—Is it loved by the gods because it is pious, or for some other reason?—No; but for this reason.—Therefore it is loved because it is pious; but it is not pious because it is loved.—So it seems.—But that which is dear to the gods and beloved of them is so because they love it.

—How could it be otherwise?—Then it follows that that which is dear to the gods, my Euthyphro, is not the definition of piety."

The remarkable thing about this conversation is the complete absence of argument on the essential point. Unlike the instances in the other dialogues, the induction here has no connection whatever with the conclusion. In fact, the induction, if carried out, would lead to exactly the opposite conclusion. Plato merely asserts that the gods love piety because it is piety. No reasons are given. He just could not imagine anyone's entertaining a different opinion.

The conclusion is of course consistent with Plato's worldview. In the *Timaeus* the Demiurge, the personal divinity who fashions this physical world out of chaotic space, receives his plan of operation from an independently existing world of Ideas. The maker of the visible world is not the maker of these Ideas. Naturally Plato argued at length to establish the theory of Ideas; but their relationship to the personal divinity seems to have been decided upon from the time of the early dialogues.

In Christianity, and even in Philo Judaeus, this is reversed. God is supreme, and any Ideas that may be required are dependent upon what God wills to think. God is the legislator, and piety is determined by his preceptive decree.

Ethics and Theology

Before this Christian view is elucidated, one example of the Platonic position in modern form should be given to heighten the contrast. Immanuel Kant, although he did not accept the theory of Ideas, made it very clear that theology cannot serve as a basis for ethics. With his categorical imperative he hoped to distinguish between a moral and an immoral act by a purely logical analysis of the maxim of the act. Ought a person, he asks, make a promise with the secret intention of breaking it? Is it permissible to make a promise solely for the purpose of avoiding a present unpleasantness?

Such questions are answered by an attempt to universalize the maxim involved. In this case the maxim would be: it is right to make a promise without intending to keep it so as to escape from a present embarrassment. Can this be universalized: Can this be made into a universal law without self-contradiction? No, says Kant, it cannot, because if everyone made insincere promises, these promises would no longer serve the purpose of avoiding embarrassment. No one would any longer be fooled by them. They work only on the assumption that they are sincere. Therefore the maxim is self-contradictory or self-defeating. This for Kant is the criterion of right and wrong. He makes no appeal to divine commands, rewards, or punishments.

On the contrary, while theology makes no contribution to ethics, ethics is a presupposition of theology. Just how seriously one should take Kant's theological assertions, and whether he believed in a personal God or not may be debatable; but if there is a theology, it would have to use ethics as its basis. A knowledge of God must be derived, if at all, from a knowledge of morality.

Kant, of course, was not a Christian. But by reason of certain historical circumstances it has been possible for Christian writers to adopt a form of Kantianism or Platonism in their defense of Christianity.

The historical circumstances are briefly the success of Christianity in the western world. Its influence is pervasive and its moral teachings have been widely accepted. To such an extent has Christian morality been accepted as the ideal that writers have argued: since Christian standards are the highest, the Christian religion must be true. The rightness of ethics proves the truth of the theology. This defense of Christianity against its enemies rests on the assumption of its moral excellence.

But if the premise be denied, what happens to the apologetics? There may have been times and places in which no one would think of denying the excellence of Christian standards. Since, however, this has not been the case in China for example, the argument could hardly have appeared convincing to the Chinese. Today China is much closer to us. Indeed there is no point in insisting on old heathen nations. English speaking philosophers daily contest the excellence of Christian morality. It is not necessary to refer to Nietzsche—he wrote in German; the humanists discussed above are equally good examples. When this fact is acknowledged, then the argument from Christian ethics must be recognized as inverted. One cannot argue the truth of Christianity on the basis of its ethics; one must defend its ethics on the basis of its theological truth. The ethics is not a premise, but a conclusion. Theology is basic.

No one with any Christian training would, I suppose, want to deprecate morality. Nevertheless, it is quite possible so to exaggerate its importance, so to misunderstand its relative place in philosophy that only confusion both moral and theoretical can result. This overemphasis on morality, so it would seem, is an important contributory cause in the rise of modernism. The authority of conscience was insisted on, a moral consciousness was developed, ethical institutions were sought for. And as these aspects of human nature—indispensable as they are—were continually brought forward, they came to usurp the position of supreme judge.

An interesting, instructive, and important example of this type of reasoning, taken from the heyday of its vigor, is found in Newman Smyth.[5] After quoting a Puritan theologian who said, "Godliness, therefore, which is the practice of divine Truth, is the measure of all intellectual truths;" Smyth continues, perhaps beyond the intention of the Puritan, and says,

"Old theology is always becoming new in the vitalizing influence of ethics. . . . It is reason enough for doubting and for restudying any traditional teaching or received word of doctrine if it be felt to harass or to confuse the Christian conscience of an age. Nothing can abide as true in theology which does not prove its genuineness under the ever renewed searching of the Christian moral sense. . . . Still less can we allow in Christian ethics any dogmatic belief which would put in bonds the Christian ethical principle itself; as, for instance, the tenet that morality is dependent upon the divine will. . . . Christian ethics cannot consent to commit suicide in any supposed interest of theology."

Newman Smyth's appeal to the observable facts of a Christian conscience leaves unanswered the difficulty of distinguishing a Christian from a non-Christian conscience. When this issue is raised, theology must enter as the decisive factor. Smyth's procedure is incapable of facing this issue because of his neglect of Biblical revelation. He must assume that somehow ethical norms can be distilled from conscience, failing to realize that these norms have never been accepted where the Biblical theology has not first been preached. And finally, his refusal to make the ethical principle itself dependent on the divine will puts him, in this respect at least, on the side of Plato and Kant.

In opposition to all this the Christian, i.e., the Biblical view is that God is the legislator. Not Law but the Lawgiver is supreme.

Divine Sovereignty

If then the personal God is supreme and all laws depend upon his ordinance, it follows that there is no superior law to restrict his sovereignty. Most people find it easy to conceive of God as having created or established physical law by divine fiat. He might have created a different kind of world, had he so desired. It does not seem to stretch the imagination much to picture a world where freezing points are so arranged that we would have to put water in the radiator to prevent the alcohol from freezing. And why could not lead, like water, expand on cooling? Nor does it bother some theologians to suppose that various details of the Mosaic ritual might have been different. Instead of requiring the priests to carry the ark on their shoulders, God might have forbidden this and ordered it to be borne on a cart drawn by oxen. But for some peculiar reason people find difficulty in applying the same consideration to ethics. Instead of recognizing God as sovereign in the moral sphere, they want to subject him to some independent, superior, Platonic law. This is inconsistent.

Yet at this point some very conscientious persons raise an apparently serious objection to the view here outlined. If this view were true, they say, honesty might not be the best policy. If morality depends purely on God's ordinance just as the laws of physics, then possibly stealing would be right and right would be wrong. Nevertheless, the fact that we have become accustomed to given ethical standards is no reason for believing that God had to make the world that way. Even if our moral opinions are correct, it is no more a reason for so believing than our knowledge of physics is for putting God under the compulsion of physical laws. Certainly in this world honesty is best. But it is best precisely because God made the world that way. Anything God does is right, because he does it; and had we no knowledge of God we could not guess what sort of moral standards he might set up for some hypothetical world not now in existence. The reason we object to stealing or to any other sin is that we have learned that it is contrary to God's ordinance. We must learn God's plan first and develop our morality afterward. We must adjust our ethics to our theology, not *vice versa*. We must argue, not from our moral standards to the truth of the Bible, but from the truth of the Bible to the morality it upholds.

A word of caution is needed here. This discussion has no particular bearing on the divine immutability. It was argued that God could have created a different physical world, had he so desired. Nothing was said, one way or the other, as to whether God could so desire. Possibly the immutability of purpose and the eternality of the decrees imply that this is the only possible world—a Calvinistic twist to a Spinozistic phrase. Yet if this is so, and if it is meaningless to suppose that God could think differently, the argument remains that morality as much as physics is what it is because God thinks this way. As the Puritans used to say, God's decree is simply God's decreeing.

Before the minimum of Biblical evidence for this view is set down, it can well be noted that the discussion is not a dead echo from an ancient Platonic past. Nor was it ended by Kant and Newman Smyth. Quite the contrary, it is alive today and will remain so for the foreseeable future.

A Contemporary Example

Just one instance will be given. Dr. Edward John Carnell writes as follows:

"If we cannot anticipate the character of God by using elements drawn from the moral and spiritual environment, then by the same token we have no way of judging the character of God's representatives, since this decision, though one step removed, involves the same difficulty. Unless we can meaningfully anticipate God's standards of rectitude, it may turn out that the book, the church, or priestly caste that is least moral on human standards is the most moral on divine standards; and we are once again left with skepticism."[6]

This is the position against which the preceding argument has been directed. In one sense the quotation contains nothing essentially new. But in another respect there is something worth noting about it. It is the statement of a professed evangelical of the twentieth century. Now, however it might have been with sincere Christians of former ages, one writing today might be expected to take note how this point of view has so frequently been used to oppose Christianity. In fact, such was the intention of John Stuart Mill, whom Dr. Carnell actually praises a few pages previously.

Then too it was precisely by this method that Mary Baker Eddy sought to refute the doctrine of the atonement. Propitiation, which Dr. Carnell defends, seemed impossible to Mrs. Eddy. "Whoever believeth that wrath is righteous or that divinity is appeased by human suffering does not understand God" (*Science and Health*, Chapter II). Can this not fairly be paraphrased, whoever believeth that wrath is righteous has not meaningfully anticipated God's standards of rectitude?

Similarly Edwin A. Burtt condemns Christ because Christ's morals are inferior to Burtt's humanistic socialism.

The possibility that the book, the church, or the priestly caste, least moral on human standards may be most moral on divine standards, is an objection without force. Consider a devout Hindu woman of the last century who, with a conscience as void of offense as Paul's when persecuting the early church, was sacrificing her infant child to her heathen god. By all her human standards she was doing right; and it appeared to her that the omission of this duty would be irreligious. Finally a Christian missionary comes to her and tries to convince her that the book, the church, and the priestly caste that she considers most moral are not so, but that by divine standards what she thinks irreligious is right. What else could a missionary do? Is this then an objection against Christianity? Indeed it is to be expected that Christian morals will differ from what the natural man anticipates.

Abraham, the Father of Us All

To make a clear contrast between the Platonic objection and the Biblical position, and to give at least a minimum of direct Biblical support to God's sovereignty in ethics, no better example can be found than that of Abraham. Abraham has become a favorite subject of discussion in recent times. Sometimes he is used to prove the superiority of Sumerian culture over that of Canaan. Human sacrifice is supposed to have been transcended in Ur, but in ruder Canaan it was still practiced. Abraham, then, raised the culture of Canaan by not sacrificing Isaac. But if this were so, Abraham's initial willingness to sacrifice Isaac would be inexplicable. Combined or uncombined with this pagan sociological motif, other authors, among whom first is Kierkegaard, see a conflict between religion and ethics. One writer says,

"Obviously, God's command to Abraham that he sacrifice his only son was an immoral one, and it embarrasses not only the modern but also troubled Abraham. And if we regard the command simply as God's testing of Abraham and thus moralize the story, we have not faced the issue raised by God's immoral command and his approval of Abraham's obedience to it."

Admittedly the writer quoted makes some statements in the sequel that modify to a degree the first impression of these sentences. But all such interpretations complicate the story of Abraham by reading into it elements that are not there. In particular, a conflict, a false conflict, between religion and ethics is produced by the presupposition that God's command to sacrifice Isaac was immoral. Where does the text make this assertion? It may be true that the Sumerians regarded human sacrifice as immoral; but the question is not one of Sumerian opinion. The question is, was God's command immoral?

The text itself tells us that God said to Abraham, "Take now thy son, thine only son Isaac, whom thou lovest, . . . and offer him for a burnt offering upon one of the mountains." Now, if Abraham had subscribed to the principles of Professor Carnell, if he had made theology subsidiary to ethics, if he had judged of this command by an "anticipation" of God's standards of rectitude, he would have concluded that this suggestion was coming, not from God, but from Satan. If this were not the voice of Satan, if one could not anticipate the nature of divine commands, then the voice that is least moral by human standards might be the most moral by divine standards; and since this cannot be true, the command to sacrifice Isaac did not come from God.

Abraham of course did not at all argue in this vein. On the contrary he recognized that it was God's voice, and therefore he was prepared to obey, no matter what the command was. No doubt God had previously forbidden human sacrifice; and so long as that command remained in force, human sacrifice was a sin. But if now, for some undetermined period of time, God commands human sacrifice, then it becomes obligatory and right. No ethical standard formulated through empirical observation, no, not even a previous command of God himself suffices for the repudiation of God's next command.

This, however, does not mean that we are left with moral skepticism, as Dr. Carnell claims. We are left with the definite commands of God. We have his complete preceptive will in the

Scriptures. Of course, if skepticism means that man without a supernatural revelation cannot establish the norms of morality, so be it. The analyses of the earlier sections are supposed to have clinched that conclusion. Neither Utilitarianism, nor Kant, nor Dewey can anticipate God's standards of rectitude. But the failure of nonrevelational ethics does not leave man without a knowledge of right and wrong. If skepticism means that man can have no knowledge, then an appeal to revelation, with its subordination of ethics to theology, is not skepticism. But everything else is.

NOTES

1. *A Christian View of Men and Things* (Eerdmans, 1952): on Utilitarianism and Kant, see chapter IV; on Brightman's theory of values, see chapter VI. Also, *Dewey* (a monograph, Presbyterian and Reformed Publishing Co., 1960).
2. Gardner Williams, *Humanistic Ethics*, p. 55.
3. William Kilpatrick, *Philosophy of Education*, pp. 97-98, 151-161.
4. cf. *The Philosophy of John Dewey*, p. 592, note; ed. by Paul Arthur Schlipp.
5. Smyth, Newman, *Christian Ethics*, 1892, republished 1922.
6. Carnell, *Christian Commitment*, p. 142.

5.

God and Evil

In the background of every religious world-view there stands a frightening spectre. An author may refrain from mentioning it; he may hope that his public will forget to think about it; but no position is complete and none can be unhesitatingly accepted until it makes a clear pronouncement on the problem of evil.

> Of man's first disobedience and the fruit
> Of that forbidden tree, whose mortal taste
> Brought Death into the world and all our woes,
> Sing heavenly muse . . .

It is not, however, the sonorous phrases of a great poet nor even the inspiration of a Muse that we need. Careful thought, clean-cut definitions, and consistency to the end are the prerequisites of progress. The aim of this chapter is to face the question of evil squarely, without dodging, and to show that, whereas various other views disintegrate at this point, the system known as Calvinism and expressed in the Westminster Confession of Faith offers a satisfactory and completely logical answer.

Historical Exposition

To bring the matter into sharp focus and to set forth the main difficulties, a representative selection will be made from the discussions of history. In antiquity evil was almost always viewed from the standpoint of some sort of religion; at the present time God is more frequently left out of the picture. Although the presuppositions of this chapter are thoroughly theistic, something will be said of non-theistic views, if only to indicate that the problem of evil does not disappear with the acceptance of secularism.

The problem, as it has usually been considered, is terrifyingly simple. How can the existence of God be harmonized with the existence of evil? There are plenty of evils. One of the Soviet secret police is quoted as boasting that he had so refined torture that he could break every bone in a man's body without killing him. And is there a God who looks down on this from on high? By those who were religiously inclined the enigma has been faced in fear and trembling; the irreligious, Voltaire, for example, with a cry of triumph have spat it forth like the poison of asps. But whatever the form, the issue is inescapable. How can the existence of God be reconciled with the existence of evil?

In early Christian times Lactantius reports its prevalence. If God is good and wants to eliminate sin, but cannot, he is not omnipotent; but if God is omnipotent and can eliminate sin, but does not, he is not good. God cannot be both omnipotent and good.

Although the Christian concept of God as omnipotent aggravates the difficulty, man's trouble with evil, his intellectual trouble with evil, did not begin with Christianity. Pain, disease, calamities, injustice, and woe have impressed people of every religion. Some religions, of which Zoroastrianism is one, concluded that the universe must be the work of two independent, conflicting deities. Neither the good god nor the evil god is omnipotent, and neither has as yet destroyed the other. On the surface, this seems to account for the mixture of good and evil in the world; but such ultimate and irreducible dualisms give rise to further riddles which many philosophers have thought equally insoluble.

Plato in his *Republic* attempted to account for evil by the assumption that God is not the cause of everything, but only of a few things—few because our evils far outnumber our goods.

In the *Timaeus* he was not quite so pessimistic, but he still held that there is an eternal and chaotic space which the Demiurge cannot entirely control. To the end therefore, it must be said, Plato retained an unreconciled dualism.

Aristotle, because his philosophy is so completely irreligious, is somewhat an exception in antiquity. He conceived God in such a way that his relation to evil, or to the moral endeavors of men, hardly mattered. The Unmoved Mover is in a sense the cause of all motion, but instead of being an active cause he causes motion by being the object of the world's desire. He exercises no voluntary control over history. Though he is constantly thinking, he does not seem to think about the world, or, at most, he knows only a part of the past and nothing whatever of the future.

Naturally, the great Christian philosopher, Augustine, grappled with the difficulty. Under Neoplatonic influence he taught that all existing things are good; evil therefore does not exist— it is metaphysically unreal. Being non-existent it can have no cause, and God therefore is not the cause of evil. When a man sins, it is a case of his choosing a lower good instead of a higher good. This choice too has no efficient cause, although Augustine assigns to it a deficient cause. In this way God was supposed to be absolved. Augustine, admittedly, was a great Christian and a great philosopher. Later in the chapter more will be said about him. But here he was at his worst. Deficient causes, if there are such things, do not explain why a good God does not abolish sin and guarantee that men always choose the highest good.

This matter of evil is not an outmoded antiquity that evaporated with Zoroaster, Aristotle, or Augustine. The twentieth century cannot evade it. Therefore a few illustrations will be selected from contemporary writers. Today, however, much of the discussion is secular in nature. Either religion is ignored, or, in some cases, Christianity is pointedly attacked.

Lucius Garvin, John L. Mothershead, and Charles A. Baylis have each written a textbook on Ethics. These books are fairly well known in American colleges today. Garvin has a very short section on Theological Ethics, with a conclusion that suggests that God is not particularly important; in the second textbook the index has no entry at all for God; and in the third it seems that God is mentioned only on one page. Nevertheless, secular ethics, although it will pay no attention to omnipotence, must still consider determinism and must say something about responsibility. An example of this type of thought will elucidate some details of the main argument as well as serve as part of an historical selection.

Professor Baylis of Duke University gives what many people will believe to be a very plausible argument. If determinism is true, he says, then a person's decisions reflect his character. The man's character causes and explains his actions. Accordingly, if we know the particular weaknesses of a man's character, we may be able, by praise, promises, threats, or punishments, to alter his character, improve the man, and so produce better decisions. Blame and punishment therefore which have the effect of reforming a person are justifiable; but retributive punishment will not be justifiable, if determinism is true. The remote causes of a man's character are far in the past and were never under his control. Therefore he is not responsible for them, and therefore retributive punishment is illegitimate. Dr. Baylis further insists that indeterminism also renders retributive punishment illegitimate; and what is worse, indeterminism can provide only a dubious justification for corrective punishment.

Another professor at Duke University furnishes an example of those who pointedly attack Christianity. The argument comes from *An Introduction to the Philosophy of Religion,* by Dr. Robert Leet Patterson.

To refer evil to a corrupt human nature, transmitted from Adam, Professor Patterson brands as "an odious doctrine which Pelagius, to his honor, anticipated modern liberals in rejecting" (p. 218, n. 3). Besides, there is a previous question. The author asks, "If it be as easy for God to create good men as to create evil men, why did not God create all men good?" (p. 173). To suppose that God created the good and the evil for his own glory, to bestow his love on the good and his wrath on the evil, is to lower God to the level of the most degenerate human tyrant. Such an idea must be decisively rejected, for, the author insists (p. 177), God cannot be thought of as immoral. Even if we believe, in the absence of all evidence, that every occurrence of evil is essential to the realization of a greater good, the fact that God could not produce the good without the previous evil indicates that God's power is limited (p. 179).

Today, then, as in the past, the existence of evil is a crucial question, and the answer frequently includes the idea of a limited deity. Many modern philosophers, such as John Stuart Mill, William Pepperell Montague, and Georgia Harkness, as well as the ancient Zoroaster and Plato, accept a finite god. But it must be clearly understood that this idea is incompatible with Christianity. The Bible presents God as omnipotent, and only on this basis can a Christian view of evil be worked out.

The idea of a finite god, although it is a non-christian expedient, has nonetheless a certain amount of merit by reason of its honesty. Professing Christians are not always so frank. In a certain Christian college the head of the Bible department used to tell his students not to discuss the subject. Indeed, this was rather clearly the policy of the institution. For the subject is controversial. It is also unedifying. And the professor should have added, it is embarrassing. For when some pointed questions were asked him, he grew irritated and replied, "I do not like the kind of questions you ask." Perhaps such colleges think that if evil is never mentioned, the students will never hear about it. They seem to forget that the secular enemies of Christianity will soon remind them and ask them controversial, unedifying, and embarrassing questions. Such an attitude of secrecy did not characterize the great Christian theologians: Augustine, Aquinas, Calvin. We may perhaps not agree with this one or that one, but like the modern secularists they were open and honest. Before we drop the idea of a finite god, however, there is one interesting consideration to mention. If the mixture of good and evil in the world rules out the possibility of a good and omnipotent God, and, if the extent of good in the world hardly allows the assumption of an infinite evil Demon, it still does not follow that there is a finite good god. A finite evil god is an equally acceptable conclusion. Instead of saying that god does the best he can, but being limited he cannot quite dominate the evil in the world, we could just as well say that god does the worst he can, but being limited he cannot quite eradicate the forces of good which oppose his will. Evidently therefore the advocates of a finite god arrive at their conclusion more by emotion than by reason.

Free Will

Because of God's omniscience, most probably, Augustine recognized that the metaphysical unreality of evil and the supposition of deficient causes were inadequate to dispose of the difficulties. Accordingly he added a theory of free will. From pagan antiquity, through the Middle Ages, on down into modern times, free will has doubtless been the most popular solution offered for the problem of evil. God is all powerful, many people will say, but he has adopted a hands-off policy and allows men to act apart from divine influence. We choose, and we choose evil, of our own free wills; God does not make us do so; therefore we alone are responsible, and not God.

This theory of free will must now be carefully examined. Is it a satisfactory theory? Do its proponents have an unambiguous concept of its chief term? Is it true that the will is free? And if it is true, does free will solve the problem of evil?

Augustine's formulation of the theory of free will, like many other of his views, did not remain unaltered. In his pagan life he had been a Manichaean: he had accepted an ultimate dualism of good and evil. After his conversion, although he had a brilliant mind, he did not immediately see the implications of the Biblical assertions so clearly as he did later in life. It took time even for Augustine to develop.

His early view of free will seems to be that all men are completely untrammeled in their decisions. Anyone can as easily choose this as that. Neither divine grace nor any other force determines a man in either direction. In his work on *Free Will* he begins by wondering how it is possible for all souls, seeing that they commit sin, to have come from God without referring those sins back to God. In other words, if God created souls which are now sinful, is not God responsible for sin? And to go further,

"I ask whether a free will itself, by which we are proved to have a power to sin, should have been given us by him who made us. For it is clear that if we were without free will we would not sin; and in this way it is to be feared that God may be adjudged the author of our evil doing" (I ii and xvi).

To avoid this conclusion, the explanation, or at least a part of it, is that without free will we could as little do good as evil. A being, such as a stone or perhaps a bug, that cannot do evil is equally incapable of doing good. The ability to do good or evil is one; and God is not to blame if man uses his freedom wrongly. Free will may indeed do wrong, but there is no right action without it. Even sin does not justify the assertion that it were better if sinners did not exist. There must be all grades of being in the world. Variety is essential. Even a soul that perseveres in sin is better than any inanimate body that cannot sin because it has no will.

One must pause, however. From the metaphysical assumption that being is *better* than non-being, does it follow that a sinner is *better off* than a stone? What would Augustine have said, if he had remembered Christ's statement, "It had been good for that man if he had not been born"? Such questions come to mind, but the exposition of Augustine's views must continue.

So far it would seem that free will is the property of all men. The very possibility of doing either good or evil requires it. But toward the end of the book Augustine introduces a thought which he expands in his later writings. Noting that men now inevitably sin and cannot avoid it, he says, "When we speak,

then, of the will free to do right, we speak of the will in which
man first was made" (III xviii). Thus it appears that no one now
has a free will.

In the *City of God* (XXII xxx) Augustine makes this point
clearer. Adam had free will in the sense that he was able not to
sin. This presumably is the popular notion of free will. Most
people seem to mean by it that a man is just as able to will one
thing as its opposite. He is free, they say, because he can choose
to obey or to disobey God's commands. But by the time that
Augustine wrote the *City of God* he had learned enough about
the Bible, and about men too, to know that in this age it is
impossible for anyone not to sin. Sin is inevitable. Therefore
the ability to do good or evil is not one. Though the unregener-
ate do evil, they cannot do good. In the future when our redemption shall have been completed and we are glorified in
heaven, another impossibility will appear. There we shall be
unable to sin. Again the ability to do good or evil is not one, for
though we shall do good, we shall not be able to do evil. There
are thus three stages in the total human drama: before the fall,
posse non peccare; and in the world to come, *non posse peccare*
but in this present world, *non posse non peccare.* Adam therefore was the only man who ever had free will—free will in the
usual sense of the term.

The phrase free will, however, had such attractive connotations that Augustine did not wish to limit it to Adam. Hence
he immediately continues, "Is God himself in truth to be denied
free will because he cannot sin?" Augustine assumes that everyone will want to call God free. One may ask the same question
also about the righteous angels. But if God and the angels have
free will, free will must be redefined so as to consist with a
denial that two incompatible actions are equally possible. Free
will must be made consistent with inevitability and therefore
will no longer bear its common meaning.

Later writers also have made a point of the fixed and determined felicity of the future state, and it might be worth a
parenthetical paragraph to pause for a reference to the puritan

John Gill. In *The Cause of God and Truth* (Part III chap. V, xiii) he writes,

"God is a most free agent, and liberty in him is in its utmost perfection, and yet does not lie in an indifference to good and evil; he has no freedom to that which is evil . . . his will is determined only to that which is good; he can do no other . . . and what he does, he does freely and yet necessarily. . . . The human nature of Christ, or the man Christ Jesus, who, as he was born without sin and lived without it all his days on earth; so was impeccable, could not sin. He lay under some kind of necessity . . . to fulfill all righteousness; and yet he did it most freely and voluntarily: which proves that the liberty of man's will . . . is consistent with some kind of necessity. . . . The good angels, holy and elect, who are confirmed in the state in which they are . . . cannot sin or fall from that happy state, yet perform their whole obedience to God, do his will and work cheerfully and willingly. . . . In the state of glorification the saints will be impeccable, cannot sin, can only do that which is good, and yet what they do, or will do, is and will be done with the utmost freedom and liberty of their wills; whence it follows that the liberty of man's will . . . is consistent both with some kind of necessity and a determination to one."

This effectively disposes of Augustine's early contention that one must be able to sin in order to do anything good; it also leaves free will in a dubious condition.

In this material from Augustine and John Gill two important points emerge. The first is that the Bible does not teach the equal possibility of two incompatible choices. Even if some perverse misinterpreter should still contend that the ability to do good or evil is one, the meaning of the denial is plain and unambiguous. The second point that emerges from the preceding discussion is, however, a matter of ambiguity. Free will has been defined as the equal ability, under given circumstances, to choose either of two courses of action. No antecedent power determines the choice. Whatever motives or inclinations a man may have, or whatever inducements may be laid before him, that might seem to turn him in a certain direction, he may at a moment disregard them all and do the opposite. This definition or description, however, is what the present writer believes to be the common notion of free will. It is not the definition found in Augustine or John Gill. Indeed these two writers do not give a formal definition of free will. Strange though it may seem to a logician, many writers do not define their terms with great care, and the reader is unfortunately left to guess at the meaning. An Arminian reading *The Cause of God and Truth* might very well wonder what its author could possibly mean by liberty and freedom. Nor would his perplexity be entirely unjustified. The Puritan speaks of a will that is both free and determined; he refers to actions that are done freely, yet necessarily; and he concludes that the liberty of a man's will is consistent with at least some kind of necessity and determination. But the Arminian reader feels himself almost necessitated to judge that this makes no sense. Are not necessity and freedom incompatible? Is it remotely possible that both could be attributed to the same action, choice, or will?

The explanation of course lies in the fact that the Arminian has a different notion of freedom from that of John Gill. And perhaps he is unaware that in the history of philosophy freedom of choice has been defined in several different ways. One should never suppose that a phrase or a term means the same thing in every book in which it occurs. Each author chooses the meaning he desires, and each reader ought to try to determine what that meaning is. To be sure, the author ought not to try to make this task difficult, and Gill and others of his day should have said more clearly what they meant. Strict definitions and strict adherence to them are essential to intelligible discussion. If one contender has one idea in mind, or perhaps no clear idea at all, while the other party to the debate entertains a different notion, or is equally vague, the result of the conversation is bound to be complete confusion. This is the elementary lesson that Socrates taught in the fifth century before Christ; but many people have not learned it yet.

In accord with common opinion the phrase free will will here henceforth be used to indicate the theory that a man faced with incompatible courses of action is as able to choose any one as well as any other. It may be necessary in quoting previous authors to use the phrase in another sense, if they so used it; but the argument of this chapter will restrict the phrase free will to the above definition. This is done in the belief that no Arminian will object. He can make no accusation that his case is prejudged by a surreptitious introduction of a Calvinistic element into the chief term. Free will is defined with all the freedom that any Arminian could desire.

It might seem that here is the proper place to ask the question, Does man have a free will? Is it true that his choices are not determined by motives, by inducements, or by his settled character? Can a person resist God's grace and power and make an uncaused decision? However, these questions will not be answered here. They will be discussed later. The next step in the argument is a slightly different one. Let us assume that man's will is free; let us assume that these questions have been answered in the affirmative; it would still remain to be shown that free will solves the problem of evil. This then is the immediate inquiry. Is the theory of free will, even if true, a satisfactory explanation of evil in a world created by God? Reasons, compelling reasons, will now be given for a negative answer. Even if men were as able to choose good as evil, even if a sinner could choose Christ as easily as he could reject him, it would be totally irrelevant to the fundamental problem. Free will was put forward to relieve God of responsibility for sin. But this it does not do.

Suppose there were a life guard stationed on a dangerous beach. In the breakers a boy is being sucked out to sea by the strong undertow. He cannot swim. He will drown without powerful aid. It will have to be powerful, for as drowning sinners do, he will struggle against his rescuer. But the life guard simply sits on his high chair and watches him drown. Perhaps he may shout a few words of advice and tell him to exercise his free will. After all, it was of his own free will that the boy went into the surf. The guard did not push him in nor interfere with him in any way. The guard merely permitted him to go in and permitted him to drown. Would an Arminian now conclude that the life guard thus escapes culpability?

This illustration, with its finite limitations, is damaging enough as it is. It shows that permission of evil as contrasted with positive causality does not relieve a life guard from responsibility. Similarly, if God merely permits men to be engulfed in sin of their own free wills, the original objections of Voltaire and Professor Patterson are not thereby met. This is what the Arminian fails to notice. And yet the illustration does not do full justice to the actual situation. For unlike the boy who exists in relative independence of the life guard, in actuality God made the boy and the ocean too. Now, if the guard, who is not a creator at all, is responsible for permitting the boy to drown, even if the boy is supposed to have entered the surf of his own free will, does not God, who made them, appear in a worse light? Surely an omnipotent God could have either made the boy a better swimmer, or made the ocean less rough, or at least have saved him from drowning.

Not only are free will and permission irrelevant to the problem of evil, but further the idea of permission has no intelligible meaning. It is quite within the range of possibility for a life guard to permit a man to drown. This permission, however, depends on the fact that the ocean's undertow is beyond the guard's control. If the guard had some giant suction device which he operated so as to engulf the boy, one would call it murder, not permission. The idea of permission is possible only where there is an independent force, either the boy's force or the ocean's force. But this is not the situation in the case of God and the universe. Nothing in the universe can be independent of the Omnipotent Creator, for in him we live and move and have our being. Therefore the idea of permission makes no sense when applied to God.

Such subterfuges must in all honesty be renounced. Consider two quotations from Calvin (*Institutes* III xxiii 8, and II iv 3).

"Here they recur to the distinction between will and permission, and insist that God permits the destruction of the impious, but does not will it. But what reason shall we assign for his permitting it, but because it is his will? It is not probable, however, that man procured his own destruction by the mere permission, without any appointment, of God; as though God had not determined what he would choose to be the condition of the principal of his creatures. I shall not hesitate therefore to confess plainly with Augustine, 'that the will of God is the necessity of things, and that what he has willed will necessarily come to pass.'"

"God is very frequently said to blind and harden the reprobate, and to turn, incline and influence their hearts, as I have elsewhere more fully stated. But it affords no explication of the nature of this influence to resort to prescience or permission. . . . For the execution of his judgments, he, by means of Satan, the minister of his wrath, directs their counsels to what he pleases and excites their wills and strengthens their efforts. Thus when Moses relates that Sihon the king would not grant a free passage to the people, because God had 'hardened his spirit and made his heart obstinate,' he immediately subjoins the end of God's design: 'That he might deliver him into thy hand.' Since God willed his destruction, the obduration of his heart therefore was the divine preparation for his ruin."

Thus the futility of free will is established. Some other theory must be sought. And in the production of that theory it will become evident that free will is not only futile but false. Certainly, if the Bible is the word of God, free will is false; for the Bible consistently denies free will. Therefore the attempt will now be made to explain evil on the basis of historic Protestantism.

Reformation Theology

So far this chapter has stated the paradox or antithesis between an omnipotent good God and the existence of evil. If free will cannot resolve the difficulty, one must turn to the opposite theory of determinism. At first determinism, instead of alleviat-

ing the situation, seems to accentuate the problem of evil by
maintaining the inevitability of every event; and not only the
inevitability, but also the further and more embarrassing point
that it is God himself who determines or decrees every action.

Some Calvinists prefer to avoid the word *determinism*. For
some reason it seems to them to carry unpleasant connotations.
However, the Bible not only speaks of predestination, usually
with reference to eternal life, but it also speaks of the foreordi-
nation or predetermination of evil acts. Therefore deliberate
avoidance of the word *determinism* would seem to be less forth-
right. This will be discussed still further later on. At the moment, however, there is a preliminary question. Do the opposing
views, free-will and determinism, form a complete disjunction?
The former holds that no human choice is determined; the
latter that all are. Is there not a third possibility? Could it not
be that some events or choices are determined and some are not?
Such a third possibility, however, could contribute nothing to
this discussion. Aside from the peculiarity of assigning a semi-
sovereignty to God and to man a semi-free will, the crux of the
conflict lies in choices that cannot be split in half. Could Judas
have chosen not to betray Christ? If he could have chosen not to
betray Christ, his moral responsibility is established, says the
Arminian; but says the Calvinist, prophecy in such a case could
have proved false. Or, again, could Pilate have decided to re-
lease Jesus? Are we prepared to say that God could not make
sure of the necessary events in his plan of redemption? Besides,
the Bible explicitly says, "Herod and Pontius Pilate with the
Gentiles and the people of Israel were gathered together for to
do whatsoever thy hand and thy counsel determined before to
be done." Here in these individual choices moral responsibility
is pitted against the success of God's eternal plan of redemption.
There is therefore no use in supposing some choices free and
others determined. The Scriptures say that this one choice was
determined ahead of time, and the whole theological and philosophical issue is found complete in this one choice.

It seems unnecessary to draw the contrast in any sharper

terms. All the elements are before us: free will, determinism, moral responsibility, prophecy, and divine sovereignty versus a finite god. What is now necessary consists of three points which will provide the outline for the remainder of the chapter. First, some extensive explanation and argument in defense of Calvinism must be given; second, a definitive and official statement of the position should be provided; and third, a few historical assertions are demanded by the wide spread ignorance of the twentieth century. These three points will be taken up in reverse order.

The low educational level of the present day, even among college people, was brought home to the present writer when he was asked to give an account of Calvinism to a group of students in a so-called Christian college. The talk was nothing more than the simplest and most elementary exposition of the famous five points. But at the end it became clear, with respect to the middle three, i.e., unconditional election, limited atonement, and irresistible grace, not only that the students had never heard of such doctrines before, but that they were shocked that any professing Christian could possibly believe them. For two or three hundred years after the Reformation there was hardly a place or a section of the people in any of the Protestant nations that did not have a rudimentary knowledge of Calvinism. They may not all have believed the doctrines, but at least they had heard them preached. In the twentieth century, however, Christian knowledge has sunk to a very low level. Calvinism of course is not totally extinguished, but many people who think of themselves as educated Christians have never heard of it. Today therefore we must insist that irresistible grace and divine determination were solid articles of the Reformation faith. Nor was it the Reformers who first discovered them.

Augustus M. Toplady, the author of that most beloved of all hymns, *Rock of Ages,* also wrote a good sized volume on the *Historic Proof of the Doctrinal Calvinism of the Church of England.* A few pages later he will be mentioned again more definitely with the main point of his book as stated in its title.

But here attention is called to his long introductory section in which he shows that Calvinism was not unknown either in the Patristic period or in the Middle Ages.

Toplady believed that the epistle of Barnabas was actually written by Barnabas. If he is mistaken in this belief, the epistle is a still more noteworthy testimony to the doctrinal character of the sub-apostolic age. The following quotation seems to reflect the idea of irresistible grace and would therefore be inconsistent with free will: "When Christ chose his own Apostles who were to preach the gospel, he chose those who were guilty above all wickedness." According to the same author Christ's death was necessary because it was prophesied. And there is a fairly clear statement of limited atonement: "Let us rest assured that the Son of God could not have suffered, but for us." To the same effect he imagines Christ answering a question with the words, "I am on the point of offering my flesh for my new people." A certain Menardus, commenting on this passage, complains that Barnabas was here mistaken because Christ did not die for a new people but for the whole world. The comment only emphasizes what Barnabas actually meant. A further negative note on free will is found in the words, "We speak as the Lord willeth us to speak. For this cause he circumcized our hearing and our hearts that we should comprehend these things."

Clement of Rome makes some very definite statements. "Since it was his will that all his beloved should be partakers of grace, he established them by his almighty power" (I Cor. 8:5). Is not this limited atonement and irresistible grace? Then again: "By the word of his majesty hath he established all things . . . Who shall say to him, What hast thou done? or who shall resist his strength? When he wills, and as he wills, he shall do all things, and nothing that he decrees shall pass away. All things are in his sight and nothing has escaped his will" (I Cor. 27:4ff.).

Ignatius begins his epistle to the Ephesians, "Ignatius . . . predestined from eternity for abiding and unchangeable glory, united and chosen . . . by the will of the Father." He introduces his epistle to the Romans with the words, "Enlightened by the will of him who has willed all things." And in opposition to free will he says, "Christianity is not the work of persuasion, but of power" (Rom. 3:3).

Perhaps it is better known, at least by those who have read some Medieval history, that the martyr Gottshalk was a strong Calvinist. Speaking of the reprobate Jews he says, "Our Lord perceived that they were predestinated to everlasting destruction and were not purchased with the price of his blood." After twenty-one years of imprisonment and torture at the hands of Bishop Hincmar for his belief in double predestination, he died A.D. 870.

Less well known is a contemporary of Gottshalk, Remigus, archbishop of Lyons. He wrote,

"Nor is it possible for any one elect person to perish, or that any of the reprobate should be saved, because of their hardness and impenitency of heart. . . . Almighty God did, from the beginning, prior to the formation of the world, and before he had made anything, predestinate . . . some certain persons to glory, of his own gratuitous favor . . . Other certain persons he hath predestinated to perdition . . . and of these none can be saved."

The Waldensians were a group whose origin Toplady puts early in the Middle Ages. He quotes from their Confession of 1508: "It is manifest that such only as are elected to glory become partakers of true faith."

A hundred years before the Reformation John Huss said, "Predestination doth make a man a member of the universal Church . . . God willeth that the predestinate shall have perpetual blessedness and the reprobate to have eternal fire. The predestinate cannot fall from grace." Obviously there is no free will here.

If Huss was burnt for the gospel, John of Wesalia was tortured because he held that

"God hath from everlasting written a book wherein he hath inscribed all his elect; and whosoever is not already written there will never be written there at all. Moreover he that is written therein will never be blotted out."

After these continental Calvinists, Toplady turns to pre-reformation Englishmen. Venerable Bede said,

"When Pelagius asserts that we are at liberty to do one thing always [i.e. to do good], seeing that we are always able to do both one and the other [i.e. free will], he herein contradicts the prophet, who, humbly addressing himself to God, saith, 'I know, O Lord, that a man's way is not his own; it is not in man that walketh to direct his own steps.'"

Thomas Bradwardine, the teacher of John Wycliffe, wrote, "What multitudes, O Lord, at this day, join hands with Pelagius in contending for free will and in fighting against thy absolutely free grace . . . Some more haughty than Lucifer . . . dread not to affirm that even in a common action their own will walks first, as an independent mistress, and that thy will follows after, like an obsequious handmaid." Again, "the will of God is universally efficacious and invincible, and necessitates as a cause. It cannot be impeded, much less can it be defeated and made void by any means whatever."

His pupil, John Wycliffe (A.D. 1324-1387), similarly declared,

"In what way soever God may declare his will by his after-discoveries of it in time, still his determination concerning the event took place before the world was made: ergo the event will surely follow. The necessity therefore of the antecedent holds no less irrefragably for the necessity of the consequent."

Dr. Peter Heylin, an Arminian historian, admits that William Tyndal "has a flying-out against free will" and taught that from predestination "it springeth altogether whether we shall believe or not believe, be loosed from sin or not be loosed; by which predestination our justifying and salvation are clear taken out of our hands and put into the hands of God only." The Arminian with his free will does not want his salvation put into the hands of God only.

Patrick Hamilton's sentence of death read:

"We, James, by the mercy of God, archbishop of St. Andrews, primate of Scotland, have found Master Patrick Hamilton many ways inflamed with heresy . . . that man hath no free will . . ."[1]

The struggles of these loyal exponents of the gospel of free grace culminated in the Protestant Reformation. At the Council of Trent the Roman church officially repudiated the doctrines that put salvation into the hands of God only. Rome chose free will and human merit. Luther and Calvin continued the apostolic teaching. In our present century of ignorance one must insist that Luther as well as Calvin rejected the Pelagian-Romish-Arminian view of man. It was Erasmus, the man who drew back from the Reformation and made his peace with Rome, who defended free will. The book that Luther wrote in reply to him is entitled *The Bondage of the Will*. In its Conclusion there is this sentence:

"For if we believe it to be true that God foreknows and foreordains all things, that he can neither be deceived nor hindered in his prescience and predestination, and that nothing can take place but according to his will, . . . then there can be no free will in man, in angel, or in any creature."

While the later Lutherans, under Melancthon's compromising spirit, which went so far as to seek reunion with Rome, abandoned many of Luther's doctrines, it must be remembered that these matters were not in dispute among Luther, Zwingli, and Calvin, nor among Ridley, Cranmer, Latimer, Bucer, Zanchius, and Knox. The same is true of the victims of Bloody Mary. Richard Woodman, who was burned at the stake with nine other martyrs at Lewes in Sussex, answered his examiners,

"If we have free will, then our salvation cometh of ourselves: which is a great blasphemy against God and his word." Richard Gibson, examined by the Bishop of London, was called upon to profess that "a man hath by God's grace a free choice and will in his doing." Gibson denied the proposition and was burned to death with two others in Smithfield. Thirty-four persons were persecuted and expelled from the towns of Winston and Mendelsham because "they denied man's free will and held that the Pope's church did err." If more evidence is desired for the Calvinism of the Reformation, there is an abundance of it in the history books and in the original writings of these faithful men.

In the non-Lutheran world the Reformation faith was first adulterated by Arminius, who, influenced by Melancthonian Lutheranism, rejected the Reformed view of free grace and retreated to a more Romish or semi-pelagian position. The Synod of Dort in 1618 condemned Arminius as a corrupter of the faith, though it did not rise to the explicit heights of the Westminster Assembly thirty years later. It is the latter's Confession that is the high water mark of Protestantism. No other creed is so detailed and so true to the Scriptures. Therefore the present day reader is requested to give exact attention to a quotation from the Westminster Confession. Though some circumscribed souls may be astonished, this is what Christianity is.

CHAPTER THREE—OF GOD'S ETERNAL DECREE

I. God from all eternity did, by the most wise and holy counsel of his own will, freely and unchangeably ordain whatsoever comes to pass; yet so, as thereby neither is God the author of sin, nor is violence offered to the will of the creatures, nor is the liberty or contingency of second causes taken away, but rather established.

II. Although God knows what may or can come to pass upon all supposed conditions, yet hath he not decreed anything because he foresaw it as future, or as that which would come to pass upon such conditions.

III. By the decree of God, for the manifestation of his glory, some men and angels are predestinated unto everlasting life, and other foreordained to everlasting death.

IV. These angels and men, thus predestinated and foreordained, are particularly and unchangeably designed; and their number is so certain and definite, that it cannot be either increased or diminished.

V. Those of mankind that are predestinated unto life, God, before the foundation of the world was laid, according to his eternal and immutable purpose, and the secret counsel and good pleasure of his will, hath chosen in Christ unto everlasting glory, out of his mere free grace and love, without any foresight of faith or good works, or perseverance in either of them, or any other thing in the creature, as conditions, or causes moving him thereunto; and all to the praise of his glorious grace.

VI. As God hath appointed the elect unto glory, so hath he, by the eternal and most free purpose of his will, foreordained all the means thereunto. Wherefore they who are elected being fallen in Adam, are redeemed by Christ; are effectually called unto faith in Christ by his Spirit working in due season; are justified, adopted, sanctified, and kept by his power through faith unto salvation. Neither are any other redeemed by Christ, effectually called, justified, adopted, sanctified, and saved, but the elect only.

VII. The rest of mankind, God was pleased, according to the unsearchable counsel of his own will, whereby he extended or withholdeth mercy as he pleaseth, for the glory of his sovereign power over his creatures, to pass by, and to ordain them to dishonor and wrath for their sin, to the praise of his glorious justice.

VIII. The doctrine of this high mystery of predestination is to be handled with special prudence and care, that men attending the will of God revealed in his word, and yielding obedience thereunto, may, from the certainty of their effectual vocation, be assured of their eternal election. So shall this doctrine afford matter of praise, reverence, and admiration of God, and of humility, diligence, and abundant consolation to all that sincerely obey the Gospel.

This official statement of the original Protestant position, of the original apostolic faith, concludes this historical section.

Missing pp. 214-230

fession declares, "They being the root of all mankind, the guilt of this sin was imputed, and the same death in sin and corrupted nature conveyed to all their posterity descending from them by ordinary generation" (VI iii). Responsibility therefore must be so defined as to make room for imputation, as well as to account for our everyday voluntary actions.

It is strange that theological literature has made so little attempt to define responsibility. It is a lack found among determinists and indeterminists alike. Admittedly some statements about responsibility are found, even some true statements; but not every true statement is a definition. Once again, if we knew precisely what we were talking about, our confusion might prove avoidable.

Now, the word responsibility looks as if it has to do with making a response. Or, accountability is to give an account. A man is responsible if he must answer for what he does. Let us then define the term by saying that a person is responsible if he can be justly rewarded or punished for his deeds. This implies, of course, that he must be answerable to someone. Responsibility presupposes a superior authority that rewards and punishes. The highest authority is God. Therefore responsibility is ultimately dependent on the power and authority of God.

Is it just then for God to punish a man for deeds that God himself "determined before to be done"? Was God just in punishing Judas, Herod, Pontius Pilate, and the others? The Scriptures answer in the affirmative and explain why. Not only is God the creator of the physical universe, not only is he the governor and judge of men, he is also the moral legislator. It is his will that establishes the distinction between right and wrong, between justice and injustice; it is his will that sets the norms of righteous conduct. Most people find it easy to conceive of God as having created or established physical law by divine fiat. He might have created a world with a different number of planets, had he so desired. Nor does it bother some theologians to suppose that God could have made different ceremonial requirements. Instead of commanding the priests to carry the ark

on their shoulders, God might have forbidded this and ordered
them to put it on a cart drawn by oxen. But for some peculiar
reason people hesitate in applying the same principle of sovereignty in the sphere of ordinary ethics. Instead of recognizing
God as sovereign in morals, they want to subject him to some
independent, superior, ethical law—a law that satisfies their
sinful opinions of what is right and wrong.

Calvin avoided any such inconsistent and unbiblical position.
In the Institutes (III xxiii 2) he says,

"how exceedingly presumptuous it is only to inquire into the causes
of the divine will, which is in fact, and is justly entitled to be, the
cause of everything that exists. For if it has any cause, then there
must be something antecedent on which it depends; which it is
impious to suppose. For the will of God is the highest rule of justice,
so that what he wills must be considered just, for this very reason,
because he wills it. When it is inquired therefore why the Lord did
so, the answer must be, Because he would. But if you go further and
ask why he so determined, you are in search of something greater
and higher than the will of God, which can never be found."

God is sovereign. Whatever he does is just, for this very
reason, because he does it. If he punishes a man, the man is
justly punished, and hence the man is responsible. This answers
the form of argument which runs: whatever God does is just;
eternal punishment is not just; therefore God does not so
punish. If the one who argues thus means that he has received
a special revelation that there is no eternal punishment, we
cannot deal with him here. If, however, he is not laying claim
to a special revelation of future history but to some philosophic
principle which is intended to show that eternal punishment is
unjust, the distinction between our positions becomes immediately obvious. Calvin has rejected the view of the universe
which makes a law, whether of justice or of evolution, instead of
the law-giver, supreme. Such a view is similar to Platonic dualism which posited a world of Ideas superior to the divine

Artificer. God in such a system is finite or limited, bound to
follow or obey the independent pattern. But those who hold to
the sovereignty of God determine what justice is by observing
what God actually does. Whatever God does is just. What he
commands men to do or not to do is similarly just or unjust.

Distortions and Cautions

The arguments so far adduced are more than sufficient for the
solution of the main problem. Further considerations could
make the exposition more complete and might remove from in-
experienced minds a number of distortions and objections that
frequently present themselves. Calvinism undoubtedly stimulates many misapprehensions, although the reason for their
frequency, as has already been seen in the discussion on puppets,
is not a point in which Arminians can take pride. At the same
time Calvinists acknowledge that they themselves have a responsibility to forestall such misapprehensions so far as possible.
The Westminster Confession and other Reformed creeds urge
caution, not so much in opposing free will, for the Reformers
were outspoken in their championship of grace in opposition to
free will, but in preaching the doctrine of election and the
divine decree. This does not condone those professors in Bible
departments who, supposing that they know better than God
what should be revealed, demand that the doctrine of the divine
decree should be suppressed in silence. But it does require that
the Scriptural passages be clearly exegeted, that the doctrine
should be logically integrated with the rest of God's revelation,
and that at least the main objections should be squarely
answered.

A recent volume, *Divine Election*, by G. C. Berkouwer, is
largely motivated by the pastoral concern to protect the congregation from the uncertainties and fear of a harsh presentation
of election, predestination, and related themes. Professor
Berkouwer is a theologian of great erudition. His volume, *The
Triumph of Grace in the Theology of Karl Barth*, is a triumph
of scholarship. Similarly *The Conflict with Rome* is a master-

piece. The book under discussion also evidences a wealth of knowledge; its doctrine is unmistakeably Calvinistic; and yet some of its hesitations and fears seem to be unfounded. Most of the dangers that he mentions have no doubt actually occurred, as in the writings of a certain Snethlage whom he mentions; these dangers could possibly be more common in Holland than in the United States; but so far as the present writer's experience goes, it would seem that the greater and far more common dangers are those of an opposite tendency.

For one thing Berkouwer thinks that it is necessary to deny that Calvinism is deterministic. The word *determinism* apparently carries some evil connotation in his mind. Unfortunately Berkouwer never clearly defines determinism. Between the lines we may gather that determinism for him automatically makes all differences within God's predetermination relative and unimportant (p. 180), so that preaching becomes useless (p. 220). There are of course various types of determinism, atheistic and mechanical as well as theistic and teleological. This, however, is a poor reason for avoiding the word *determinism*. On the contrary, a uniform avoidance of this term might suggest to the congregation that the pastor does not really believe that God controls every event; and this unfortunate result would surely be more serious than any mistake arising from the word *determinism*. Sinful human nature is much more apt to deny or to circumscribe God's authority in favor of human independence than it is to exaggerate the power of God. Pastoral caution and care therefore lead rather in the opposite direction.

Berkouwer also cautions against ascribing absolute power to God, against asserting God's superiority to all law, and against calling his decisions arbitrary. In each case, however, there is a sense in which these terms can be used of God as well as a sense in which they are objectionable. Perhaps Occam's idea of absolute power is not correct, yet Berkouwer admits that there is no law superior to God and that in this sense God is indeed "Ex-lex." When discussing the parable of the employer who paid his laborers the same wage regardless of the time they worked, Berkouwer says that this was not "arbitrary"—it was "good." So it was; but Berkouwer's concern seems centered more on words than on their meaning.

Berkouwer also shows himself to be suspicious of the concept of causality, largely because the idea of cause tends to "a metaphysical determinism which leaves no room for variation and differences but which subsumes everything under the one causality of God" (p. 178). This is an empty objection, if ever there was one; and the discussion leaves much to be desired because Berkouwer admits that "it is inherently difficult to give any answer that in itself would be transparent to reflective and reasonable thinking. On the one hand, we want to maintain the freedom of God in election, and on the other hand, we want to avoid any conclusion which would make God the cause of sin and unbelief" (p. 181).

Berkouwer, in spite of his Calvinism and his many truly fine statements of the Reformed position, is so embarrassed by his imaginary difficulties that once he even stumbles into what I take to be an historical blunder. He writes, "What Jacobs says of Calvin—that in his preaching and commentaries the election of God is repeatedly discussed, while rejection is not mentioned —can be said with as much validity of the Reformed confessions" (p. 194). This sentence in its context seems to mean that the Reformed confessions do not even mention reprobation. This is not true; and we hope that Berkouwer intended to say something else, but merely failed to express it clearly. That the ostensible meaning, however, is not true is undeniable. Earlier in this chapter a part of the Westminster Confession was quoted, and the reader's attention is again called to the third, fourth, and seventh sections of chapter three.

It is not by a strained analysis of the concept of causality that Berkouwer can avoid calling God the cause of sin or can contribute to the prevention of misapprehensions. There are indeed two mistaken conclusions that should be guarded against, not so much for the purpose of protecting Calvinistic congregations from anxiety and insecurity, as Berkouwer believes, but in order to save Arminians from the blunders they have fallen into. In connection with the phrase, God is the cause of sin, something yet needs to be said about causality, and, second, something needs to be said about God's holiness.

Berkouwer had complained that the attempt to explain the divine decree in terms of causality prevented the acknowledgment of differences and variations within the divine decree and therefore eliminated these distinctions in the historical process. Even though Berkouwer admits that there are two types of causality, he still concludes that "every discussion of causality fails, must fail" (p. 190).

The question is slightly complex. One part of it has to do with the necessity of means, or secondary or proximate causes. God does not do everything, he hardly does anything, immediately. For this reason the Westminster Confession, to which Berkouwer pays insufficient attention, has a phrase about secondary causation.

It is human nature, depraved human nature, to attempt to avoid responsibility for wrong doing. In seeking to excuse himself for an evil act, a man may assign the blame to his tempter, as Adam and Eve did, or to compelling and extenuating circumstances, or to something else more remote and ultimate. The insincerity of this procedure becomes apparent when we notice that men do not try to avoid praise and honor by referring their good acts to ultimate causes. They wish to escape blame, but they are willing, only too willing, to accept compliments. The Christian view, however, is clearly expressed in David's great confession. David did not complain, I have sinned a great sin, but alas, I was born sinful and could not help it; so, do not blame me too much. On the contrary David said, I have sinned a great sin; and what makes it all the worse is that I was born that way; I could not help it, for I myself am evil. Repentant David placed the blame, not on his mother, nor on Adam, nor on God, even though all of these are causes in the chain of causation leading to his sin. Repentant David placed the blame on the immediate cause of his act—himself. The doctrine of creation, with its implication that there is no power independent of God, does not deny but rather establishes the existence of secondary causes. To suppose otherwise is unscriptural and to avoid the notion of causality is illogical.

Berkouwer's contention that an original, all inclusive, universal decree of causation removes other distinctions is also untenable. He is afraid that the principle of causality would conflict with the very Scriptural position that guilt is the judicial ground of condemnation. Now, this is an important factor, a most important factor for pastoral caution. The majority of people, both inside and outside the Church, are immersed in practical details and their vision seldom rises to more general theological principles. They need the point emphasized that God condemns people for their sins. In particular, evangelistic endeavor cannot omit the fact of sin. But Calvinism does not make any such omission. Nor is there any inconsistency. The doctrines of election and reprobation do not conflict with the fact that God's punishment is visited on no one who is not a sinner. The sinner deserves his punishment because he is evil and has done evil. No innocent person suffers. To be sure, Calvinism also insists that there are no innocent persons, except Christ of course. All are dead in sin. Salvation is a free unmerited gift. Sin alone has merited wages, and those wages are death. All this Calvinism proclaims without compromise. There is nothing in the divine decree that is inconsistent with acknowledging sin as the judicial ground of punishment. Berkouwer's claim that the concept of cause removes particularities from the divine decree is therefore untenable.

There are admittedly other details whose discussion might obviate various misunderstandings. To consider them all, even if they were not repetitious, would require a length and minuteness incompatible with the present plan. There is, however, one extremely important topic that cannot be omitted. Does the view here defended make God the cause and author of sin? Berkouwer asks this question also; and so has everyone else. Let it be unequivocally said that this view certainly makes

God the cause of sin. God is the sole ultimate cause of everything. There is absolutely nothing independent of him. He alone is the eternal being. He alone is omnipotent. He alone is sovereign. Not only is Satan his creature, but every detail of history was eternally in his plan before the world began; and he willed that it should all come to pass. The men and angels predestined to eternal life and those foreordained to everlasting death are particularly and unchangeably designed; and their number is so certain and definite that it cannot be either increased or diminished. Election and reprobation are equally ultimate. God determined that Christ should die; he determined as well that Judas should betray him. There was never the remotest possibility that something different could have happened.

"Whatsoever the Lord pleased, that did he in heaven and in earth" (Psa. 135:6). "All the inhabitants of the earth are reputed as nothing, and he doeth according to his will in the army of heaven and among the inhabitants of the earth, and none can stay his hand, or say unto him, What doest thou?" (Dan. 4:35). "I form the light and create darkness; I make peace and create evil; I the Lord do all these things" (Isa. 45:7). "The Lord hath made all things for himself; yea, even the wicked for the day of evil" (Prov. 16:4). "Thou wilt say then unto me, Why doth he yet find fault? For who hath resisted his will? Nay, but, O man, who art thou that repliest against God . . . Hath not the potter power over the clay, of the same lump to make one vessel unto honor and another unto dishonor?" (Rom. 9:19-21). "Behold therefore the goodness and severity of God" (Rom. 11:22).

One is permitted to ask, however, whether the phrase 'cause of sin' is the equivalent of the phrase 'author of sin.' Is the latter phrase used to deny God's universal causality? Obviously not, for the same people who affirm causality deny the authorship. They must have intended a difference. An illustration is close at hand. God is not the author of this book, as the Arminians would be the first to admit; but he is its ultimate cause as the Bible teaches. Yet I am the author. Authorship therefore is one

kind of cause, but there are other kinds. The author of a book
is its immediate cause; God is its ultimate cause.

This distinction between first and secondary causation, explicitly maintained in the Westminster Confession, has not always been appreciated, even by those who are in general agreement. John Gill, for example, who is so excellent on so much,
failed to grasp the distinction between the immediate author
and the ultimate cause. For this reason there are some faulty
passages in his otherwise fine work. Such is the difficulty of the
problem and so confused are the discussions from the time of
the patristics to the present day, that some of the best Calvinists
have not extricated themselves completely from scholastic errors. Not only Berkouwer, but even Jonathan Edwards, in spite
of Calvin, still spoke about God's permission of sin.

When accordingly the discussion comes to God's being the
author of sin, one must understand the question to be, Is God
the immediate cause of sin? Or, more clearly, Does God commit
sin? This is a question concerning God's holiness. Now, it should
be evident that God no more commits sin than he is writing
these words. Although the betrayal of Christ was foreordained
from eternity as a means of effecting the atonement, it was
Judas, not God, who betrayed Christ. The secondary causes in
history are not eliminated by divine causality, but rather they
are made certain. And the acts of these secondary causes, whether
they be righteous acts or sinful acts, are to be immediately referred to the agents; and it is these agents who are responsible.
God is neither responsible nor sinful, even though he is the
only ultimate cause of everything. He is not sinful because in
the first place whatever God does is just and right. It is just and
right simply in virtue of the fact that he does it. Justice or
righteousness is not a standard external to God to which God
is obligated to submit. Righteousness is what God does. Since
God caused Judas to betray Christ, this causal act is righteous
and not sinful. By definition God cannot sin. At this point it
must be particularly pointed out that God's causing a man to
sin is not sin. There is no law, superior to God, which forbids

him to decree sinful acts. Sin presupposes a law, for sin is law-lessness. Sin is any want of conformity unto or transgression of the law of God. But God is "Ex-lex."

True it is that if a man, a created being, should cause or try to cause another man to sin, this attempt would be sinful. The reason is plain. The relation of one man to another is entirely different from the relation of God to any man. God is the creator; man is a creature. And the relation of a man to the law is equally different from the relation of God to the law. What holds in the one situation does not hold in the other. God has absolute and unlimited rights over all created things. Of the same lump he can make one vessel for honor and another for dishonor. The clay has no claims on the potter. Among men, on the contrary, rights are limited.

The idea that God is above law can be explained in another particular. The laws that God imposes on men do not apply to the divine nature. They are applicable only to human conditions. For example, God cannot steal, not only because whatever he does is right, but also because he owns everything: there is no one to steal from. Thus the law that defines sin envisages human conditions and has no relevance to a sovereign Creator.

As God cannot sin, so in the next place, God is not responsible for sin, even though he decrees it. Perhaps it would be well, before we conclude, to give a little more Scriptural evidence that God indeed decrees and causes sin. II Chron. 18:20-22 reads: "Then there came out a spirit and stood before the Lord, and said, I will entice him. And the Lord said unto him, Wherewith? And he said, I will go out and be a lying spirit in the mouth of all his prophets. And the Lord said, Thou shalt entice him, and thou shalt also prevail: go out and do even so. Now therefore, behold, the Lord hath put a lying spirit in the mouth of these thy prophets, and the Lord hath spoken evil against thee." This passage definitely says that the Lord caused the prophets to lie. Other similar passages ought easily to come to one's remembrance. But that God is not responsible for the sin he causes is a conclusion closely connected with the preceding argument.

Another aspect of the human conditions presupposed by the laws God imposes on man is that they carry with them a penalty that cannot be inflicted on God. Man is responsible because God calls him to account; man is responsible because the supreme power can punish him for disobedience. God, on the contrary, cannot be responsible for the plain reason that there is no power superior to him; no greater being can hold him accountable; no one can punish him; there is no one to whom God is responsible; there are no laws which he could disobey.

The sinner therefore, and not God, is responsible; the sinner alone is the author of sin. Man has no free will, for salvation is purely of grace; and God is sovereign.

Deo Soli Gloria

"I am the Lord, and there is none else; there is no God beside me. I form the light and create darkness; I make peace and create evil; I the Lord do all these things. Woe unto him that striveth with his Maker! Shall the clay say unto him that fashioneth it, What makest thou? Thus saith the Lord, the Holy One of Israel, I have made the earth and created man upon it; I, even my hands, have stretched out the heavens, and all the host of them have I commanded . . . O, the depth of the riches both of the wisdom and knowledge of God! How unsearchable are his judgments and his ways past finding out. For of him, and through him, and to him, are all things; to whom be glory for ever. Amen."

NOTES

1. Of these quotations by Toplady I have verified those I could easily find. Others are relatively inaccessible. Since Toplady often gives the Latin text, one may hope that he has been accurate. If in some place he has made a mistake, it is still proved that the five points did not originate with Calvin, much less with the Synod of Dort.

2. For further argument, see Jonathan Edwards, *Miscellaneous Observations*, Part II, chap. 3; 1811 edition, Vol. VIII, p. 384.

3. Georgia Harkness, *Conflict in Religious Thought*, pp. 233-234.

4. The Resurrection of Theism, p. 174.